Pre-publication REVIEWS, COMMENTARIES, EVALUATIONS . . .

"**D**rs. Hecker and Sori have again collected a cornucopia of helpful strategies. The format is easy to use, pick a page and apply the idea with your clients to deepen the therapy experience."

—**Jon Carlson, PsyD, EdD, ABPP**
Distinguished Professor,
Governors State University

"**A** comprehensive collection of practical interventions of seasoned and talented clinicians who share their inspired experiences and resourceful knowledge in easy to use ways. The book not only covers all members of families who get involved in psychotherapy but also focuses on specific problem domains. This book belongs on the desk of every clinician and trainee. It is full of wisdom and joy."

—**Volker Thomas, PhD**
Associate Professor of Marriage
and Family Therapy in the Department
of Child Development and Family
Studies at Purdue University

"**L**orna and Catherine have done it again! The fruits that can be picked from this tree of clinical wisdom are substantial. The artful landscape and clinical scope the editors cover is impressive. Each of the contributors plants their ideas in well tilled theoretical ground, arrange colorful clinical vignettes, and illuminate pathways for further reading for both clinician and client. There is a wide variety of contributors assembled in this book and each of them presents their ideas in a way that can serve as a catalyst for seeding the reader's own creativity and resourcefulness. Whether seasoned clinician or budding student intern, this notebook can provide a solid source for watering your own ideas and tools for tending your own therapeutic gardens."

—**Timothy F. Dwyer, PhD**
McCormick Tribune Foundation
Chair in Marital and Family Therapy,
MSMFT Program Director,
The Family Institute at Northwestern
University

"**T**his book surpasses the first volume in every way. It is a treasure chest of useful, validated, clinical interventions that fit a broad array of situations. The contributors come from all areas of practice. Clinicians of all levels will find themselves returning again and again to this book."

—**Joseph L. Wetchler, PhD**
Professor and Director,
Marriage and Family Therapy
Program, Purdue University,
Calumet

The Therapist's Notebook, Volume 2
More Homework, Handouts, and Activities for Use in Psychotherapy

HAWORTH Practical Practice in Mental Health
Lorna L. Hecker, PhD
Senior Editor

101 Interventions in Family Therapy edited by Thorana S. Nelson and Terry S. Trepper

101 More Interventions in Family Therapy edited by Thorana S. Nelson and Terry S. Trepper

The Practical Practice of Marriage and Family Therapy: Things My Training Supervisor Never Told Me by Mark Odell and Charles E. Campbell

The Therapist's Notebook for Families: Solution-Oriented Exercises for Working with Parents, Children, and Adolescents by Bob Bertolino and Gary Schultheis

Collaborative Practice in Psychology and Therapy edited by David A. Paré and Glenn Larner

The Therapist's Notebook for Children and Adolescents: Homework, Handouts, and Activities for Use in Psychotherapy edited by Catherine Ford Sori and Lorna L. Hecker

The Therapist's Notebook for Lesbian, Gay, and Bisexual Clients: Homework, Handouts, and Activities for Use in Psychotherapy by Joy S. Whitman and Cynthia J. Boyd

A Guide to Self-Help Workbooks for Mental Health Clinicians and Researchers by Luciano L'Abate

Workbooks in Prevention, Psychotherapy, and Rehabilitation: A Resource for Clinicians and Researchers edited by Luciano L'Abate

The Psychotherapist as Parent Coordinator in High-Conflict Divorce: Strategies and Techniques by Susan M. Boyan and Ann Marie Termini

The Couple and Family Therapist's Notebook: Homework, Handouts, and Activities for Use in Marital and Family Therapy by Katherine A. Milewski Hertlein, Dawn Viers, and Associates

The Therapist's Notebook for Integrating Spirituality in Counseling: Homework, Handouts, and Activities for Use in Psychotherapy edited by Karen B. Helmeke and Catherine Ford Sori

The Therapist's Notebook for Integrating Spirituality in Counseling II: More Homework, Handouts, and Activities for Use in Psychotherapy edited by Karen B. Helmeke and Catherine Ford Sori

Interactive Art Therapy: "No Talent Required" Projects by Linda L. Simmons

Therapy's Best: Practical Advice and Gems of Wisdom from Twenty Accomplished Counselors and Therapists by Howard Rosenthal

The Christian Therapist's Notebook: Homework, Handouts, and Activities for Use in Christian Counseling by Philip J. Henry, Lori Marie Figueroa, and David R. Miller

The Therapist's Notebook, Volume 2: More Homework, Handouts, and Activities for Use in Psychotherapy by Lorna L. Hecker, Catherine Ford Sori, and Associates

The Group Therapist's Notebook: Homework, Handouts, and Activities for Use in Psychotherapy edited by Dawn Viers

Introduction to Complementary and Alternative Therapies edited by Anne L. Strozier and Joyce Carpenter

The Therapist's Notebook, Volume 2

More Homework, Handouts, and Activities for Use in Psychotherapy

Lorna L. Hecker
Catherine Ford Sori
and Associates

The Haworth Press, Inc.
New York

For more information on this book or to order, visit
http://www.haworthpress.com/store/product.asp?sku=5550

or call 1-800-HAWORTH (800-429-6784) in the United States and Canada
or (607) 722-5857 outside the United States and Canada

or contact orders@HaworthPress.com

PUBLISHER'S NOTE
The development, preparation, and publication of this work has been undertaken with great care. However, the Publisher, employees, editors, and agents of The Haworth Press are not responsible for any errors contained herein or for consequences that may ensue from use of materials or information contained in this work. The Haworth Press is committed to the dissemination of ideas and information according to the highest standards of intellectual freedom and the free exchange of ideas. Statements made and opinions expressed in this publication do not necessarily reflect the views of the Publisher, Directors, management, or staff of The Haworth Press, Inc., or an endorsement by them.

Identities and circumstances of individuals discussed in this book have been changed to protect confidentiality.

Written permission to publish the vignette in Chapter 6 was given by the mother. The family's characteristics were sufficiently disguised to avoid recognition and guarantee anonymity.

Chapters 6, 13, 21, 24, 27, and 28 first appeared in the *Journal of Clinical Activities, Assignments & Handouts in Psychotherapy Practice,* 1(1), 5-18; 2(3), 23-29; 2(1), 33-42; 1(3), 3-13; 2(4), 15-39; and 2(3), 31-37, respectively. Copyright 2001 and 2002 The Haworth Press, Inc.

Faces artwork in Handouts 2.2 and 2.3 appear courtesy of Paul A. Benning.

Cover design by Kerry Mack.

Library of Congress Cataloging-in-Publication Data

Hecker, Lorna L.
    The therapist's notebook, volume 2: more homework, handouts, and activities for use in psychotherapy / Lorna L. Hecker, Catherine Ford Sori, and associates.
        p. cm.
    Includes bibliographical references and index.
    ISBN: 978-0-7890-2802-0 (soft : alk. paper)
    1. Psychotherapy—Problems, exercises, etc. I. Sori, Catherine Ford. II. Title. III. Title: Therapist's notebook two.
    [DNLM: 1. Psychotherapy—methods. WM 420 H449t 2007]
RC480.5.H3482 2007
616.89'14076—dc22
                                                                                                2006035939

We dedicate this book to clients who reveal to us their deepest thoughts and darkest moments—to clients who show us their greatest resiliencies and abilities to heal.

CONTENTS

About the Editors   xi

Contributors   xiii

Preface   xix

Acknowledgments   xxi

SECTION I: COUPLES

Chapter 1. Couples Drawing Together   3
    Shannon B. Dermer and Kimanne Foraker-Koons

Chapter 2. Finding a Connection   11
    Sophia Treyger, Melanie Frey, and Belinda Stepnowski

Chapter 3. Interrupting Couple Negativity   21
    Josephine Bonomo

Chapter 4. Counseling Couples with Choice Theory and Reality Therapy:
    The Structured First Interview   29
    Patricia A. Robey

Chapter 5. Blossoming Relationships: Using Creativity in Couple Counseling   37
    Nancy L. A. Forth and Atsuko Seto

SECTION II: CHILDREN, ADOLESCENTS, AND FAMILIES

Chapter 6. Hugging, Holding, Huddling, and Cuddling (3HC): A Task Prescription
    in Couple and Family Therapy   47
    Luciano L'Abate

Chapter 7. Bridging Game for Ill and Well Siblings   57
    Catherine Ford Sori and Nancee M. Biank

Chapter 8. Connecting Spaces: Experiential Encounters for Families   69
    Scott A. Edwards and Erica J. Weekes

Chapter 9. The Feeling Head   75
    Adam Zagelbaum

Chapter 10. The Gingerbread Figure Activity   81
    George W. Bitar and Faith Drew

Chapter 11. The Creative Career Constellation   87
    Adam Zagelbaum

Chapter 12. Props: Therapeutic Use of Common Objects   93
    Joe M. Utay

SECTION III: ADULTS

Chapter 13. Client Family-of-Origin Interviews with Parents: Questions That
    Support Discovery and Connection   105
    Fred P. Piercy

Chapter 14. Externalizing Problems: It's in the Bag   109
    Margaret L. Keeling

Chapter 15. Putting Pressure on Procrastination   115
    Howard G. Rosenthal

Chapter 16. The Situation Trigger Worksheet   119
    Kolleen L. Simons

Chapter 17. Active Imagination   125
    Marita Delaney

Chapter 18. Discovering Hidden Immigrants   131
    Elise Cole

SECTION IV: GROUPS

Chapter 19. Creating a Special Place   139
    Lorna L. Hecker and Catherine Ford Sori

Chapter 20. Say It with Flowers: An Innovative Group Therapy Activity
    for Adults and Children   147
    Jolene Oppawsky

Chapter 21. Taking Out the Trash   151
    René A. Jones

SECTION V: TRAUMA AND ABUSE RECOVERY

Chapter 22. Exploring Relationships: An Eco-Map Activity for Adult Survivors
    of Incest   159
        Abigail T. Christiansen, Andrea K. Wittenborn, Günnur Karakurt,
        Syidah Abdullah, and Chunhong Zhang

Chapter 23. Using Art and Metaphor in Spiritual Restoration After Trauma   169
    Lisa A. Hollingsworth, Mary J. Didelot, and Caryn Levington

Chapter 24. Writing the Script for Survivor Therapy   177
    Mary Bratton

SECTION VI: DIVORCE AND STEPFAMILIES

Chapter 25. Dos and Don'ts of Divorced Parents   187
    Lorna L. Hecker and Catherine Ford Sori

Chapter 26. Stepfamilies   193
    Catherine Ford Sori and Lorna L. Hecker

Chapter 27. Encouraging Children's Stories of Divorce   199
    Nancee M. Biank and Catherine Ford Sori

Chapter 28. Using Movie Clips to Facilitate Discussion in the Postdivorce Family   223
    Christie Eppler and Christopher Latty

SECTION VII: SPIRITUALITY

Chapter 29. How to Defeat a Giant: Using Spiritual Stories to Empower Children   229
    Donald J. Olund

Chapter 30. Spiritual Play Genogram   237
    Catherine Ford Sori

SECTION VIII: THERAPIST TOOLS

Chapter 31. Family Strengths and Concerns Assessment   251
    Belinda Stepnowski

Chapter 32. Therapy Intake Form   261
    Lorna L. Hecker and Catherine Ford Sori

Chapter 33. Quick Depression Assessment   273
    Catherine Ford Sori and Lorna L. Hecker

Chapter 34. The Tiger Woods Analogy: The Seven-Minute Active Listening Solution   277
    Howard G. Rosenthal

Index   281

ABOUT THE EDITORS

Lorna L. Hecker, PhD, LMFT, is a professor of marriage and family therapy at Purdue University Calumet in Hammond, Indiana, where she is faculty in the marriage and family therapy master's program in the Department of Behavioral Sciences. She teaches graduate courses in ethics and couples therapy. She is also the director of the Purdue University Calumet Couple and Family Therapy Center. She is a clinical member of the American Association of Marriage and Family Therapy (AAMFT) and an AAMFT Approved Supervisor. She is a licensed marriage and family therapist, and maintains a small private practice in Hammond, Indiana. Her clinical interests include divorce, trauma recovery, and couples counseling. She co-authored (with Catherine Ford Sori, PhD, and Associates) *The Therapist's Notebook for Children and Adolescents: Homework, Handouts and Activities for Use in Psychotherapy* (Haworth). She also edited (with Joseph Wetcher) *An Introduction to Marriage and Family Therapy* (Haworth). Dr. Hecker is the senior book program editor of Haworth's Practical Practice in Mental Health: Guidebooks for In-Patient, Out-Patient, and Independent Practice. Dr. Hecker was the founding editor of the *Journal of Clinical Activities, Assignments & Handouts in Psychotherapy Practice*. She has also published articles in the *Journal of Marital & Family Therapy,* the *American Journal of Family Therapy,* and the *Journal of Family Psychotherapy.*

Catherine Ford Sori, PhD, is an associate professor of marriage and family counseling at Governors State University in University Park, Illinois; and associate faculty at the Chicago Center for Family Health. Her special interests include training issues related to children in family therapy, children and families facing illness and bereavement, and integrating spirituality in therapy. Dr. Sori was the Director of Children and Family Services at the Cancer Support Center in Homewood, Illinois. She is frequently invited to present on topics pertaining to children, families, illness, bereavement, and family play therapy. Dr. Sori received her PhD in marriage and family therapy from Purdue University, and practiced for several years at Samaritan Counseling Center in Munster, Indiana. Her publications include journal articles in the *Journal of Marital and Family Therapy*; *The Family Journal*; *Journal of Clinical Activities, Assignments & Handouts in Psychotherapy Practice*; *Journal of Couple & Relationship Therapy*; *American Journal of Family Therapy*; and the *Journal of Family Psychotherapy*. Dr. Sori co-authored (with Lorna L. Hecker, PhD, and Associates) *The Therapist's Notebook for Children and Adolescents: Homework, Handouts and Activities for Use in Psychotherapy* (Haworth); *The Therapist's Notebook for Integrating Spirituality in Counseling, Vols. I & II* (with Karen Helmeke, PhD) (Haworth); and *Engaging Children in Family Therapy: Creative Approaches to Integrating Theory and Research in Clinical Practice*. She also developed the training program for Kids Support, a national training program for the treatment of cancer in the family. She is on the editorial boards for the *Journal of Couple & Relationship Therapy* and the *Journal of the Illinois Counseling Association*. Dr. Sori is a licensed marriage and family therapist and a clinical member of AAMFT as well as an AAMFT Approved Supervisor, and is a member of the American Counseling Association.

The Therapist's Notebook, Volume 2
© 2007 by The Haworth Press, Inc. All rights reserved.
doi:10.1300/5550_a

CONTRIBUTORS

Syidah Abdullah, MS, is currently completing a doctorate in marriage and family therapy at Purdue University. Her clinical interests involve working with individuals, couples, and families from an emotionally focused theoretical framework and using a feminist lens. Her research interests focus on the connection between adult attachment styles, rates of marital infidelity, marital satisfaction, and marital stability. Her other interest involves working with African-American couples and the impact of racism and prejudice on romantic relationships. She is a former facilitator of an incest survivors' support group.

Nancee M. Biank, MSW, LCSW, is the Director of Children and Family Services at Wellness House, Hinsdale, Illinois, a nonprofit organization that offers psychosocial support to cancer patients and their families, where she developed the groundbreaking Family Matters Program for children who have a parent with cancer. She has written numerous articles on children and illness, death, and divorce. Ms. Biank is also in private practice and is co-founder of Partners in Transition in Hinsdale.

George W. Bitar is a licensed marriage and family therapy associate and a licensed professional counselor intern. George is a doctoral candidate in the marriage and family therapy program at Texas Tech University.

Josephine Bonomo, MS, LMFT, is a doctoral candidate in the marriage and family therapy program, Department of Child Development and Family Studies, at Purdue University. Her clinical work has focused on conduct disordered youth and their families, marital therapy, and abused and neglected children. Her research interests include juvenile sex offender treatment, change processes in family therapy, and supervision and mentoring.

Mary Bratton, MS, is a licensed professional counselor and a diplomate of the American Psychotherapy Association. She maintains a private psychotherapy practice at Cary Counseling Center in Cary, North Carolina, where she specializes in the treatment of adult survivors of childhood abuse and trauma. As Director of Intervention Resources, she also provides training and consultation services. Mary is the author of numerous professional journal articles and two books, *A Guide to Family Intervention* (1989, Health Communications, Inc.) and *From Surviving to Thriving: A Guide to Stage II Recovery for Survivors of Childhood Abuse* (1999, The Haworth Press).

Abigail T. Christiansen, MS, is a graduate student in marriage and family therapy at Purdue University in West Lafayette, Indiana. She is a student member of the American Association for Marriage and Family Therapy, the National Council on Family Relations, and the American Psychological Association. She previously researched the intersection of work and marriage. She cofacilitated an adult incest survivors' support group for two years.

Elise Cole received her master's degree in marriage and family therapy from George Fox University in Portland, Oregon. She is a doctoral student in the marriage and family therapy program at Virginia Tech University. Prior to attending Virginia Tech, she spent two years prac-

The Therapist's Notebook, Volume 2
© 2007 by The Haworth Press, Inc. All rights reserved.
doi:10.1300/5550_b

ticing family therapy. The primary clinical populations she has worked with include young children, teenagers, and their families. She is a white American who grew up in Kenya, East Africa. She is interested in finding culturally appropriate ways to apply marriage and family therapy principles to populations overseas.

Marita Delaney is an associate professor of counseling and school psychology at Western New Mexico University, where she is coordinator of the master's in counseling program at the Gallup Graduate Studies Center. She is a licensed psychologist and a certified supervisory-level school psychologist. Her interests include Jungian psychology and community mental health. She has worked as a clinical psychologist in schools on the Navajo reservation and community mental health centers in northwestern New Mexico for the past ten years.

Shannon B. Dermer is an assistant professor at Governors State University. She received her PhD in marriage and family therapy from Kansas State University in 1998 and a master's in psychology in 1994 from Illinois State University. She has published on using technology in teaching and therapy, a feminist critique of solution-focused therapy, and multiple chapters on parenting and play therapy. Her interests include supervision, postmodern therapies, feminism, couple therapy, and technology in teaching and therapy.

Mary J. Didelot, PhD, is an associate professor of graduate counseling and development at Purdue University Calumet. She is also Department Chair of the graduate program in secondary education. She has numerous national and international publications and presentations in the areas of logotherapy, spirituality, and leadership. In addition, Dr. Didelot engages in private practice and consultation.

Faith Drew is a doctoral candidate in the marriage and family therapy program at Texas Tech University. Faith is a licensed marriage and family therapy associate and a licensed professional counselor intern.

Scott A. Edwards, PhD, LMFT, is Director of Internships and an assistant professor in the marriage and family therapy department at Seattle Pacific University in Seattle, Washington. In addition to teaching and supervising within a COAMFTE-accredited program, he provides therapy to couples and families. He received his bachelor's degree in psychology from Cornell University in 1991 and his master's degree in marriage and family therapy from Auburn University in 1996. In 2001, Dr. Edwards received his PhD in marriage and family therapy from Virginia Polytechnic Institute and State University.

Christie Eppler, PhD, is an assistant professor in school counseling in the School of Education of Seattle Pacific University. Her clinical training covers the complete age span of children and youth as demonstrated by two years counseling with children and families in an elementary school setting, four years of clinical work with teens and their families at a community-based clinic, and one year counseling college students. Her current work focuses on teaching and qualitatively researching family advocacy in K–12 settings, using narratives when counseling K–12 students, and exploring resiliency during times of transition.

Kimanne Foraker-Koons is a master's candidate in marriage and family counseling at Governors State University in University Park, Illinois. She worked with local psychologists to design and create Ident dolls, used to help sexually and physically abused children. With a background in law enforcement, she assisted in creating Lock Out Child Krime (L.O.C.K.), an organization responsible for changing, improving, and strengthening state and federal laws pertaining to child molesters and the victims of child molestation. She co-authored a chapter in *The Therapist's Notebook: Resources for Working with Children.*

Nancy L. A. Forth, PhD, is a counselor educator and an assistant professor with the counselor education department at Central Missouri State University. Dr. Forth primarily teaches clinical courses as well as providing supervision to master's-level counselors in training. Dr. Forth is a licensed professional counselor and a national certified counselor, a member of the American Counseling Association and the Association for Counselor Education and Supervision, and has varied clinical experience. Her interests and completed works surround the use of creativity in clinical practice and supervision.

Melanie Frey is a student at Purdue University Calumet working toward a master's degree in marriage and family therapy. She is a therapist intern at the Samaritan Counseling Center. Ms. Frey has worked with a variety of clientele including couples, individuals, and families with various concerns. In addition, she is conducting a research project analyzing how parental psychological symptoms of anxiety and depression or marital satisfaction affect the parent's perception of the child's behavior.

Lisa A. Hollingsworth, PsyD, is an associate professor and Department Chair of Graduate Counseling and Development at Purdue University Calumet. She has numerous national and international publications and presentations in the areas of logotherapy and spirituality. In addition, Dr. Hollingsworth maintains a private practice.

René A. Jones is currently in private practice in marriage and family therapy and sex therapy. She holds two master's degrees, one from Purdue University Calumet in marriage and family therapy and the other from the University of Pennsylvania in human sexuality education.

Günnur Karakurt, MS, received her master's degree from Middle East Technical University, Ankara, Turkey. She is currently working toward her doctorate at Purdue University. Her interests include emotion-focused family therapy and culture, development of affect regulation in families, the role of the regulation of feelings in violence, sexual abuse, externalizing and internalizing behaviors, jealousy, extramarital relationships, and relationship stability. Günnur cofacilitated a female adult survivors of incest support group for more than a year.

Margaret L. Keeling, PhD, is an assistant professor and director of clinical training in the marriage and family therapy doctoral program at Virginia Polytechnic Institute and State University, Blacksburg, Virginia. Her research and clinical interests include developing innovative treatment approaches for populations who underutilize therapy or who have limited access to therapeutic services. She has traveled widely, particularly in Asia, and recently conducted a clinical training workshop in Jakarta, Indonesia, along with Dr. Fred Piercy, to introduce family therapy theory and practice ideas to mental health workers preparing to assist tsunami survivors in the Indonesian province of Aceh.

Luciano L'Abate, PhD (Duke), is a fellow of Divisions 12 and 43 of the American Psychological Association and professor emeritus of psychology at Georgia State University in Atlanta. He is a diplomate and former examiner of the American Board of Professional Psychology and fellow and approved supervisor of the American Association for Marriage and Family Therapy; author and co-author of over 250 papers, chapters, and book reviews in professional journals and author, co-author, editor, and co-editor of thirty-eight books (two additional books are in press and three book proposals are under editorial review). His work has been published in Argentina, China, Denmark, Finland, Canada, Germany, Italy, Japan, Korea, and Poland.

Christopher Latty, PhD, is an assistant professsor in the human development family studies area in the College of Human Environmental Studies at Central Michigan University. He completed his marriage and family therapy education and clinical training at Michigan State University.

Caryn Levington, PsyD, is a professor of psychology at William Rainey Harper College. She is also director of the college's health and psychological services. Dr. Levington has numerous national and international publications and presentations in the areas of existentialism and philosophy. In addition, she participates in consulting.

Donald J. Olund, MA, LPC, is currently a marriage and family counselor at Lifework Counseling Center, Downers Grove, Illinois. He received a bachelor's degree in psychology and his master's degree in marriage and family counseling from Governors State University. He was selected student speaker for commencement services at Governors State University and is a member of Chi Sigma Iota. Professional interests include specializing in marriage and family counseling, helping families adjust to life cycle changes, particularly those with parent and adolescent transitions, and he also specializes in integrating spirituality and counseling. Prior to entering professional counseling, he served twenty years in pastoral ministry.

Jolene Oppawsky, PhD, is a diplomate psychotherapist and approved clinical supervisor, a University of Phoenix faculty member and clinical supervisor in the master's program in counseling, Tucson, Arizona.

Fred P. Piercy, PhD, is a professor and department head of human development at Virginia Tech. Dr. Piercy joined Virginia Tech in August 2000 after twenty-five years teaching family therapy, the last eighteen of which were at Purdue University. He is an active researcher and has worked in a variety of mental health settings. Dr. Piercy has written over 160 published articles, five books, and thirty-five funded grants. He is the co-editor of *Research Methods in Family Therapy, Second Edition* (with Douglas Sprenkle, Guilford Press, 2005) and *Handbook for the Clinical Treatment of Infidelity* (with Katherine Hertlein and Joseph Wetchler, The Haworth Press, 2005), and co-author of *Family Therapy Sourcebook* (with Douglas Sprenkle, Joseph Wetchler, and Associates, Guilford Press, 1986, 1996) and *Stop Marital Fights Before They Start* (with Norman Lobsenz, Berkley Press, 1994. He has collaborated extensively with colleagues from the University of Indonesia and Atma Jaya University (in Jakarta, Indonesia) and was the principle investigator of a World AIDS Foundation–funded project in Indonesia.

Patricia A. Robey, MA, LPC, NCC, RTC, is a senior faculty member of the William Glasser Institute. She has taught the concepts of choice theory and reality therapy in the United States, Canada, Europe, and Asia, addressing the application of these ideas in the fields of counseling, corrections, education, business, and health care as well as to individuals interested in personal growth and development. Ms. Robey is a lecturer at Governors State University, where she teaches master's-level students in counseling. As a counselor at Oak Lawn Family Services in Illinois, she works with individuals, groups, families, couples, and children. She is currently pursuing her doctorate in counselor education at Northern Illinois University.

Howard G. Rosenthal, EdD, is a professor and program coordinator of Human Services at St. Louis Community College at Florissant Valley. He is the author of two best sellers, the *Encyclopedia of Counseling* (Brunner-Routledge) and *Favorite Counseling and Therapy Techniques* (Brunner-Routledge), as well as a number of other books, including the first-ever *Human Services Dictionary* (Brunner-Routledge). Counselors nationwide use his materials to pass state licensing and national board certification exams. His book, *Therapy's Best: Practical Advice and Gems of Wisdom from Twenty Accomplished Counselors and Therapists* (Haworth), includes interviews with some of the top therapists in the world.

Atsuko Seto, PhD, is an assistant professor and community counseling program coordinator with the Department of Counselor Education at the College of New Jersey. She is a licensed professional counselor and a national certified counselor, and has experience in counseling children and their families, including providing crisis interventions. Dr. Seto primarily teaches Introduction to Marriage and Family Therapy, practicum, and internship courses as well as providing individual supervision to master's-level counselors in training. Her interest areas in research and publication include creativity in counseling, counseling Japanese families, cross-national couples, and multicultural counseling and training. Dr. Seto is a member of the American Association for Marriage and Family Therapy and the International Association of Marriage and Family Counselors.

Kolleen L. Simons currently works in private practice serving both adolescents and adults. She is a former law enforcement officer who continues to work with crime victims and rape surivors.

Belinda Stepnowski currently works at Southlake Center for Mental Health in Merrillville, Indiana, as a community assistance specialist and case manager in the Partial Hospitalization Program. She is currently seeking a master of science degree in child development and family studies with a specialization in marriage and family therapy at Purdue University Calumet in Hammond, Indiana. Her research focus involves determining if positive factors such as happiness and relationship satisfaction can buffer against the act of infidelity in a relationship.

Sophia Treyger is currently a student at Purdue University Calumet working toward a master's degree in marriage and family therapy. She does therapy at the Success Center in Lansing, Illinois. She has worked with developmentally disabled children and their families for close to four years before seeking a degree in couple and family therapy. Her clinical interests include working with couples, sex therapy with individuals and couples, families in which incest has occurred, sexual abuse and rape, and working with adolescents. Her research interests include positive sexual identity formation among queer women.

Joe M. Utay, EdD, LPC, NCC, LMFT, is a faculty member in the Department of Counseling at Indiana University of Pennsylvania, where he teaches and is Internship Coordinator for the counseling program. He is also Director of Counseling and Evaluation Services for Total Learning Centers in Wexford, Pennsylvania, where his roles include school psychologist, counselor, and family therapist working with children, adolescents, adults, couples, families, and groups. Dr. Utay is a clinical member of the American Association for Marriage and Family Therapy.

Erica J. Weekes is a graduate student in the marriage and family therapy program at Seattle Pacific University in Seattle, Washington. She received her bachelor's degree in psychology from St. Olaf College in 2004. Erica has previous experience facilitating experiential therapy and high adventure groups. Currently, she provides therapy as a marriage and family therapy intern at Renton Area Youth and Family Services in Seattle, Washington, where she works with children, adolescents, and their families.

Andrea K. Wittenborn, MS, is a doctoral candidate in marriage and family therapy at Purdue University in West Lafayette, Indiana. She is a student member of the American Association for Marriage and Family Therapy and the American Psychological Association. Andrea cofacilitated an adult incest survivors' support group for one year. Her previous work includes examining attachment and affect regulation in couple relationships, especially in the context of emotion-focused therapy.

Adam Zagelbaum, PhD, is an assistant professor at Governors State University in the school counseling master's degree program. He received his bachelor's degree in psychology from the University of Florida in 1996, a master's degree in counseling psychology from the University of Southern Mississippi in 1998, and a counseling psychology doctorate in 2005 from Ball State University. He has been licensed as a school counselor in Indiana and Washington. Previous works include *A Review of the School Counseling Literature for Themes Evolving from the Education Trust Initiative* (Professional School Counseling, 2003) and *Increasing Adolescent Awareness of At-Risk Behaviors via Psychosocial Drama* (The Arts in Psychotherapy, 2004).

He has also presented at multiple regional and national conferences regarding similar topics in adolescent growth, development, conflict management, and mental health.

Chunhong Zhang, PhD, is a recent graduate from the marriage and family therapy program of Purdue University, West Lafayette, Indiana. Her previous work includes research and clinical work in family therapy with Alzheimer's disease, family therapy with sexual minority youth, family group therapy with incarcerated adolescents, and cross-cultural application of emotionally focused couple therapy. She has presented her work at local, regional, and national conferences. Her current research interests focus on work and family interface, family resiliency, and marriage and family therapy training and supervision.

Preface

Most therapists recognize that therapy is a blend of art and science. Seasoned therapists recognize that theory must be augmented by creativity, and they ultimately must do what works. This includes interventions, psychoeducational handouts, homework, and field-tested activities. They also acknowledge that while they are in the trenches, they are often in the trenches by themselves, and when they reach for ideas, they often reach to their bookshelves. The *Therapist's Notebook: Handouts and Activities for Use in Psychotherapy* (Hecker, Deacon, & Associates, 1998) was originally designed to put ideas at clinicians' fingertips when they needed homework, handouts, or activities for use in psychotherapy. Apparently, therapists reached for the *Therapist's Notebook* often, and the demand called for us to compile *The Therapist's Notebook, Volume 2: More Homework, Handouts, and Activities for Use in Psychotherapy*.

To meet this need, we pulled together a cadre of talented therapists from numerous disciplines who shared their therapy acumen. They have brought therapy activities, homework, psychoeducational ideas, handouts, and interventions once again to your bookshelves. These authors understand the need to be theoretical, creative, and practical in therapy. They understand that clients must be understood and respected, that clients may share dark feelings in therapy, or conversely that clients and therapists may sometimes need to have fun in therapy. Our authors understand that the creative synergy between client and therapist can in and of itself be healing. This book offers opportunities for that synergy.

In this book, the client populations you may see in your practice are covered: couples, children, adolescents, families, adults, and groups. In addition, common issues that most clinicians encounter in their treatment are covered: trauma and abuse recovery, divorce and stepfamilies, spirituality, illness, intimacy, communication, expression of feelings, career development, addictions, procrastination, family conflict, dreams, immigration, relaxation and visualization, and body image. In addition, we also provide some therapist tools that are ready to use, such as a very thorough family strengths and concerns assessment, a therapy intake form, a quick depression assessment, and a training activity to promote active listening.

The book offers readers a myriad of theoretical perspectives, including cognitive behavioral, narrative therapy, solution focused, choice theory and reality therapy, REBT (Rational-Emotive Behavior Therapy), strategic family therapy, experiential, art, and play therapies, couples approaches including Gottman and emotionally focused therapy, medical family therapy, Jungian, family-of-origin therapy, and adventure-based therapy. However, many of the creative interventions written from a specific theoretical perspective can be easily adapted to fit a clinician's preferred theoretical approach. In addition, several chapters include activities that are empirically derived.

ORGANIZATION OF THE BOOK

In the table of contents, we have attempted to group the thirty-four chapters according to their primary topic, but there is much overlap, and many chapters easily could have been listed under several categories. The eight sections are Couples; Children, Adolescents, and Families; Adults; Groups; Trauma and Abuse Recovery; Divorce and Stepfamilies; Spirituality; and Therapist Tools.

In *The Therapist's Notebook, Volume 2* most chapters follow the same format: first is the title and name of the author, followed by the type of contribution contained in the chapter, which is either an activity that can be used by clinicians in session, a homework assignment they can give to clients, a handout to be used in therapy, or perhaps some combination of the three. Many chapters have handouts that guide clinicians in utilizing the activities or interventions, or can be given to clients to use as homework. A few chapters have a slightly different format because they were originally published in the *Journal of Clinical Activities, Assignments & Handouts in Psychotherapy Practice,* which gave birth to this book series.

Next is the Objectives section that contains a short summary of the purpose of the chapter, which is followed by the Rationale for Use section. In the Instructions section that follows, the authors offer a clear description on how to implement the activity, handout, or homework in session. A brief vignette supplements the chapters and offers readers rich insight into how to use the activity, handout, or homework assignment. (Note: All the names of clients and important identifying information in the Brief Vignette sections have been changed to protect client confidentiality.) The next two sections are Suggestions for Follow-Up and Contraindications, which offer guidance and suggestions on how to expand on the material contained in the chapter. Finally, this book expands on the typical references found in most of the literature, as three different types of reference sections are offered. After the References section is the Professional Readings and Resources section, which offers clinicians a helpful list of additional resources for further study. Then Bibliotherapy Sources for Clients offers clinicians a list of sources that may be shared with clients. These sources include helpful books for adults, parents, and children, Web sites, and videos. Many readers tell us that they found the lists of resources included at the end of the chapters in *The Therapist's Notebook, Volume 2* quite useful to themselves and clients.

Many chapters contain a handout (or handouts) at the end. These have been designed to use with clients in implementing the activity or homework assignment, or as a resource for the clinician.

We believe that this volume offers readers a unique collection of tried and true tools for practical yet creative use in the therapy room. We hope that it inspires you to do your best work, that it helps you heal clients, and that it will never gather dust on your bookshelf.

REFERENCE

Hecker, L., Deacon, S., & Associates. (1998). *The Therapist's Notebook: Handouts and Activities for Use in Psychotherapy.* Binghamton, NY: The Haworth Press.

Acknowledgments

We would like to acknowledge our many wonderful and knowledgeable contributors who made this book possible. We also want to acknowledge the people behind the scenes who toiled to make this book a reality: Michelle Mannino, Julie Ramisch, Kathy Schultz, Jessica Roberson, Heather Paul, and the good people at Haworth Press. Thanks go out to Mike Flannery for his ongoing support. A special thanks to our families and friends whose love and support sustains us. A hug for Aaron (alias Mr. Krikkit) and Noah (alias Jeff).

We appreciate our friendship foundation on which this book was built. We appreciate those in our lives who offer support and turn shadowy days into light.

Special thanks to John and Jonathan.

The Therapist's Notebook, Volume 2
© 2007 by The Haworth Press, Inc. All rights reserved.
doi:10.1300/5550_d

SECTION I:
COUPLES

Couples Drawing Together

Shannon B. Dermer
Kimanne Foraker-Koons

Type of Contribution: *Activity, Handout*

Objectives

Couples Drawing Together is an activity based on research describing successful relationships and on the experiential premises of fun, spontaneity, and honest communication. Clients are asked to draw answers to a series of questions designed to assess basic knowledge about their partner and to express how they think and feel about him or her. The goal is to assess the detail and accuracy of clients' information about one another, assist clients in expressing themselves freely and honestly, explore their feelings of respect and affection for one another, and increase overall positive sentiment in the relationship. The activity is meant to be a playful way to share aspects of each individual and the relationship.

Rationale for Use

The rationale for Couples Drawing Together is based on research about couples and couple therapy. John Gottman and Susan Johnson are two leaders in the study of relationships and couple therapy. Gottman (1999) focuses on strengthening relationships during nonconflictual times and the matching of emotional styles, whereas Johnson (1996) focuses on sharing emotions and normalizing attachment needs. The activity, Couples Drawing Together, is congruent with the goals of both Gottman's and Johnson's approaches. In addition, the activity is based on the experiential premises of processing emotion in the moment and injecting spontaneity, action, and fun into sessions.

Gottman's Sound Marital House Theory

According to John Gottman's (1999) research on relationships, the foundation of a happy, stable relationship is a strong friendship. Creating a bond based on mutual respect and enjoyment of each other's company during nonconflictual times creates a buffer against negativity during relational conflict (Gottman, 1999, 2000). Having current information about one's partner's life, expressing fondness and admiration, and being open to connecting with one's partner rather than distancing are all variables in creating a robust relationship.

Two key foundational aspects of creating a strong relationship, according to Gottman (1999, 2000, 2004), are *love maps* and the *fondness and admiration system*. Love maps are the amount of space people have dedicated in their minds to their partners. Couples who have strong love maps have detailed, current knowledge of a partner's daily happenings, hopes and dreams, and likes and dislikes (Gottman, 2004). In addition to love maps, the fondness and admiration system is strong in stable, happy couples. This system consists of the amount of regard, appreciation, esteem, warmth, caring, and love each person feels for the other. The ability to interpret actions in a positive or neutral manner involves a recursive relationship with the fondness and admiration system.

A couple's fondness and admiration for each other may be expressed in many different ways, both verbally and nonverbally. For example, they may express positive feelings through direct, verbal communication such as, "Honey, I'm always amazed at how clever you are." In addition, their fondness and admiration may be expressed through physical affection (e.g., hugging, kissing, touching, eye contact) and indirectly through how they talk about each other to family, friends, and co-workers. Gottman (1999) believes that as long as there is a trace of fondness and admiration, then there is hope for a relationship.

Johnson's Emotionally Focused Therapy

Susan Johnson's work is based on a combination of attachment theory, systems theory, and experiential therapy. The goal is to create a strong, positive emotional bond between the couple that allows each to be emotionally vulnerable within a safe context (Johnson, 1996). Congruent with attachment theory, she believes both children and adults need to create reliable, safe, secure, loving attachments (bonds) to others. These relationships are a source of security, protection, and comfort. For children, the attachment figure is usually a parent and for adults it is usually a committed partner or spouse. The pathway to creating these emotional bonds in adult relationships is through being able identify and express one's own attachment needs and to be accessible and responsive to a partner's needs.

Basically, Johnson (1996) believes the key to building a strong relationship is the ability to recognize and share one's primary emotions within the context of a safe relationship. Primary emotions are biologically based emotions (i.e., love, sadness, fear, joy, anger) that help people monitor and regulate attachments. Infants are born with the ability to express these primary emotions. However, over time people sometimes learn to use the expression of secondary emotional responses as a way to protect themselves from getting hurt, or because the expression of certain emotions is more culturally acceptable. For example, a husband who missed his wife when she was away on business may express anger at her for neglecting him and the children. The primary emotion may have been sadness, but admitting sadness may have made him feel vulnerable and open to possible rejection. In addition, society tends to send the message to men that anger is more acceptable than sadness. People sometimes get so adept at fitting into cultural norms and protecting themselves from getting hurt that secondary emotions emerge automatically.

Despite messages from society to the contrary, needs, desires, and expression of primary emotions are healthy and adaptive for both men and women. Couples sometimes need to be trained to be in the moment (consistent with experiential therapy) in order to be comfortable recognizing and sharing their attachment needs. Being in the moment requires that people are able to be present focused and identify and share feelings that are occurring at a particular moment (rather than discussing cognitively what they have felt in the past). Virginia Satir (1976), a leader in experiential family therapy, called this *congruence* or emotional honesty. This involves congruence between what people actually feel and how they verbally and nonverbally communicate feelings as they are feeling them. Satir (1976) believed that the freedom to see the world, oneself, and other people as they are, rather than how they "should" be, and being free to take risks on one's own behalf, are essential to one's health. Similarly, Johnson (1996) believes that the key to a happy, stable relationship is one in which both partners can identify, share, and accept the honest expression of primary emotions. In other words, each partner is willing to take the risk of being vulnerable with the other person.

Drawing Gottman and Johnson Together

Couples Drawing Together allows therapists to assess couples' love maps, fondness and admiration, and their ability to be spontaneous and playful. In addition, the format of the activity encourages couples to be open and honest, to be vulnerable to one another, to connect with one another, to be in the moment, to express their affection, and to be playful. Depending on the therapist's theoretical orientation, the activity can be used to highlight emotional, cognitive, and behavioral aspects of the clients' interactions during the activity.

A couple's knowledge about each other, their affection level, and their ability to be vulnerable may be assessed through pencil-and-paper instruments and interviews rather than an activity. However, utilizing a playful, interactive approach has several advantages over traditional assessment formats. Although counselors may readily think of playfulness as a technique to use with children, it can also be helpful with adults (Sori, 2000). These types of activities promote spontaneity, communication, and interaction while decreasing defensiveness (Gil, 1994). "Play can bring people together in a common, pleasurable task, which inherently promotes disinhibition and enjoyment" (p. 41). Playful activities in couple therapy allow therapists and distressed couples to inject humor into sessions and discuss potentially painful subjects in a nondefensive manner.

Although serious subjects are broached in couple therapy, it does not always have to be done seriously. Couples Drawing Together provides an avenue for assessing love maps, ability to communicate, and the fondness and admiration system in a manner that encourages spontaneity, fun, connection, and open expression of feeling. The therapist creates a safe, enjoyable environment in which couples share their views and feelings.

Instructions

For Couples Drawing Together, the therapist will need a white board or chalk board and the appropriate writing utensils. If possible, provide each client with his or her own board or utilize one large board and draw a line down the middle to divide the space (if you want to save pictures, use a large pad of drawing paper for each client or take pictures of the activity). The couple will be asked to draw various objects, ideas, or perceptions (see questions listed in the handout at the end of the chapter) on his or her drawing space. For example, clients may be asked to draw out three things they think their partner admires about them.

The therapist should ask clients at the beginning of the session if they are willing to do an activity to find out how well they know each other. Explain that they both will be asked to draw their responses to a series of questions. Assure clients that it doesn't matter whether they can draw well or not. They will have up to one minute to draw an answer and will have a little time to explain the drawing.

During the game there are a few guidelines. The therapist should ask each person to briefly explain his or her drawing. In addition, each partner can comment on the other person's drawing and ask questions. However, this is not the time for extended conversations. The therapist should actively structure the conversations to limit the time spent on discussion, interrupt overly negative exchanges, and help the couple express their feelings about the drawings. If a couple wants to discuss a topic in more detail, the therapist should restate the issue and assure the couple that they can discuss it in the next session.

Depending on the length of the session, the therapist may or may not have time to go through all of the questions on the handout. Based on the therapist's knowledge of the couple, he or she may want to go through the handout before the session and mark which questions are the most appropriate or important to ask the couple. There needs to be enough time to explain the game, spend three minutes on each question (one minute to draw and two minutes to briefly discuss the drawings), and have ten minutes at the end of session to debrief about the process of the game. If anything about the content was particularly surprising, upsetting, or positive, the therapist should let the couple know that these things will be more thoroughly discussed in the next session. Alternatively, the therapist may want to schedule a session that is longer than usual so that these topics can be processed in more detail immediately after the activity.

Brief Vignette

Linda and Carolyn sought couples counseling because they were drifting apart. They have been together for eight years, had a commitment ceremony six years ago, and adopted a newborn two years ago. Linda and Carolyn lived in the same household, but stated that they felt like "two ships that pass in the night." The couple stated they had lost touch with each other due to the daily stresses and strains of life.

They reported that they used to discuss issues often and were very affectionate, but had distanced in the last year. Linda tended to bring up "hot topics" that Carolyn worried could escalate into an argument, so Carolyn retreated to the bedroom to listen to music or read. In addition, the couple indicated there had been a dramatic decline in display of nonsexual and sexual affection in the past six months.

Despite the decline in discussions, physical affection, and sexual interaction, the couple still displayed much fondness and affection for each other. Their affection and respect for each other were evident as they recalled the beginning of their relationship with warmth and laughter. In addition, during sessions Linda and Carolyn showed mutual support for expressing each other's emotions and feelings. They each paid attention while the other was speaking, would often reach out to hold each other's hands, and comforted each other when upsetting topics were discussed. Both Linda and Carolyn asserted they still cared deeply for each other and wished to stay committed. They felt, however, that the pattern that had developed needed to change in order for the relationship to progress further.

After three sessions, the cotherapists decided to use Couples Drawing Together as an intervention with the couple. During the first few sessions, it had already been established that the couple had a strong friendship, were open to humor, and could express affection for each other within a safe environment. However, over the past year they had gotten into a pattern of distancing and avoidance out of hurt or fear of conflicts escalating. In trying so hard to protect each other and their relationship from conflict, it was having the paradoxical effect of eroding their relationship. The cotherapists decided to utilize the game as a way to further assess the couple, update their cognitive love maps, continue to strengthen their fondness and admiration system, highlight their strengths as a couple, help them express their thoughts and emotions in a safe environment, and inject some fun into their interactions.

In the fourth session, Linda and Carolyn played Couples Drawing Together on a large chalkboard. Neither was particularly artistic, but they enjoyed trying to draw the best they could. They laughed at each other's answers and attempts at drawing. They would tease each other about their stick figure drawings, ask each other why they chose a particular answer, and sometimes explain why they disagreed with their partner's answer.

At times the session took a serious tone, especially when the couple was asked to draw each other's favorite way of showing physical affection. Linda drew the two of them cuddling on the couch and Carolyn drew a picture of two stick figures on top of each other in bed. While discussing their pictures, Carolyn started to tear up and explained that they had not had any kind of sexual activity in more than six months. The therapists asked if sex would be an okay topic to discuss next session and the couple agreed.

During the debriefing, the couple laughed and playfully made fun of each other's pictures. They also stated that they were surprised at how serious the game had been at times. Carolyn started to tear up again and Linda took her hand. Both stated that the game had been fun and challenging. They were looking forward to discussing some of the topics that had surfaced during the game. Both clients were complimented for their participation.

In addition, they were asked if, besides sex, there were any other topics they would like to make sure to discuss next session. Carolyn stated that she would also like to discuss their views of the world. Linda had drawn Carolyn's view as all dark and with squiggly lines. During the game, Linda explained that she thought Carolyn viewed the world as rather dark and chaotic. Carolyn agreed with this view but said it was something that she wanted to change.

Her view hadn't always been like that. It had changed since she went on hormone replacement therapy after a hysterectomy approximately eighteen months ago. She explained that she felt different ever since the operation and like her life and body were out of control, but she had only minimally discussed these issues with her doctor. She stated, "It's like when the house is a mess, it affects my whole day or week and it distracts me to know that things are out of order. I feel like my body and my relationship have been a mess for a while and I want to get things back in order. The house is still there—it's just covered by a bunch of clutter."

The therapist assured them that they would discuss sex and "getting their house back in order" next time. In addition, the therapist asked Carolyn to make an appointment with her physician for a checkup and discuss any physical changes she felt had occurred since the hysterectomy and discuss the possible physical, sexual, and mental side effects of the hormone replacement therapy. The therapist explained that the body, mind, and relationships all affected one another and so it was important to pay attention to each.

Suggestions for Follow-Up

The process of the game can be discussed in follow-up sessions. The therapists may comment on the couple interaction during the game to reinforce helpful interactions and to correct unhelpful ones. For example, the therapist may point out how the couple was critical of each other during the game and have them practice expressing complaints without criticism. Discussion of answers can be used to add to love maps and to stimulate conversation around the fondness and admiration system. Questions 7-13 overtly focus on the fondness and admiration systems and the other questions focus on knowledge of each other. The couple should discuss in more detail information they didn't know or that the partner disagreed with, and what they liked and admired about each other.

The therapist should help coach couples on how to share their answers in a way that encourages discussion rather than shutting it down because of defensiveness and self-protection. Clients need to become comfortable expressing and listening to wants, desires, and needs. The drawings provide a springboard for these discussions. Various therapeutic models can be used to accomplish this, but we suggest Gottman's (1999) or Johnson's (1996) models discussed previously. Gottman (1999) would help the couple to strengthen their relational friendship through working on cognitive love maps, increasing their fondness and admiration, having them be open to bids for attention from the partner, being open to influence from the partner, complaining rather than criticizing, helping them negotiate problems that are fixable, and accepting problems that are related to differences in worldviews and are therefore not fixable. Johnson (1996) would focus more on having the couple identify and embrace their attachment needs, become vulnerable with a partner and accept a partner's vulnerability, help them identify and express primary emotions, soften the clients' views of each other, help them express their need and desire for each other, reinterpret their struggles as trying to get their attachment needs met, and help the couple to express their attachment needs in a way that is more likely to bring a partner closer rather than pushing him or her away.

For couples who already have a strong relational friendship or who are already good at openly expressing feelings and accepting a partner's expression of feelings, therapists can use the opportunity to reinforce client strengths and point out how those strengths correlate with healthy relationships. If a couple struggles with the activity, then the therapist can use the debriefing time after the game and in subsequent sessions to highlight strengths and coach clients in areas that need improvement. Although the game should be completed in one session, discussion of the game may occur throughout subsequent sessions.

Contraindications

Couples Drawing Together should be used with clients where the therapist is confident the couple are able to express at least some fondness and admiration and have at least basic, current knowledge about each other. If they are extremely negative or contemptuous of each other, the game may be misused as another way to insult a partner. This activity is meant to enhance or highlight knowledge and affection, not create them. Therapists should avoid using these types of games if there is a recent history of violence in the relationship or with couples who will use the game as a means for showing contempt for each other.

References

Gil, E. (1994). *Play in family therapy.* New York: Guilford.

Gottman, J. M. (1999). *The marriage clinic: A scientifically based marital therapy.* New York: W.W. Norton.

Gottman, J. M. (2000). *The seven principles for making marriage work.* New York: Three Rivers Press.

Gottman, J. M. (2004). (Ed.). *The marriage clinic: Casebook.* New York: W.W. Norton.

Johnson, S. M. (1996). *The practice of emotionally focused marital therapy: Creating connection.* New York: Brunner/Mazel.

Satir, V. (1976). *Making contact.* Millbrae, CA: Celestial Arts.

Sori, C. F. (2000). *Training family therapists to work with children in family therapy: A modified Delphi study.* Unpublished doctoral dissertation, Purdue University.

Professional Readings and Resources

Dattilio, F. M. (1998). *Case studies in couple and family therapy: Systemic and cognitive perspectives.* New York: Guilford.

Gottman, J. M. (1999). *The marriage clinic: A scientifically based marital therapy.* New York: W. W. Norton.

Gottman, J. M. (2000). *The seven principles for making marriage work.* New York: Three Rivers Press.

Gottman, J. S. (2004). (Ed.). *The marriage clinic: Casebook.* New York: W. W. Norton.

Gurman, A. S., & Jacobson, N. S. (2002). *The clinical handbook of couple therapy* (3rd ed.). New York: Guilford.

Johnson, S. M. (2004). *The practice of emotionally focused marital therapy: Creating connection.* New York: Brunner/Mazel.

Bibliotherapy Sources for Clients

Gottman, J. M. (2000). *The seven principles for making marriage work.* New York: Three Rivers Press.

Gottman, J. M. (2002). *The relationship cure: A 5 step guide to strengthening your marriage, family, and friendships.* New York: Three Rivers Press.

HANDOUT 1.1

*COUPLES DRAWING TOGETHER

Instructions: You will each be asked to draw, at the same time, the answers to some questions. You will have up to one minute to draw your answer and you each will have a little time to explain your drawing. Please do not worry about your artistic ability—the goal is more about speed than artistry.

1. Draw your partner's favorite piece of clothing.
2. Draw your partner's favorite holiday.
3. Draw your partner's least favorite holiday.
4. Draw your partner's family.
5. Draw your partner's view of the world.
6. Draw your partner's view of passion.
7. Draw three things your partner does well.
8. Draw three things your partner does that make you laugh.
9. Draw two things your partner did for you last week that made you smile.
10. Draw two things your partner has done that make you proud.
11. Draw your partner's best physical feature.
12. Draw your partner's best quality.
13. Draw your favorite activity to do with your partner.
14. Draw a scene from your partner's favorite movie.
15. Draw your partner's favorite sleeping position.
16. Draw your partner's favorite way of showing affection.
17. Draw your partner's biggest fear.
18. Draw your partner's dream car.
19. Draw your partner's dream house.
20. Draw your partner's favorite time or place to fall asleep.

*This handout is based on concepts developed by Gottman (1999).

Dermer, S. B., & Foraker-Koons, K. (2007). Couples drawing together. In L. L. Hecker, C. F. Sori, & Associates, *The therapist's notebook, volume 2: More homework, handouts, and activities for use in psychotherapy* (pp. 3-9). Binghamton, NY: The Haworth Press.

Finding a Connection

Sophia Treyger
Melanie Frey
Belinda Stepnowski

Type of Contribution: *Activity, Handouts*

Objectives

This chapter describes an emotionally focused activity that can be utilized when a therapist is conducting couple therapy. The purpose of this activity is for a couple to identify and distinguish their emotions within their relationship and to delve into the emotions that are generally not shared in a relationship. In order to help a couple explore and identify these emotions, the activity educates the couple about secondary versus primary emotions (Johnson, 2004). Primary emotions are biologically based and are usually our first responses to a situation. Secondary emotions are built on primary emotions and involve more thought and interpretation. They are the emotions more readily shown and expressed (Johnson, 2004).

This activity provides a way for clients to talk about their emotional experience, while their partner actively listens to their needs in the relationship. The overarching goal of the activity is for the couple to find comfort in sharing their primary emotions with their partner; in addition, partners are encouraged to actively listen and express their needs within the relationship. It is hoped that each partner finds comfort, security, and connection with their partner after completing the activity.

Rationale for Use

Emotions can be very difficult to talk about for some clients. It is sometimes particularly difficult to show outwardly the emotions that we feel on the inside. This activity is useful because it provides clients with explicit examples of types of emotions they may be feeling during arguments, discussions, or situations that occur within their relationship. The activity also promotes active listening by requiring the couple to listen and respond to emotions and needs that their partner is expressing. Finally, the activity promotes the safety of the client who is expressing emotions and needs within the relationship. After completing this activity, the couple may feel safe to discuss some of their underlying emotions that may have felt threatening for them to discuss or display before.

Instructions

Give partners the Finding a Connection packet to complete in session (see Handouts 2.1-2.5).

The Therapist's Notebook, Volume 2
© 2007 by The Haworth Press, Inc. All rights reserved.
doi:10.1300/5550_02

Step 1: Ask the clients to read the first page individually and then write down the corresponding answers to each question without discussing their responses with each other. Write what the argument was about and how it began; describe the argument using a dialogue; and then write what stopped or ended the argument. Once each individual completes this page, the therapist begins discussing each partner's responses. Each partner's response is discussed at length to help the therapist and couple identify and externalize the interactional pattern underlying the arguments.

Step 2: On the second page, each partner independently circles the pictures that depict the feelings that he or she usually expresses to the other during interactions or arguments. These are deemed the external feelings or secondary emotions. The therapist asks each individual to describe his or her reactions to the partner when the partner is expressing secondary emotions. This gives each partner an opportunity to hear what the other's triggers are, for example. It also gives each one an opportunity to vent his or her feelings.

Step 3: For the third page, each partner independently circles the pictures that depict the feelings he or she does not want the other to see. These are deemed the internal feelings or primary emotions. The therapist explains to the couple that these are the feelings that many people experience but are reluctant to share with their partner due to mistrust or fear of being vulnerable. The therapist gives each person an opportunity to express his or her primary emotions while gauging the reaction of the partner. Each partner is asked to listen while the other speaks about his or her experience using primary emotions during arguments. The therapist speaks at length with partners about their experiences and helps the couple understand their interactional pattern in terms of their primary emotions. Helping the couple see their pattern and their partner in a new light are the keys to building trust between the members.

Step 4: For Worksheet A, each partner first writes down the feelings he or she wants the partner to know but is afraid to express openly.

Step 5: Still using Worksheet A, each partner fills in the blanks describing his or her primary and secondary emotions, and the details of the interactional pattern. Using the script in the worksheet, the therapist instructs them to recite to their partner their primary emotions during arguments.

Step 6: After each partner has expressed his or her primary emotions, the therapist asks the couple to describe their experience when hearing each partner express primary emotions. Both partners are asked to describe what they would like the other to do or say when he or she is describing his or her primary emotions.

Step 7: For Worksheet B, each partner independently writes down how he or she can help the other work toward his or her needs for the relationship.

Step 8: Next, the couple discusses each list and works together to prioritize their needs. The therapist guides the couple to discuss their needs in terms of their primary emotions. The couple are encouraged to work collaboratively to support each other's needs.

Step 9: The final step in the activity is for the couple to brainstorm solutions that will help them support each other in meeting their individual needs. If necessary, the therapist will redirect the couple to their pattern and primary emotions when the couple get stuck during discussion.

Brief Vignette

Delia and Dave decided to enter therapy because Dave had suspicions that Delia was cheating on him. Delia exclaimed wholeheartedly that she was faithful, but Dave had difficulty believing her. Since Dave accused Delia of cheating, she became suspicious that Dave was cheating on her. The therapist learned in the second session that Delia had attempted suicide several months before and was hospitalized. She said that at the time of the attempt she was extremely depressed and hopeless because Dave had threatened to leave her on several occasions. This further increased her suspicions that he was cheating on her. The couple had three children together and the prospect of Dave leaving her made her anxious because of the inevitable financial and emotional burden that would ensue. She believed that if Dave left her, he would disappear from her and his children's lives.

The couple constantly snapped at each other during the first and second sessions and there was little opportunity for each individual to hear the other out. Furthermore, their therapist believed that their conversations together were going in circles. Consequently, the therapist decided to utilize the Finding a Connection activity over a span of eight sessions.

The therapist instructed each individual to look at the first page of the activity and to complete it independently. When each individual was done, the therapist gave each person an opportunity to state the facts of an argument they usually have. Although the page was completed independently, both descriptions of an argument were strikingly similar. They both chose an argument they had had earlier in the week. The therapist learned that an argument usually began when Delia was working late. Dave would call to ask her when she would be home. If Delia was not home when she specified, Dave would call her again and ask her when she would be home, using an angry tone. Delia would answer him angrily and hang up the phone. After Delia would arrive home, Dave would angrily ask her, using profanity, where she had been and Delia would answer that it was "none of his frigging business." This would trigger Dave to become enraged and he would begin screaming at her. He would curse at her, accuse her of being with another man, and threaten to leave her. At his point, Delia would usually begin to attend to the children while Dave would storm out of the house without telling her where he was going and when he would return. Dave would usually return later in the evening when everyone was asleep, crawl into bed with Delia, and try to have sex with her. Delia would usually tell him to leave her alone and that she was too tired to have sex. The next day the couple would go about their business like nothing had happened.

The therapist learned that this was a typical argument between them. She also learned that when either one tried to talk about his or her feelings, the other would shut down and walk away. The therapist surmised that their pattern consisted of one person trying to talk to the other while the other person withdrew. Both Delia and Dave took turns pursuing each other and distancing from each other. The therapist presented their pattern and they agreed that that is what was happening.

The therapist then instructed the couple to go on to the next page. Each person was asked to circle the pictures that depicted how each expressed external feelings to the other while in an argument. What did the partner see? Both circled "angry" and "enraged," and Dave circled "suspicious." The therapist discussed with the couple that often these are the emotions that people see during an argument. The discussion also covered what it was like for each partner when he or she was at the receiving end of such displays of emotion.

The following page gave the couple independently the opportunity to circle the feelings that each had on the inside; feelings that are usually not expressed to a partner. Delia circled "depressed," "overwhelmed," "sad," and "frightened." Dave circled "anxious," "suspicious," "depressed," "jealous," and "lonely." The therapist praised each individual for being honest about his or her internal emotions. They then had a discussion about what their pattern could mean to them in this new light. The therapist presented the possibility that each person's efforts to try to get close to the other had the opposite effect and in turn it would exacerbate the distancer-pursuer cycle. The therapist then gently suggested that perhaps each person was trying to protect the other from his or her true feelings so as not to burden the other. Through questioning of what their feelings meant to each one of them, the therapist learned that expressing their primary emotions was very painful for both of them, and each assumed that the other would not be able to handle the intense emotions.

Following this discussion, the couple, once again independently, completed Worksheet A. This gave them the opportunity to structure their thoughts so that they could present their thoughts and emotions to their partner. After completing the page, each partner turned to the other and expressed his or her primary emotions while the other listened. This segment of the session was markedly different from their previous interactions. Each allowed the other to speak and each listened to the other. A fruitful conversation ensued after each person spoke. For example, when Delia expressed to Dave that she was afraid of what would happen to her without him there, he put his hand on her leg and said, "Don't worry, I will always be with you because I love you." The therapist asked if they could use therapy to begin to talk about being more truthful with each other regarding any affairs and they agreed it would be a safe place to do so. The therapist also validated how difficult it is to express such painful emotions, especially when trying to protect your partner.

The final page of the activity, Worksheet B, consisted of the couple coming up with solutions that would help them support each other during this emotional time. They had a lot of planning to do and both agreed that they would try to be honest with each other and not keep painful information from each other.

The activity is useful in grounding therapy by letting each individual express independently his or her ideas and feelings about the situation, and helps the therapist structure discussions. The activity guides the discussions and helps the therapist to identify important breakthroughs during discussions, such as when a partner begins to soften (Johnson & Denton, 2002). The activity is useful to clients because it is user friendly and allows partners the freedom to navigate their emotions without worrying about what their partner might be thinking or feeling. Finally, the activity is a wonderful catalyst for discussions regarding patterns, primary emotions, and solutions.

Suggestions for Follow-Up

Once couples are given the opportunity to explore their relational conflict issues and patterns associated with the argument process, partners will be able to change negative interactional positions into more constructive expressions. As their interactions are restructured, they will be able to have a better understanding of each other and, in turn, create bonding events. If they are successful in this endeavor, the new positions and cycles of interaction will be consolidated. They can also continue to facilitate new solutions to other past problems in the relationship. If the discussion is unproductive, it is suggested that the couple strive to engage in dialogues that are free from negative affect and focus on their accomplishments as a couple. Moreover, a therapist can help support partners in the endeavor of resolving concrete issues that have been detrimental to the relationship.

Contraindications

The Finding a Connection activity can be used with couples regardless of race, ethnicity, gender, or sexual orientation. It can be utilized with clients who are experiencing minor conflict in their relationship or whose conflicts are gridlocked (Gottman & Silver, 1999). However, it is contraindicated for couples with severe domestic violence and when each partner needs to be seen individually. Once domestic violence has ceased and each individual feels safe to speak in the presence of the other, couple therapy can resume. If deemed appropriate, the therapist can begin to use the activity during couple therapy.

The activity may also be contraindicated for individuals who have experienced severe trauma or abuse in the past. This activity may inadvertently elicit trauma reactions as each individual completes it. Trauma reactions such as posttraumatic stress symptoms must be addressed appropriately before focusing on couple conflict. However, Johnson (2002) has utilized EFT (Emotionally Focused Therapy) with couples who have experienced trauma. Therapists who decide to use this activity should proceed with care and address any issues of trauma when and if they come up during the course of the activity or therapy.

References

Gottman, J. M., & Silver, N. (1999). *The seven principles for making marriage work: A practical guide from the country's foremost relationship expert.* New York: Three Rivers Press.

Johnson, S. M. (2002). *Emotionally focused couple therapy with trauma survivors: Strengthening attachment bonds.* New York: Guilford.

Johnson, S. M. (2004). *The practice of emotionally focused couple therapy: Creating connection.* New York: Guilford.

Johnson, S. M., & Denton, W. (2002). Emotionally focused couple therapy: Creating secure connections. In A. S. Gurman & N. S. Jacobson (Eds.), *Clinical handbook of couple therapy* (pp. 221-250). New York: Guilford.

Professional Readings and Resources

Johnson, S. M. (2002). *Emotionally focused couple therapy with trauma survivors: Strengthening attachment bonds.* New York: Guilford.

Johnson, S. M. (2004). *The practice of emotionally focused couple therapy: Creating connection.* New York: Guilford.

Johnson, S. M., & Denton, W. (2002). Emotionally focused couple therapy: Creating secure connections. In A. S. Gurman & N. S. Jacobson (Eds.), *Clinical handbook of couple therapy* (pp. 221-250). New York: Guilford.

Bibliotherapy Sources for Clients

Gottman, J. M., & Silver, N. (1999). *The seven principles for making marriage work: A practical guide from the country's foremost relationship expert.* New York: Three Rivers Press.

Markman, H. J., Stanley, S. M., & Blumberg, S. L. (2001). *Fighting for your marriage: Positive steps for preventing divorce and preserving a lasting love, new and revised.* San Francisco, CA: Jossey-Bass.

HANDOUT 2.1

FINDING A CONNECTION

Think of an argument that you seem to have often or one that you have had recently with your partner. EACH PARTNER DOES THIS ALONE UNTIL FURTHER INSTRUCTIONS ARE GIVEN.

- What was the argument about?

- How did the argument begin? What was the trigger that led to the argument? A trigger could be a word, a look, a feeling, or a gesture. For example: Crystal slams the door and this irritates Susan. Crystal then starts to criticize Susan for not calling her to cancel dinner, and so on.

- Pretend that someone was watching you on television or in a movie. What would the argument look like? Write out a small clip of what was said during the argument in the form of a dialogue or a screenplay. Also include any behaviors that happened during the argument (such as crying, raised voice, sighing, rolling eyes, etc.). An example of such an argument would be: Rita: Why do you have to drive so fast? Craig: Quit nagging me. I drive fine. Rita: You know that I get really upset when you drive so darn fast. Are you trying to kill me? Craig: Chill out! Rita: Don't tell me to chill out. Stop the car. STOP THE CAR!

- How did the argument end? Who or what stopped it from continuing? What was it like between you after it ended? What was it like between that time and the next argument?

Treyger, S., Frey, M., & Stepnowski, B. (2007). Finding a connection. In L. L. Hecker, C. F. Sori, & Associates, *The therapist's notebook, volume 2: More homework, handouts, and activities for use in psychotherapy* (pp. 11-20). Binghamton, NY: The Haworth Press.

HANDOUT 2.2

EXTERNAL FEELINGS

Circle the FEELINGS your partner SEES when you are arguing; the FEELINGS you choose to show your partner or the mask you wear when you are arguing.

Treyger, S., Frey, M., & Stepnowski, B. (2007). Finding a connection. In L. L. Hecker, C. F. Sori, & Associates, *The therapist's notebook, volume 2: More homework, handouts, and activities for use in psychotherapy* (pp. 11-20). Binghamton, NY: The Haworth Press.

HANDOUT 2.3

FEELINGS ON THE INSIDE

NOW, circle the feelings you experience hidden behind the mask; the feelings you do not want your partner to see, but rather the feelings you experience deep down inside.

Treyger, S., Frey, M., & Stepnowski, B. (2007). Finding a connection. In L. L. Hecker, C. F. Sori, & Associates, *The therapist's notebook, volume 2: More homework, handouts, and activities for use in psychotherapy* (pp. 11-20). Binghamton, NY: The Haworth Press.

HANDOUT 2.4

WORKSHEET A

- Look at the feelings you circled on the previous page—the feelings on the inside. When you are arguing, these are the feelings that you likely want your partner to know but you may be afraid to tell him or her. Please list those feelings that you have circled in the space below.

- Please fill in:

  When we are arguing about _____ (fill in topic), I feel _____ (fill in with the external feelings).

  What I am really feeling behind my mask is _____ (fill in with the feelings) behind your mask—the feelings on the inside) because _____ _____ (fill in why you feel those feelings behind your mask; think about what is most important to you in your life).

  When we argue about _____ (fill in topic), what I really want from you is _____ (fill in what you want or need from your partner; something you want to tell him or her but find it hard to do).

- Say the following to your partner:

  I have something to tell you and I would like you to listen to me because it is difficult for me to say it.

  When we argue about _____ (fill in topic), what I really want from you is _____ (fill in the behavior you want instead of the behavior you get from your partner).

- Give your partner the opportunity to tell you what he or she wants to say and what you should do in response (e.g., just sit and listen).

- What was it like for you to hear your partner tell you how he or she feels behind his or her mask (refer to the feelings on the inside)? How do you see your partner now?

Treyger, S., Frey, M., & Stepnowski, B. (2007). Finding a connection. In L. L. Hecker, C. F. Sori, & Associates, *The therapist's notebook, volume 2: More homework, handouts, and activities for use in psychotherapy* (pp. 11-20). Binghamton, NY: The Haworth Press.

HANDOUT 2.5

WORKSHEET B

- List several ways you could help your partner work toward his or her needs in the relationship.

    1.

    2.

    3.

    4.

    5.

    6.

    7.

- Discuss the list you have just made with your partner and work TOGETHER to prioritize the needs in order of importance.

- Finally, think about which would be the most beneficial solution for you and your relationship and communicate this to your partner.

Treyger, S., Frey, M., & Stepnowski, B. (2007). Finding a connection. In L. L. Hecker, C. F. Sori, & Associates, *The therapist's notebook, volume 2: More homework, handouts, and activities for use in psychotherapy* (pp. 11-20). Binghamton, NY: The Haworth Press.

Interrupting Couple Negativity

Josephine Bonomo

Type of Contribution: *Homework, Handouts*

Objectives

The objective of this exercise is to teach families or couples how to interrupt potentially escalating negative interactions. The therapist and clients work together to devise specific methods to intervene in common problematic couple patterns. Clients learn the methods in session with the goal of using them at home.

Rationale for Use

Literature in the couple and family fields clearly supports the need for interrupting negativity and slowing down common negative interactional patterns (Gottman, 1999; Johnson, 1996; Robbins, Alexander, & Turner, 2000). Whether the goal of interrupting negativity is to teach new behaviors, help encourage emotional softening, or provide new perceptions, interrupting negative interactional patterns appears to be an essential therapeutic change mechanism (Diamond & Liddle, 1999; Fincham & Beach, 1999; Gottman, 1999; Jacobson & Christensen, 1996; Stuart, Broderick, & Gurman, 1980). However, although there are very specific ways that therapists' behaviors can influence the interruption of such patterns during sessions, probably one of the most difficult tasks in therapy is having clients learn how to do this independently from therapy. There is a clear need for skills to transfer from the therapy room to the home so that clients do not require the therapist's presence. This exercise is meant to help clients learn how to interrupt negativity and slow down common negative interactional patterns when they are outside the therapy room.

Instructions

For best results in couple therapy, John Gottman (1999) has directed therapists to work with couples in three important ways. The first is to increase positive interaction between the spouses. Next is to increase positivity during conflict, and last, the goal is to decrease negativity within the couple relationship. Commonly, with regard to the last of these goals, couples become mired in negative interactional patterns, many of which contain an escalating pattern. This intervention targets this last goal: decreasing negativity between partners by teaching clients how to interrupt themselves or each other when mired in negative interchanges.

It is important to note that while the therapist may have the general idea of the process of the intervention, the exercise must be created with the client for it to be salient to the client. In other words, although the therapist may have a direction in mind as to the general goal of the interven-

The Therapist's Notebook, Volume 2
doi:10.1300/5550_03

tion, it must be designed with the client in a way that fits the client's unique needs. Therefore, while designing the intervention is a collaborative process, it also provides the therapist a flexible means to a specific goal.

In addition, this intervention should be done only after assessing for safety issues within the couple, such as domestic violence. Then a balanced therapeutic alliance should be developed and the problem definition and goals of therapy delineated. These therapeutic factors must be in place for several reasons. First, both members of the couple should feel that the therapist understands each of their perspectives on the problem. A client who experiences a good working therapeutic relationship is probably more likely to participate in the change process (Tallman & Bohart, 1999). Also, by defining the problem and goal of therapy in a safe, therapeutic environment, the therapist is preparing a focused path toward achieving a common goal so that the client may be more likely to be invested in the change process (Tallman & Bohart, 1999).

As with all good interventions, the exercise should be modified as needed as therapy progresses. Modifications should be considered and based on both the therapist's and client's assessment of progress toward the goal of interrupting negativity. For instance, the therapist may feel that the client may need more practice in the therapy room before practicing at home. Or clients may feel that they need more examples to rely on during the intervention.

The intervention consists of three steps.

Step 1: Explain to the client the rationale for the intervention.

There are many ways to explain the rationale, depending on the client's expectations of therapy and learning styles. Therefore, with some clients it may be helpful to discuss some of the research and literature that support the need for interruption of negativity. With clients who expect a directive therapist, it may be helpful to discuss the intervention as a type of prescription that needs to be done to alleviate symptoms. Ensuring that the client is ready to try the intervention is essential, and a verbal agreement is often a helpful way to proceed with an understanding that everyone has a part in the solution.

In addition, discussing the physiological reactions that occur during negative interactional processes (Gottman, 1999) might help better explain the purpose of the intervention and make the exercise more meaningful. Teaching clients that their bodies predict trouble by giving off an alarm (defined as a diffuse physiological arousal, or DPA, by Gottman, 1999) during negative interactions may be instrumental in interrupting common escalating patterns. Since DPA triggers a fight-or-flight response, clients will be less likely to be open to what their spouses are trying to communicate. In turn, this causes the common patterns of negativity between clients. Hence, teaching clients how to self-soothe in order to decrease their DPA will help them become more open to communication and less likely to fall into old patterns. The goal of self-soothing exercises is to decrease DPA and may include teaching clients how to breathe through anxiety, visualize a peaceful environment, or relaxing the most tense parts of their bodies (e.g., jaw, hands, face).

Step 2: Explain the exercise.

It is important to stress to the clients that the exercise requires the couple or family members to slow down or interrupt negativity when they see it starting. This can be done in two basic ways: words and actions. At this point, therapists can use examples that they have already used during therapy to illustrate the usefulness of the intervention. For an example of a cue word, a therapist might say, "I've noticed that it's helpful when things start to get heated between you when I whisper to you, Dwayne, 'listen.' It slows you down and you respond differently to your wife." For an example of a cue action, a therapist might say, "I have noticed that when I make a time-out signal with my hands, you both stop and wait." The key to this exercise is to brainstorm with the clients several possible methods of slowing down or interrupting negativity under either category. See the handout for examples that could be useful.

Step 3: Ensure understanding of the exercise.

Next, the therapist highlights the importance of the exercise and uses methods to help clients remember it. For some clients it may be helpful for the therapist to write the plan out (see handouts), while others might feel empowered by writing it out themselves. For some, having them write it out might be more empowering. Ask how they might best remember the intervention during the week. Having clients practice the intervention with the therapist, as awkward as that might feel, is often a good way to help coach or model the exercise. Practicing is often the best way to work through potential problems with the implementation of the exercise. Finally, suggest a specific day of the week or ask them to try the intervention once over a week's span. This might help ensure that they complete the exercise, and as well as letting them know that it is an obtainable intervention.

Brief Vignette

A newlywed couple of two years came to therapy complaining of communication problems. The wife defined the problem as the husband's lack of sensitivity when she wanted to talk to him about something that had upset her. She described his behaviors as shutting down, getting a glazed look in his eyes, and making excuses that he had to leave to make a phone call or to run an errand. She reported feeling very lonely and far away from him. The husband defined the problem as the wife's constant need to overprocess everything. He described her behaviors as being hypersensitive to anything he did that did not feel affectionate enough to her. He reported feeling very tired of trying to be supportive of her, and feeling like he would never be successful.

After discussing the possible meanings of the interactions between them and the emotional ramifications of their behaviors for their relationship, the therapist and the couple decided that a good goal would be to break the pattern of negativity that escalated hurtful emotions. This couple was very interested in the rationale for the exercise, so Step 1 was discussed in great detail. It appeared that the main difficulty in their patterns in regard to negativity was the beginning of their discussions. Therefore, the focus of the exercise was on how to start a discussion without their usual patterns of negativity, or in Gottman's (1999) terms, to soften harsh start-ups.

Step 2 took quite a bit of structuring as the wife tended to be extremely enthusiastic while the husband tended to reject all ideas. Therefore, the couple and the therapist decided to set some rules for possible words and actions to use. Some of the rules included making sure that word cues had to be brief (not more than ten to fifteen words) and did not have to include an emotional word, or that actions did not have to be affectionate and could be seen as humorous. The couple decided that having only a few cue phrases would be best at first, and each having different phrases would be a better fit for them. The wife decided that the best way for her to stop herself from escalating and overwhelming her husband with her emotions would be to say, "I miss you and we'll connect very soon." She said that this gave her sufficient emotional expression and still stated her hope that they would talk soon. The husband decided that when he was feeling overwhelmed the best way to manage his anxiety would be to state, "I want to do this well." He said this reminded both of them that he did not want to ignore her emotions but he wanted to do it when he could listen to her better by being in a more fully present and engaged state. The couple decided that they would try to take a break for a couple hours before coming back together to use communication skills to discuss the problem at hand. By interrupting the negativity at the onset of their discussions, they were better able to talk through the issue at hand.

Step 3 consisted of much practicing and coaching during the session and refining the exercise when they found certain things did not work as smoothly at home. For instance, the wife found waiting a few hours was too long for her, so the husband agreed to try a break for an hour instead. The husband reported that saying "I can't do this now" as a way to interrupt a potential negative pattern fit him better, but this phrase felt more hurtful to the wife. She compromised by accepting this cue as long as she could express more of her hurt in her phrase (such as "I am really hurt and need you right now and feel so sad"). The actual words did not matter as much as the process of slowing down and interrupting their escalating interactions.

At termination, the couple reported and displayed benefits from treatment by having less negative communication episodes and more frequent positive interactions. The wife expressed feelings of relief and comfort that she was secure in her husband eventually coming back to discuss what was most important to her. She reported her fear of losing him had diminished and that she had learned the importance of soothing herself during her anxious times. The husband also expressed feelings of relief that getting space was not a failure on his part and that he could hold conversations that made him feel helpful. Both spouses' behavioral changes in interrupting the negativity between them allowed for an increase in positive exchanges. For instance, when the husband would take time-outs, he would briefly jot down his feelings of devotion for her that he read to her before they came back together to talk. Doing this set a conciliatory tone for the discussion as well as soothing the wife's anxieties that she might be losing him. Also, the wife began inviting her husband for weekly date nights, where daily stressors were not allowed to be discussed. During these date nights, they both reported feeling like they were getting to know each other again.

Suggestions for Follow-Up

This exercise is not a panacea for communication problems and is only meant to facilitate more meaningful dialogue. The exercise has the simple yet complex goal of interrupting negativity before it happens or during escalating interactions. There is need for communication skill practices to work in conjunction with this exercise.

Therapists should take care to ensure that both members of the couple have a part in the exercise. While negativity can easily be defined as one person's problem, it is a relational process and therefore each person has a part in the problem and in the solution.

Therapists might want to consider having a plan if a relapse does occur. The plan might include discussing the rationale for the exercise, talking about why the exercise has not been working, and ways to practice again. A relapse prevention plan might also be considered, which could include possible risk factors clients can observe, such as feelings of resentment or trying to talk themselves out of sharing their feelings. The client may also consider regular checkups with each other and the therapist to discuss the progress of their communication in relation to the exercise and ways to continue to refine it.

Contraindications

Therapists should assess for couple or family violence to ensure client safety. Using this intervention with clients who are powerless in a domestic violence situation is contraindicated.

References

Diamond, G. S., & Liddle, H. A. (1999). Transforming negative parent-adolescent interactions: From impasse to dialogue. *Family Process, 38,* 5-26.

Fincham, F., & Beach, S. (1999). Conflict in marriage. *Annual Review of Psychology, 50,* 47-78.

Gottman, J. M. (1999). *The marriage clinic: A scientifically based marital therapy.* New York: Norton.

Jacobson, J. S., & Christensen, A. (1996). *Integrative couple therapy: Promoting acceptance and change.* New York: Norton.

Johnson, S. M. (1996). *Creating connection: The practice of emotionally focused marital therapy*. New York: Brunner/Mazel.

Robbins, M. S., Alexander, J. F., & Turner, C. W. (2000). Disrupting defensive family interactions in family therapy with delinquent adolescents. *Journal of Family Psychology, 14*(4), 688-701.

Stuart, R. B., Broderick, C., & Gurman, A. S. (1980). *Helping couples change: A social learning approach to marital therapy*. New York: Guilford.

Tallman, K., & Bohart, A. C. (1999). The client as a common factor: Clients as self-healers. In M. A. Hubble, B. L. Duncan, & S. D. Miller (Eds.), *The heart and soul of change: What works in therapy* (pp. 91-131). Washington, DC: American Psychological Association.

Professional Readings and Resources

Gottman, J. M. (1999). *The marriage clinic: A scientifically based marital therapy*. New York: Norton.

Johnson, S. M. (1996). *Creating connection: The practice of emotionally focused marital therapy*. New York: Brunner/Mazel.

Bibliotherapy Sources for Clients

Gottman, J. M., & Silver, N. (1999). *The seven principles for making marriage work: A practical guide from the country's foremost relationship expert*. New York: Random House.

Wahlroos, S. (1995). *Family communication*. New York: McGraw-Hill.

HANDOUT 3.1

INTERRUPTING COUPLE NEGATIVITY

Things to REMEMBER:

- This will be hard to do in the heat of the moment.
- Breathe.
- Slow down.
- Take a time-out if you need one.
- You are both trying the best that you can.

Things you can SAY TO YOURSELF:

- Listen!
- Breathe.
- Your turn will come to speak.
- What is he or she trying to tell me?
- Concentrate on the issue at hand.
- This can be worked out.
- Take your time to understand.
- I want him or her to know that I am scared.
- I want him or her to know that I really care.
- I can keep calm.
- We can work this out.
- What is he or she really saying?
- Be patient with yourself and with him or her.
- One thing at a time.
- I am committed to making this work.
- I want him or her to know that I care.

Bonomo, J. (2007). Interrupting couple negativity. In L. L. Hecker, C. F. Sori, & Associates, *The therapist's notebook, volume 2: More homework, handouts, and activities for use in psychotherapy* (pp. 21-28). Binghamton, NY: The Haworth Press.

Things you can SAY OUT LOUD:

- Let's stop.
- Let's not fight.
- Stop.
- I love us.
- Please.
- No more.
- I miss you.
- I don't want to hurt you.
- I feel I'm losing you.
- I'm scared.
- I'm so hurt.
- This is making me sad.
- I need a time-out/break.
- I'm not sure what to do or say right now.
- Let's sit with this for awhile and come back to it in an hour.
- You are so important to me.

Things you can DO:

- Make a time-out signal.
- Raise your hand.
- Make a peace sign.
- Place your head in your hands.
- Sit on the floor together.
- Breathe in and out slowly a couple of times.
- Count to ten slowly.
- Close your eyes and imagine a peaceful scene.
- Say a favorite self-affirming phrase or quote.
- Touch your wedding ring to remind you of your commitment to each other.

Bonomo, J. (2007). Interrupting couple negativity. In L. L. Hecker, C. F. Sori, & Associates, *The therapist's notebook, volume 2: More homework, handouts, and activities for use in psychotherapy* (pp. 21-28). Binghamton, NY: The Haworth Press.

Things you can DO TO HELP YOU LISTEN:

- Take deep breaths.
- Focus on what the other is saying.
- Stay calm and summarize what is being said.
- Take brief notes of major points for discussion.
- Pay attention to the issue at hand.
- Concentrate on relaxing your body.
- Pay attention to words that the other is repeating.

Things you can SAY TO HELP YOU LISTEN:

- Help me understand.
- Can you tell me more?
- I am trying hard to understand your experience.
- Can I clarify what I think you are saying?
- It is really important for me to hear you out.
- Do I have it right that you mean. . . .
- I need to take a break right now, but I do want to hear what you have to say.
- I want to figure this out and I need your help.

Things NOT TO DO:

- Do not interrupt.
- Do not jump to conclusions.
- Do not think of all the bad experiences of the past.
- Do not try to hurry this process.
- Do not think of how you can quickly escape.
- Do not tense your body (clenched fists or locked jaw) or hold your breath.
- Do not give off negative body signals such as rolling your eyes, sighing, tapping your foot, or crossing your arms.
- Do not look away from partner.
- Do not say the things or words you know might trigger a negative response (e.g., the word "divorce" or calling the other "controlling").
- Do not be silent when it is your turn to speak.
- Do not prepare your response while the other is still speaking.
- Do not be impatient with yourself or your partner.
- Do not think this is easy.
- Do not forget your commitment to the relationship.
- Do not give up.
- Do not think of what you want to say next.

Bonomo, J. (2007). Interrupting couple negativity. In L. L. Hecker, C. F. Sori, & Associates, *The therapist's notebook, volume 2: More homework, handouts, and activities for use in psychotherapy* (pp. 21-28). Binghamton, NY: The Haworth Press.

4

Counseling Couples with Choice Theory and Reality Therapy: The Structured First Interview

Patricia A. Robey

Type of Contribution: *Activity, Handout, and Homework*

Objectives

The objective of this chapter is to provide the therapist with a structured format to use in the first session with a couple. The format is designed to engage each member of the couple in taking responsibility for his or her part in the problem and in its resolution. At the conclusion of the structured interview, the couple will have begun to make the shift from an external to an internal locus of control and will leave the session with a plan for behavioral change that can be implemented immediately. As a result, the couple will begin the process of learning to work cooperatively, rather than competitively.

Rationale for Use

All therapists are aware that there is no guarantee that a client, couple, or family will return for a second counseling session. Therefore, it is imperative that clinicians make the most out of the time they have with clients in the first session. The process of reality therapy focuses on what is happening in the present and avoids spending much time with symptoms and complaints rather than working toward the desired outcome (Glasser, 1998). Because sessions may be limited, in the first session the reality therapist will ask clients to evaluate the effectiveness of their behavior and how their behavior is helping or hurting their relationships. The therapist teaches clients that they can only control their own behavior and that their effort to control their partner is what is ruining their relationship.

In his book *Getting Together and Staying Together: Solving the Mystery of Marriage,* Dr. William Glasser stated that individuals who are having difficulty getting along with each other are doing so because they are using external control behaviors in an attempt to change their partners. "Employing external control, unhappily married people keep thinking: *It's not me, it's my partner who's the cause of my misery. And it's my obligation to do everything I can to change the way my partner behaves toward me*" (Glasser & Glasser, 2000, p. 15). Glasser has identified a list of behaviors he calls the Seven Deadly Habits of external control: (1) criticizing, (2) blaming, (3) complaining, (4) nagging, (5) threatening, (6) punishing, and (7) bribing or rewarding to control. He suggests that the continued use of these behaviors over time is what destroys relationships. Instead of the deadly habits, Glasser encourages the use of Seven Caring Habits: (1) listening, (2) supporting, (3) encouraging, (4) respecting, (5) trusting, (6) accepting, and (7) always negotiating disagreements.

The Therapist's Notebook, Volume 2
doi:10.1300/5550_04

Using the structured reality therapy process in the first session of counseling helps clients understand that they can only control themselves and leads them from the deadly habits of the problem to the caring habits of the solution. Because each individual takes turns responding to the questions, each feels heard. Although each is able to express his or her perception of the problem, neither is blamed by the therapist. Instead, both are expected to take responsibility for the solution.

Instructions

This intervention is adapted from *Choice Theory: A New Psychology of Personal Freedom* (Glasser, 1998, pp. 179-182).

As with all therapy, the therapist begins by introducing himself or herself and establishing a relationship with the clients. The clients are told that the session will involve a series of questions and that each question must be answered satisfactorily before the therapy can continue.

The intervention is as follows:

1. Are you here because you want to save the relationship?

This question begins to create a climate for solving the problem rather than focusing on symptoms. It helps to collapse the conflict between the couple by finding the area of agreement between them. Both clients must answer yes to this question before moving on to Question 2. If one or both answer no, then the purpose of the counseling changes.

2. Briefly, what do you see as the problem with the relationship?

Each client is allowed to briefly express his or her perception of what is wrong with the relationship. Usually this involves each blaming the other for the problems. Ask each to avoid interrupting, and assure them that each will have an opportunity to state his or her case. This helps each person to release feelings of frustration and pain. Note, however, that the therapist does not allow this to go on for more than a few minutes. The therapist must carefully monitor this process so that it does not become an outpouring of blaming, complaining, accusing, criticizing, and threatening (although this is what many people expect and want to do in counseling).

3. Whose behavior can you control?

Evaluation of behavior and acceptance of personal responsibility for one's actions are at the core of the reality therapy process. This is not a hard question, yet many people resist the answer—which is that they can only really control themselves. Often clients will claim they can control their spouses, children, employees, or others through the use of coercion. The therapist must then challenge this perception; even though a person is coerced, that person still can choose to resist or disobey. The answer to this question—"I can only control myself"—is crucial to this process. Clients must realize that no matter what they do, the only person they can control is themselves. This sets the stage for making personal change toward the solution of the problem.

4. Tell me one good thing about the relationship as it exists now.

This is often a difficult request for the clients. They are usually so involved with the problem that they have forgotten why they joined together in the first place. The therapist must be patient, but insist that each find some answer to this request. Responses that "the relationship would be fine if only he or she would . . ." must be rejected.

Most couples are able to come up with a few things that are good about the relationship. If they couldn't, they would likely be in divorce proceedings rather than counseling. As the clients talk about the good things in their relationship, they will begin to release some of the anger and hostility they were experiencing. The answer to this request shifts the focus from the problem to potential sources for solutions. Usually the clients are very pleased by what their partners have to say in response to this direction.

5. What is one thing you are willing to do this week that will help your relationship? This must be something you can do yourself and will not depend on anything your partner does.

This question helps the clients create a plan for change that will help their relationship. The idea that each person chooses something he or she can do in spite of the other's behavior emphasizes the idea that we can only control our own behavior, though we may hope to influence another by what we choose to do. This is a good time to teach clients about the deadly and caring habits, and to ask each to identify what caring habit he or she might choose in the next week to improve the relationship. A helpful tool is to give the clients the handout included at the end of this chapter, or a card with the deadly habits listed on one side and the caring habits on the other. This card can be carried in a wallet, while the handout can be posted on the refrigerator at home. These tools provide cues for self-evaluation of behavior when the clients are not in session.

The therapist may need to be patient here, as the clients may struggle with their desire to choose a caring behavior only if their partner will do something first. The therapist must remind each partner that the behavior must occur regardless of what the other partner does. If a person chooses a behavior and the partner states that the behavior will not be helpful, then the person must try again. For example, a partner who chooses to go golfing rather than nag his wife about her cooking will not necessarily help the relationship.

When each agrees on a plan for the week, it is assigned as homework.

6. During the week, I would like you to think of other things you could do that would help build the relationship. If you can do it, go ahead, but I want to caution you about doing too much in this first week. Bring your idea to counseling next week and we will talk about it.

This assignment is optional. It gives each member a positive task to focus on and is something they can look forward to sharing in the next session. Advising the clients not to do too much is a paradoxical intervention that may encourage them to be more active than they might have otherwise.

Glasser (1998) suggests that the therapist teach the couple how to manage their problems at home through the use of the solving circle. When the couple has a problem that influences the relationship, one or both of them can request a meeting of the solving circle. The circle is a metaphor for the relationship and when the couple is working within the solving circle, they are working within the context of the relationship and for the sake of the relationship, rather than for the sake of each individual. Within the circle, only caring habits are used. If the couple cannot agree to focus on what is best for the relationship, the circle is broken for that time and they must arrange an appointment to meet again when each is willing to focus on the relationship rather than on himself or herself.

Brief Vignette

Katie (twenty-six) and Patrick (twenty-eight) were a working-class couple, both of Irish descent. They had been living together for four years and were the parents of a one-year-old boy, Colin. Katie requested counseling because she was unhappy with the way that Patrick was treating her and Colin. Patrick agreed to come to counseling to "get Katie off my back."

The tension between Katie and Patrick was evident as they entered the room and chose chairs opposite each other. The therapist greeted them and explained who she was, her theory of counseling, and how she worked with couples. The therapist told them that, while she would listen to their problems, she was more interested in helping them identify their hopes and wishes for the relationship and to help them learn new ways of interacting that would help them become closer if that was their wish. The therapist explained that she was optimistic that they could have a good relationship and that she looked forward to working with them in this process.

Katie and Patrick seemed a bit more comfortable after the therapist joined with them and appeared curious about the process in which they would be involved. The therapist began the structured interview by asking the first question.

Both agreed that they would like to save the relationship, though Patrick expressed some reservation that it could be saved. The therapist asked him again if that was what he wanted and expressed the importance of his commitment to the process. Patrick stated that he wanted the relationship to be a success, especially since there was a child involved.

Katie jumped at the chance to answer the question regarding what was wrong with the relationship. As the therapist had anticipated, Katie blamed Patrick for the troubles they were having. "As soon as Colin was born, Patrick changed. He is at work all the time and when he comes home he doesn't want anything to do with me or with the baby. He screams at me to clean the house and complains that I don't do anything all day. He has no idea what it's like to take care of a baby and a house. Plus, he never gives me any money. He treats me like an incompetent child and I don't like it!"

Patrick had his turn to vent. "I work hard all day and when I come home I want to relax. I don't want to have to deal with diapers or a messy house. How hard can it be to take care of a little kid, anyway? And I'm sick of her nagging at me to be with Colin. What am I supposed to do with him? He just sits there anyway; he can't talk or do anything with me. On top of everything, she wants me to watch Colin while she goes out with her friends. What does she need to go out for? Then she expects me to stay awake with Colin while she's out drinking! I don't think so!"

"Wow, I can see that you both are feeling very frustrated and overwhelmed right now," the therapist said. "I am so glad you came to counseling and that you are committed to working this out. Now let me ask you something, and I want both of you to answer this question carefully. Whose behavior can you control in all of this?"

Katie replied, "Patrick tries to control me, but I refuse to let him! I am not his mother and I won't act like it!"

Patrick responded, "Nobody can control her, that's for sure!"

The therapist repeated the question. "So, who can you each control?"

After a brief period of silent resistance to this question, each reluctantly admitted that he or she could only control himself or herself.

"Okay, now I am going to ask you a question that may be a tough one for you to answer right now," the therapist said. "I want you each to tell me something that is good about your relationship."

Each looked to the other to answer first. The therapist could see them struggling to respond to her request. The therapist knew that this was a surprise and that they expected that they would be talking about what was going wrong, not what was going right. The therapist also knew that it would be risky for each of them to admit that they appreciated something about the other. Or worse, what if the partner couldn't say something good about the relationship? Neither wanted to be the first to become vulnerable. The therapist waited patiently.

Finally Katie softened. "He really does work hard and makes sure that we have all the stuff we need. But . . ."

The therapist interrupted, knowing the "but" would precede a criticism. "Thanks, Katie. Feel free to add some other good things about Patrick and your relationship as you think of them. Patrick?"

"Well, she is a good mother," he replied. "And she can be pretty sexy when she wants to be."

Katie looked surprised. "I'd be interested more often if you didn't come home so late," she said.

The therapist could see that this could quickly become problem focused if she didn't intervene. "Remember that I want you both to keep focused on the positives in your relationship right now. It sounds like you both have things about one another that you appreciate. Katie, you appreciate that Patrick takes good care of you and Colin. And Patrick, you appreciate that Katie is a good mom and that she can be very sexy. Is there anything else you'd like to add?"

Katie said, "We used to have a lot of fun together before Colin was born."

Surprisingly, Patrick added, "I miss those times."

This was a good time to transition to the next question.

"We are getting close to the end of our time together today, but before you go, I have a very important question for you," the therapist said. "What is one thing that each of you can do during this next week that will help your relationship? Keep in mind that it has to be something you can do yourself, that doesn't rely on anything the other person does."

Katie had an idea right away. "I could get my mom to babysit, I think. Then we could go out together on Friday like we used to."

"I could live with that," Patrick replied, "but I don't know if I can get off work."

"You and your job!" Katie pouted. "It always comes first!"

"Remember," the therapist said, "that what you plan has to rely only on what you can do and can't depend on what your partner does. We want this to be a positive plan for making your relationship better."

Patrick sighed. "Okay, I'll get off work. But don't complain when my paycheck is short next week."

"I won't!" Katie replied. "And I will try not to be so crabby this week."

"That's a good idea, Katie," the therapist said. "But let's make your plan for something you will do, rather than for something you won't do. So, when you feel crabby, what will you do instead of directing it toward Patrick?"

"Hmmm, that's a good question. I guess I could think up something to compliment him on instead of complain about."

"How would you feel if Katie did that, Patrick?" the therapist asked.

"That would be great," he replied. "I hope it happens."

"Well, you both agreed that you can control yourselves. If you do these things, I can almost guarantee that your week will be better than it has been. But it is no miracle. It requires commitment and work on both your parts. However, I feel optimistic that you can do this. You both want to see the relationship work and that's a good start."

Katie and Patrick were able to put their plan into action that week and had a fun night out. In the next session they discussed the caring and deadly habits and the therapist asked them to evaluate which they used more often in their relationship. The therapist introduced the idea of the solving circle and when to use it. As sessions continued, Katie and Patrick learned how to communicate with each other more effectively. They took time out for fun. They also identified individual needs that had to be addressed. Katie wanted to go back to school and the couple had to adjust to her new schedule and distractions.

The sessions were not always easy or smooth. As with all couples, Katie and Patrick brought different needs and wants to their relationships that were not always compatible. However, they learned to work with their differences and to allow each other the space to grow both separately and together. Many sessions were heated, but each session ended with a renewed commitment to the relationship and plans for behavior that brought them closer together.

Suggestions for Follow-Up

Therapeutic sessions involve educating clients as well as counseling them (Glasser, 1998). The therapist should teach clients to recognize and eliminate the deadly habits and to practice the caring habits. The solving circle and the structured interview can be taught to couples and used by couples at home as well as in counseling sessions.

Choice theory explains that all behavior has purpose (Glasser, 1998). People behave to get what they want, which satisfies one or more of their basic needs. Teaching clients choice theory concepts helps them to understand their own behavior and the behavior of others. Teaching choice theory to clients is considered to be part of the reality therapy process. In this way, clients are able to generalize what they have learned in counseling to other areas of their lives.

Contraindications

As with all couples counseling, care must be taken to provide an environment of safety and trust. If there is evidence of abuse in the relationship, the therapist must evaluate whether couples counseling is the best answer for both the clients.

References

Glasser, W. (1998). *Choice theory: A new psychology of personal freedom.* New York: HarperCollins.

Glasser, W., & Glasser, C. (2000). *Getting together and staying together: Solving the mystery of marriage.* New York: HarperCollins.

Professional Readings and Resources

Crawford, D. K., Bodine, R. J., & Hoglund, R. G. (1993). *The school for quality learning.* Champaign, IL: Research Press.

Erwin, J. (2004). *The classroom of choice.* Alexandria, VA: Association for Supervision and Curriculum Development.

Glasser, W. (1992). *The quality school.* New York: HarperCollins.

Glasser, W. (1998). *Choice theory: A new psychology of personal freedom.* New York: HarperCollins.

Glasser, W. (2000). *Counseling with choice theory: The new reality therapy.* New York: HarperCollins.

Glasser, W. (2000). *Every student can succeed.* San Diego, CA: Black Forest Press.

Ludwig, S. A., & Mentley, K. W. (1997). *Quality is the key: Stories from Huntington Woods School.* Wyoming, MI: KWM Educational Services.

Myers, L., & Jackson, D. (2002). *Reality therapy and choice theory: Managing behavior today, developing skills for tomorrow.* Lanham, MD: American Correctional Association.

Wubbolding, R. E. (1988). *Using reality therapy.* New York: Harper & Row.

Wubbolding, R. E. (1998). Client inner self-evaluation: A necessary prelude to change. In H. Rosentahl (Ed.), *Favorite counseling and therapy techniques* (pp. 197-198). Washington, DC: Taylor and Francis.

Wubbolding, R. E. (2000). *Reality therapy for the 21st century.* Philadelphia: Brunner-Routledge.

Bibliotherapy Sources for Clients

Buck, N. S. (2000). *Peaceful parenting.* San Diego, CA: Black Forest Press.

Glasser, W., & Glasser, C. (2000). *Getting together and staying together: Solving the mystery of marriage.* New York: HarperCollins.

Wubbolding, R. E., & Brickell, J. (2001). *A set of directions for putting and keeping yourself together.* Minneapolis, MN: Educational Media Corporation.

ASK YOURSELF:
IS WHAT I'M ABOUT TO DO GOING TO BRING US CLOSER TOGETHER
OR PUSH US FARTHER APART?

SEVEN DEADLY HABITS

(1) Criticizing

(2) Blaming

(3) Complaining

(4) Nagging

(5) Threatening

(6) Punishing

(7) Bribing or rewarding to control

SEVEN CARING HABITS

(1) Listening

(2) Supporting

(3) Encouraging

(4) Respecting

(5) Trusting

(6) Accepting

(7) Always negotiating disagreements

(Adapted from Glasser & Glasser, 2000, p. 15)

Robey, P. A. (2007). Counseling couples with choice theory and reality therapy: The structured first interview. In L. L. Hecker, C. F. Sori, & Associates, *The therapist's notebook, volume 2: More homework, handouts, and activities for use in psychotherapy* (pp. 29-36). Binghamton, NY: The Haworth Press.

5

Blossoming Relationships:
Using Creativity in Couple Counseling

Nancy L. A. Forth
Atsuko Seto

Type of Contribution: *Activity, Handout*

Objectives

Couples who attend therapy often have difficulty communicating to each other their wants, desires, fears, and concerns in a manner that nurtures intimacy. In addition, when the relationship is based upon assumptions and demands rather than clear understanding of these issues, the relationship may become strained. The purpose of this activity is to offer a safe environment and a manner for couples to explore, describe, and express thoughts and feelings to each other.

Rationale for Use

Healers of all persuasions have recognized the power of the arts as they use them to assist individuals in releasing unhealthy feelings and thereby to feel complete again (Gladding, 1985). In more recent years, therapists have realized the value of employing creative arts in therapy (e.g., Dermer, Olund, & Sori, 2006; Gil, 1994). First, many clients show incongruence between their inner thoughts and feelings and how they express these to others, which may hinder growth attempts. Use of the arts offers the opportunity for clients to gain awareness of this incongruence (Levick, 1983) and gain insight. Increasing insight often results in clients discovering their situation as different than they had previously experienced and generally not as hopeless as previously believed. Finally, using creative arts honors the uniqueness of clients while offering a range of creative ways for clients to express themselves in an enjoyable, stimulating, and informal manner (Gladding, 1998).

Incorporating creative interventions into couple and family therapy is imperative to meet the needs of diverse populations (Murray & Rotter, 2002). The extent to which individuals are resilient and receptive to stressors may be associated with the level of creativity they possess (Carson & Becker, 2003). Carson and Becker explain how couples may experience stressors to varying degrees as they experience changes according to life transitions, as well as unexpected challenges. Therefore, innovative interventions can encourage individuals to listen to their inner voice in order to foster optimal relationships.

The following activity was inspired by the work of Blisard, Cantrell, and Perryman (2000), who initially utilized flowers in a six-week group-counseling program. Using items found in nature such as flowers, pine cones, and small rocks adds the dimension of comfort, beauty, and simplicity, which promotes inspiration, self-reflection, and self-acceptance (Fausek, 1997).

doi:10.1300/5550_05

This innovative technique was modified to be used in couple therapy by changing the specific facilitative questions in the process portion of the activity that address barriers as well as hopes within the context of an intimate relationship.

Instructions

After gathering the supplies and preparing two arrangement bases for the activity (see handout), introduce the activity to the couple by explaining that this activity can offer them an opportunity to better understand and express themselves through the use of flowers and other objects found in nature. Inform the couple that each of them will create their own individual arrangement. Ask the couple to take a moment to envision their marriage, including wants, desires, fears, or concerns they have about their relationship. Direct the couple to choose an object, which they believe represents this vision, and then place it in their respective arrangement base. The therapist should also state that clients may choose items that they believe represent themselves, their partner, and concerns; and they may be drawn to an object name, scent, color, size, shape, texture, and so on. As a way to avoid clients judging their own or their partner's choices, it is essential that the therapist tell clients there is no right or wrong way to make the arrangements. After both partners appear satisfied with their arrangements, the process portion begins.

Process and Evaluation

The therapist begins the process by telling clients, "Share with your partner what you selected and the reason you chose your objects." As seen in the brief clinical vignette that follows, the therapist explores meanings, such as distance, height, color, and so on of the chosen objects. After both partners share their choices and meanings, the therapist invites "wonderings" about each other's arrangements, asking clients to speak directly to each other.

For evaluation, ask the couple what this experience was like and what they will take from the activity. Discussing how the couple can incorporate concepts such as creativity, playfulness, and spontaneity outside of therapy can also be beneficial. Finally, to promote continued work outside the session, ask the couple what they plan to do with their arrangements.

Brief Vignette

The following vignette and figures illustrate how the activity can be used in couple therapy to foster self-reflection and exploration. As the couple engages in a creative intervention, their defensiveness and fears diminish, which allows them to openly share their feelings and thoughts. Kevin, a forty-year-old accountant, and Angela, a thirty-year-old middle school teacher, sought couples therapy prior to their wedding, which was six months away. Angela had been married in the past, which she described as a verbally abusive relationship. She suggested the couple seek counseling so that they know their decision to marry was right. Kevin had never been married and desired to start a family. After a few sessions to build a rapport with this couple, the therapist discussed an idea of exploring their feelings and thoughts on marriage through the use of flowers and other objects found in nature. The couple agreed to participate in this activity during next session.

THERAPIST: As we talked about in the last session, I would like the two of you to use this session as an opportunity to explore your thoughts and feelings regarding marriage. Take a moment to think about what you envision the future to be in your marriage. When you are ready, go ahead and choose flowers or objects that represent what you just envisioned, including things that represent each other and your hopes and concerns. You might also find yourself being drawn to size, color, shape, scent, or a texture of the flowers and objects.

[Angela and Kevin take time to create their respective arrangements.]

THERAPIST: Angela, could you tell Kevin about your arrangement? What flowers and objects did you choose to describe each of you, as well as all hopes, desires, and concerns that come to your mind when you think about your marriage?

ANGELA: Sure. I chose daisies for you and me (Figure 5.1). Mine is a little bit shorter than yours because you are taller and bigger than I am, but I also see you as more mature and dependable than I am. You have been there for me when things were rough. I chose the same flower because we have a lot in common, like we both want children, we want to support each other's career, and we want to be close to our families. I chose baby's breath for my hopes and desires for us. I want our marriage to be based on honesty, and the color white represents that. I also want us to have a few children so that we have a large family that is filled with love and laughter. Around the foundation [flower foam], I put a few rocks to represent our family and friends. They are people whom we can count on when we need support. I don't know what these flowers are called, but I chose them to represent my fears. Like I said before, I really want this marriage to be right for us. I know you tell me on a daily basis how much you love me and that you will be caring and faithful. I think I believe you, but I still get worried about how each of us will change over the years.

FIGURE 5.1. Angela's arrangement.

THERAPIST: I noticed that your fear is widely spread out and placed between your hopes and the two of you as a couple. I'm curious about that.

ANGELA: My fears are all over the place, like these flowers. I find myself being worried about the "what ifs" and not even enjoying the relationship. I sometimes act as if our relationship is over and realize that I am not even married yet!

KEVIN: I didn't realize how scared Angela is.

THERAPIST: Kevin, go ahead and talk more to Angela about that.

KEVIN: Well, I didn't know how scared you are about the whole thing—how each of us will change as we marry. I am not a perfect guy, but I will be faithful to you, and I have been so. If I give you any impression that I am not being honest with you, then I want you to tell me that. I love you.

ANGELA: I love you, too. I want you to know that it's not you. It just that I am so happy to find you, and at the same time I anticipate something awful happening in our relationship—like you would turn into an abusive man. I think that is why I placed you and me right next to each other in my arrangement. I need your support so that I can deal with my fears.

FIGURE 5.2. Kevin's arrangement.

KEVIN: I will do my best to support you in our marriage. You are very important to me and you help me be a better person. Like I tried to tell you in my arrangement here (Figure 5.2). Well, mine looks a little bit strange, so don't laugh. I chose the foundation and a carnation for you. I know this foundation may not be really appealing to you, but that is not why I chose it. I chose the foundation because I feel grounded when I am with you. I never felt this way with anyone else in my life. You are also beautiful inside and out like this carnation. I loved the color because it is soothing. I guess you help me calm down when I am stressed out at work. I chose a pine cone for myself. Ideally, I wanted the pine cone to be bigger than the foundation, but that is okay. The point I wanted to make was that I am right next to you. I also see myself as a pretty well-balanced guy, and this pine cone represents that balance. The rose is our future together—bright and with many hopes. We already have a house that is big enough to have children. I want us to have children, so I chose these small purple flowers for them.

THERAPIST: I noticed that you chose a rosebud for your future with Angela instead of a fully blossomed one. Any thoughts?

KEVIN: Well, I wanted to focus my hopes on our marriage. Many exciting things are already happening, but some hopes are yet to come—like having kids.

ANGELA: [looking very pleased] I like how you chose a rosebud for our future. It looks beautiful as it is, but it will be even more beautiful when it blossoms.

THERAPIST: It sounds to me like both of you value honesty as the core of your relationship. You also sound very excited at the prospect of raising children. I am curious about any concerns you have. . . . Kevin, any thoughts?

KEVIN: Oh, yes, concerns. I didn't choose a particular object for that. I chose the thorns on the rose for my concerns. I know this sounds silly, but I sometimes worry about my age. I wonder about being too old to be a dad to our kids. I guess, ever since my knee replacement, I am more aware of my physical limitations. I don't think about it all the time, but it is on my mind. So my worry is like the thorns on this rosebud—they get you when you least expect it.

ANGELA: I know your knees really bother you. It's frustrating for you not being able to run like you used to. Yes, we might be older parents than others, but I think we will be great ones. I know you will be a great father.

KEVIN: Yeah, I hope I will. I just need to stay in good shape.

ANGELA: Besides, you chose a pine cone to represent you. Without pine cones, there will be no pine trees. You are the root of our family. Without you, there will be no "us."

KEVIN: Wow, that is a lot of pressure, but I guess that is okay. I need to stay healthy for my family, and that is good motivation.

The session continued by focusing on finding ways to work through the fears Kevin and Angela are bringing to their relationship as well as exploring the couple's strengths in relation to their hopes and desires (i.e., qualities that make them loving parents). The therapist encouraged Angela and Kevin to think about the roots of their fears (i.e., repeating the same mistake or being too old to start a family) and how their fears have manifested as sources of potential strain in their relationship. Through their explorations, the couple discussed how each of them needs to take ownership of his or her own fear while also learning to become the best support for each other.

The therapist also asked the couple what it was like for them to hear the description of each one by the other. Doing so created the opportunity to verbally share their deep appreciation for each other and highlighted the importance of doing so in their relationship. Furthermore, the therapist asked the couple what insight and meaning they gained from this experience. Kevin responded by saying that he was suspicious about the activity first but was pleasantly surprised as he felt at ease when talking about his fear as represented by thorns. Kevin also stated that he had a better understanding of Angela's fear and acknowledged the importance of verbally expressing his commitment to the relationship. Angela said it was a relief to openly talk about her fear in Kevin's presence without being defensive. She learned that she no longer has to pretend, and that she can work though her fear with Kevin's support. Angela also decided to practice a healthier lifestyle in order to support Kevin in tackling his fear. At the end of the session, the therapist asked the couple to think about what they want to do with their arrangements. The couple decided to take their arrangements home and use them as decorations. A few weeks later, the couple told the therapist that they decided to take a few flowers from both arrangements and dry them. They hoped to place these dried flowers in a picture frame as a reminder of their commitment and love for each other.

Suggestions for Follow-Up

The next session should include the therapist asking if they became aware of any further thoughts, feelings, or changes in their relationship that had occurred since the activity session. Session time should be spent processing these two questions, and depending upon this process outcome, existing therapeutic goals may be evaluated or new goals may be established. If a recurring theme is observed, enactments (Minuchin, 1981) may be used to allow the couple to discuss and gain a deeper understanding of the roles each plays in the marital dyad. As a culminating activity, final session time could also be used for the couple to cocreate an arrangement, thereby exhibiting growth in their relationship.

Contraindications

As with most counseling techniques, there are contraindications before and while using this technique when counseling couples. One consideration is the degree to which clients are able to engage in self-exploration and expression. Since various factors such as family of origin, cultural and social contexts, and individual personality may influence clients' ability in this process, it is essential that the therapist understand each client's comfort level in using creative arts and their receptiveness to insight-oriented counseling. Finally, some clients may be allergic to flowers and other objects used in this technique.

References

Blisard, P., Cantrell, N., & Perryman, K. (2000). *Floratherapy handbook.* Fayetteville, AR: Waliski Enterprise.

Carson, D. K., & Becker, K. W. (2003). *Reaching new heights with individuals, couples, and families.* Binghamton, NY: The Haworth Press.

Dermer, S., Olund, D., & Sori, C. F. (2006). Integrating play in family therapy theories. In C. F. Sori (Ed.), *Engaging children in family therapy: Creative approaches to integrating theory and research in clinical practice* (pp. 37-65). New York: Routledge.

Fausek, D. (1997). *A practical guide to art therapy groups.* Binghamton, NY: The Haworth Press.

Gil, E. (1994). *Play in family therapy.* New York: Guilford.

Gladding, S. T. (1985). Counseling and the creative arts. *Counseling and Human Development, 18,* 1-12.

Gladding, S. T. (1998). *Counseling as an art: The creative arts in counseling* (2nd ed.). Alexandria, VA: American Counseling Association.

Levick, M. F. (1983). *They could not talk and so they drew.* Springfield, IL: Charles C Thomas.

Minuchin, S. (1981). *Family therapy techniques.* Cambridge, MA: Harvard University Press.

Murray, P. E., & Rotter, J. C. (2002). Creative counseling techniques for family therapists. *Family Journal: Counseling and Therapy for Couples and Families, 10,* 203-206.

Professional Readings and Resources

Arge, N. A., & Mirviss, S. (1998). *Therapy techniques using the creative arts.* Ravensdale, WA: Idyll Arbor.

Carson, D. K. (1999). The importance of creativity in family therapy: A preliminary consideration. *Family Journal: Counseling and Therapy for Couples and Families, 7*(4), 326-334.

Coleman, V. D., & Farris-Dufrene, P. M. (1996). *Art therapy and psychotherapy: Blending two therapeutic approaches.* Washington, DC: Accelerated Development.

Hammond, L. C., & Gantt, L. (1998). Using art in counseling: Ethical considerations. *Journal of Counseling and Development, 76,* 271-276.

Sween, E. (2000). Using the metaphor of teamwork in narrative couples therapy. *Journal of Systemic Therapies, 19*(3), 76-82.

Bibliotherapy Sources for Clients

Gottman, J. M., & Silver, N. (1999). *The seven principles for making marriage work.* New York: Three Rivers Press.

Howell, P., & Jones, R. (2002). *World class marriage: How to create the relationship you always wanted with the partner you already have.* Encinitas, CA: HJ Books.

Levine, J. R., & Markman, H. J. (2001). *Why do fools fall in love: Experiencing the magic, mystery, and meaning of successful relationships.* New York: Jossey-Bass.

McCarthy, B., & McCarthy, E. J. (2004). *Getting it right the first time: Creating a healthy marriage.* New York: Brunner-Routledge.

Perry, S. K. (2003). *Loving in flow: How the happiest couples get and stay that way.* Naperville, IL: Sourcebooks.

Savage, E. (2000). *Breathing room: Creating space to be a couple.* Oakland, CA: New Harbinger.

HANDOUT 5.1

SUGGESTED SUPPLIES, PREPARATION, AND COST

Suggested Supplies

- Assorted fresh flowers and greenery (at various stages of development including buds, open blossoms, and fading blooms)
- Pine cones
- Small sticks
- Small rocks and pebbles
- Seashells
- Other objects found in nature that can appeal to both males and females
- Index cards
- Two disposable plastic plates (twelve inches in diameter)
- Floral foam (for fresh flowers)
- Floral moss
- Floral pins
- Scissors

Preparation

1. After gathering supplies, soak floral moss in warm water for approximately ten minutes (or until moss becomes fully hydrated).
2. Cut floral foam into two 3" × 3" × 3" blocks and hot glue each block to a disposable plastic plate.
3. Attach soaked floral moss to floral foam blocks on the two plates with approximately four floral pins each.
4. Arrange flowers and other objects on a table.
5. Since some clients may be drawn to a particular object because of its name (e.g., client choosing a snapdragon because he believes his partner often snaps at him), write names of flowers or objects on index cards and place cards next to the specific items.
6. Some clients may want to adapt objects. Therefore, add scissors to the table.

Cost

The cost of supplies used in activities is often a consideration. Although numerous items are listed, there are many ways to make this activity cost effective. First, pine cones, small sticks, small rocks and pebbles, wildflowers, seashells, and other like objects are readily available at no cost to the individual who practices taking walks in nature for exercise and self-care. Second, therapists may choose to grow their own flowers, purchase them at discount stores, or request that clients bring them and other objects to the session. Another suggestion is to cut the length of the flower stems. Using shorter flowers results in smaller arrangements, consequently using fewer materials and lowering costs. Finally, as seen in the list of suggested supplies, this activity requires flowers at various stages of development. Since florists generally discard flowers that are beyond their peak blooms, it is recommended that therapists work closely with a florist, as they will often donate these flowers.

Forth, N. L. A., & Seto, A. (2007). Blossoming relationships: Using creativity in couple counseling. In L. L. Hecker, C. F. Sori, & Associates, *The therapist's notebook, volume 2: More homework, handouts, and activities for use in psychotherapy* (pp. 37-44). Binghamton, NY: The Haworth Press.

SECTION II:
CHILDREN, ADOLESCENTS, AND FAMILIES

6

Hugging, Holding, Huddling, and Cuddling (3HC): A Task Prescription in Couple and Family Therapy

Luciano L'Abate

Type of Contribution: *Homework, Handout*

Objectives

The purpose of this homework activity is to introduce the importance of extensive touching, hugging, holding, huddling, and cuddling (3HC) in intimate (committed, close, and prolonged) relationships. It seems that 3HC is so important in showing and sharing affection that it should receive more attention than it has received heretofore from the couple and family therapy community.

Rationale for Use

After examining theory-derived clinical applications of 3HC as a task prescription for couples and families (L'Abate, 2000b), it seemed that this topic needed concrete, practical expansion and applications. This task prescription is too important to relegate it just to theory.

3HC represents four levels of embracing as reciprocal but sequential acts, starting with hugging, between intimates according to a variety of dimensions. They are similar to the extent that all four represent one form of affectionate contact between two or more individuals obtained through mutual embrace. However, all four acts differ in terms of: (1) target persons being hugged, held, huddled, and cuddled (partner, parent, child, friend, lover, acquaintance, etc.); (2) intensity (weak, strong); (3) duration, to the extent that: (a) hugging lasts from a few seconds to about a minute, (b) holding can last from a few seconds to four to five minutes, (c) huddling can last over five minutes, and (d) cuddling can last from a few minutes to hours; (4) frequency (once or more often a day, every other day, weekly, monthly, once in a blue moon); (5) goal or intent (manipulative, validative, affectionate, seductive, sexual, etc.); and (6) context (immediate/delayed, public/private).

On the other hand, hugging also is often used as a relatively insignificant greeting in our culture, much like shaking hands. It is now a perfunctorily routinized, relatively superficial form of affectionate greeting and salutation for people who like each other. Its frequent use relegates hugging to an act that is trivial and tangential, having little meaning in itself. It is so very frequently used in greeting someone affectionately that there is little to use clinically with couples and families. Outside of the initial, usually short-lived, embrace, there are few indications that this behavior persists once the initial welcome is completed. There are, of course, various types of hugging (affectionate, greeting, formal, impersonal, passionate, sexual, and so on), just as there are different kinds of holding (maternal, paternal, parental, etc.). Little if any clinical use-

doi:10.1300/5550_06

fulness can be attached to just hugging. More than just hugging is needed to make a long-term difference in couples and families.

Consequently, hugging is too short-lived to derive clinical applications for couples and families. Longer periods of time, implied in holding, huddling, and cuddling, will be necessary to obtain desirable results. Furthermore, presently, hugging has become a taboo behavior for teachers, physicians, and mental health professionals because of its possible sexual overtones (Anderson & Murray, 1999; Coverdale, Bayer, Chiang, & Moore, 1996; Felmlee, 1999; Warren & Messer, 1999). In this litigious era, it is too risky to perform it, especially between individuals of different gender and of different ascribed power status, like professionals and patients. Nonetheless, hugging is the preliminary prerequisite for subsequently sequential holding, huddling, and cuddling, hence 3HC.

These considerations leave extensive 3HC as a prescribable task. This task prescription means, of course, "benign holding" in contrast with "forced holding," a coercive task prescription assigned in the therapist's office with parents of omnipotent children (L'Abate, Johnson, & Weeks, 1979). Forced holding, on the other hand, has never been prescribed outside of the therapist's office, and should not be performed outside that office under any circumstances. 3HC is benign to the extent that it is achieved voluntarily by consensus of two or more parties involved in the embrace. It is not and should not be achieved by coercion or any other kind of subtle or unsubtle communication.

Cuddling in itself usually has such a benign connotation that it does not need qualification at this juncture. Hence, the combination of sequential 3HC prescribable tasks with couples and families needs to be demonstrated in the professional's office initially but prescribed for home use after the initial office demonstration.

This generic prescription, therefore, is designed to improve the emotional climate of couple or family relationships. It is derived directly from a theory of personality socialization in the family (L'Abate, 1986, 1994, 1997) that makes being emotionally available and physically present the cornerstone of love and intimacy. It does not require perfection, performance, production, or problem solving. Its importance in child development has been studied and stressed repeatedly (Field, Harding, Soliday, & Lasko, 1994; Gupta & Schork, 1995; Linderman & Stewart, 1999). However, in spite of the alleged importance of both holding and cuddling in intimate relationships, very few references could be found about their being prescribed in couple or family therapy. In fact, no reference could be found about holding and cuddling as prescriptions in couple and family therapy in classical treatises (Gurman & Kniskern, 1981, 1991; Mikesell, Lusterman, & McDaniel, 1995).

Instructions

A detailed handout for 3HC with couples and families gives the instructions necessary to carry out this task at home. This intervention should be performed in an accessible family living area: if at all possible, bedrooms should be avoided simply because of the possible sexual connotations of the room.

3HC is meant to last from a minimum of ten to a maximum of twenty minutes, as often as partners or family members are willing to perform it (once a day, every other day, twice a week). They can use a timer or alarm clock to log how long it lasted. Telephone calls or other interruptions should be ignored and a minimum of light allowed, minimizing external sources of interference and maximizing concentration on the task at hand. Depending on the age of the children, for instance, complete darkness could be frightening. Specific instructions for this task are contained in Handout 6.1. It would be a desirably responsible, professional act to obtain a signed informed consent from caretakers after demonstrating this task in the professional's office. Professionals should refrain at all costs from participating in the office demonstration.

It must be stressed from the outset that 3HC should be performed without any behavior that crosses the line from affectionate to sexual. Therefore, it should take place sitting down on a sofa, if at all possible, not in the bedroom, unless that is the only place available. The floor might be more appropriate than the bedroom, especially the caretakers' bedroom. Talk should be kept to a minimum and only for instrumental purposes, such as feedback at the end of the task prescription. 3HC should be interrupted immediately if sexual feelings and behaviors are coming to the surface, especially in couples. The crucial difference between affection as an indication of unconditional love and sex as a completely different expression of love should be discussed with partners before prescription, or if it should enter into the task prescription.

Supposedly, according to stereotyped notions of sex and affection, men prefer sex over affection, while women prefer affection over sex (Felmlee, 1999). Many women like to be held and cuddled more often and more intensely than they like sex. Clear gender differences in this area need to be found to validate my strictly clinical and therefore impressionistic, possibly stereotyped conclusions. Women want concrete, frequent, and lasting shows of affection such as 3HC more than sex. Men seem to value sex more than affection because to some of them, not all of them of course, being affectionate may represent being soft, even weak, and worst, vulnerable. At least in the past, men were socialized for invulnerability. You do not win wars or progress in the marketplace of job competition by being soft, cuddly, and vulnerable. Possible sex differences based on stereotypes should be discussed with partners to ensure that this task is not confused with sensate focus or any other sexually oriented prescription. This task must be demonstrated in the therapist's office before prescription for home use. However, the therapist must not, in any way, shape, or form, participate in it.

Often clients (partners, parents, and children) are interested in solving the referral question. However, it should be stressed that this task is generic in nature and not oriented toward solving any specific problem. The prescribed task should be accurately chosen in view of the referral question. For instance, if a couple or family indicates that the immediate context and emotional climate of the relationship are barren and void of affection, holding and cuddling can be prescribed in addition to whatever specific intervention is taking place to deal with the referral question. It would make no sense to prescribe this task with a couple or family who are demonstrably affectionate and physically close, as shown by frequent touching and reports of frequent holding and cuddling. However, in this author's clinical experience, very few couples and families engage in frequent holding and cuddling, even relatively functional ones.

The task typically needs to be justified and explained, especially if it flows directly from what has been learned about the couple or the family's emotional climate. It may not seem directly related to the symptom or to the referral question. Hence, it becomes very important for the professional to develop an ad hoc rationale that fits into a couple or family mythology. Of course, like any prescription, it should be qualified as an experimental procedure that needs to be tried out for at least three to four weeks before discarding it as not useful. ("I don't know whether it will help or not. However, let's see what happens after you have tried it out for a couple of weeks.")

A prescribable task needs to be straightforwardly simple, concrete, easy to administer, and easy to follow for all respondents, regardless of age, gender, ethnicity, socioeconomic status, and educational background. Of course, 3HC fulfills these criteria beautifully. These behaviors cannot be any more simple, concrete, and seemingly easy to administer. However, this apparent simplicity should not in any way lull professionals into thinking that it can be administered without resistance from certain couples and families. This resistance may well represent a cultural taboo about behaviors taking place between adults. However, this is more often than not an excuse and a specific indication about fear of intimacy and its existence in the couple and family. Obsessive compulsives and those with character disorders, for instance, are often very resistant to the idea of prolonged hugging and holding. This resistance suggests that this very pattern of holding and cuddling may be a missing ingredient in many family functionalities and dys-functionalities.

Resistance to any task prescription is the best way to discover how a couple or family really functions, above and beyond talk. This prescription is a good way to discover how intimate respondents are and how intimate they want to be. They may claim they want intimacy, but when faced with a task of this kind, the claim may give way to anxieties, fears, and traumatic memories. This, like all task prescriptions, is diagnostic. It helps to find how couples and families really function or fail to function. Years ago, I saw a young, attractive couple who were having trouble with sex and sexuality because of the wife's family-of-origin strong taboo about touching. Family members were allowed to hug only at funerals. One can imagine what connotations hugging had for this young wife. In fact, this is the very case that started me thinking about the need for more 3HC.

If administered in a timely and appropriate fashion, the outcome of this prescription should be visible within a relatively short time, three to four weeks after its initial administration. Therefore, it is crucial for professionals to recommend that written notes be taken by both partners or parents immediately after termination of the task, describing what was done, how long it lasted, and what was said by everyone involved, especially children. I have insisted for a long time on the importance of written homework assignments (L'Abate, 1986, 1994). By the same token, I have also stressed the importance of nonverbal behavior (L'Abate, 1997, 1999) as demanded by this prescription. Without written feedback, it would be difficult to evaluate whether this task is helpful or not. Like any task administration, how it is accomplished tells how the couple or family is functioning or malfunctioning. It could be completed well. It could be completed halfway, or not at all. In any case, how a task is performed furnishes useful information to professionals.

As already suggested, two provisos should be kept in mind, one before and the second after the administration of this task. In the first place, this prescription should be introduced very tentatively, because: (1) the evidence to support it is still strictly anecdotal, and therefore this prescription is at a pre-experimental stage; and (2) one cannot be at all sure that it will generalize outside my experience. ("I do not know and I am not sure whether this task will work. How about trying it for a couple of weeks to see what happens? Would you be willing to carry it out after I explain to you what it is? Let me show it to you right here in my office and let's see what you feel about it.")

In the second place, even if the task is not successful, it should provide fertile grounds to find reasons why it was not. If it was successful, the therapist should express complete surprise and healthy skepticism about its success (Weeks & L'Abate, 1982), questioning whether it was as successful as the couple or family claims it was, or whether it would last long. ("It is probably a fluke. I doubt whether it will last long. Why don't we try for another two weeks to find out whether this is not a temporary escape into health? Is that okay?")

To illustrate how this prescription has been used, the following case study is presented.

Brief Vignette

This family of very low socioeconomic status and education consisted of a single mother, Maribel, with three children with three different fathers. Maribel, a rather large, tall woman in her middle thirties, worked as a hospital assistant without any financial help or availability from the three fathers of the children. The children ranged in age from thirteen to four. Dwayne, the oldest son, was a towering figure already over six feet tall. Earnest, the Identified Patient (IP), was eleven years old, and was referred by the school for inattention and sudden rages at himself in the classroom. The "baby" in the family, LaKeisha, was four years old. Both boys were very affectionate with LaKeisha and took care of her while the mother remained at work. Earnest's behavior in school produced frequent calls to the mother at work that were not appreciated by her supervisor.

A typical problematic exchange would include Earnest not paying attention to a teacher, whereby he subsequently complained that he had not understood what the teacher was saying and had asked the teacher to repeat the explanation. The teacher demanded he pay attention, resenting and not fulfilling his repeated requests for repetition of instructions. As a result of the teacher's refusal to satisfy his requests, Earnest would become angry and refuse to complete homework assignments, consequently producing a call from the teacher to the mother. These phone calls had occurred at least two to four times a week since the start of school weeks earlier. In spite of these problems, Earnest maintained a B average in most of his courses, except arithmetic. At home Dwayne and Earnest were reminded frequently by the mother about chores to be completed, with each child being responsible for a specific number of chores.

The mother as well as the boys lavished a great deal of attention and affection on the youngest daughter. However, when inquiring about affection with or toward the older boys, Maribel demurred, explaining that they seemed to want too much affection from her, wanting to kiss and hug her very often. She stated she was too busy to devote any time to them in this manner. Furthermore, she believed they were old enough not to need her affection. The validity of this statement was met by loud protestations from the two older boys, who stated very clearly and strongly their need for affection from her. Her response was to admonish them for wanting affection when they had not completed their chores, responsibilities that ultimately were still left to her to complete or remind them to complete. Her love, therefore, was conditional on their performance and production.

Maribel described her childhood as being one without affection, where her mother was too busy surviving to give her and her siblings any affection. The therapist asked the mother if this inadequate affection might relate to her having three different fathers for her children. She stated she never thought about this possibility. The mother was congratulated for being an outstanding mother given that she was able to support herself and take good care of the children, who were always well fed, adequately dressed, and attending school.

During one of the three initial evaluation interviews, Earnest seemed to be very tense but alert and verbally articulate, explaining his behavior at school as a problem with the teacher, with statements such as: "He does not like me." Earnest skillfully avoided taking responsibility for his inattention and for getting mad at himself because of his need to be error free. Dwayne also expressed dismay of being made fun of by his classmates for his height. Therapy initially addressed the instrumental issues about who did what and when at home and the results of the actions. In addition, a call was placed to the teacher with whom Earnest was having trouble. It became apparent through the interviews that Earnest remained rather sad and preoccupied. Maribel still had to remind him repeatedly of his chores and responsibilities in the house. The possibility was contemplated to allow use of the television contingent on completion of homework and household chores. Eventually, mother, Dwayne, and LaKeisha were asked to step out of the therapy session and Earnest was asked directly, "What are you afraid of?" In response, he began to sob, stating, "I am afraid of losing my mother . . . I am afraid of losing my family."

At this point, it became clear that the 3HC task could be administered according to the steps outlined in the handout, that is, every day, after Maribel came home from work for two weeks (this is the frequency of therapy sessions for this family). Both older children were very enthusiastic about the administration of this task, because of their previously stated need to be more affectionate with their mother. As a demonstration, after being instructed to hug, hold, huddle, and cuddle with each other, they enthusiastically jumped from their seats and joined Maribel on the sofa, hugging her from both sides with LaKeisha staying on top of all of them. When it was explained how the task should be practiced, the family agreed to practice it every day for the next two weeks.

After two weeks, they reported being together ten times out of the fourteen prescribed times because of intervening holidays and work-related problems. Earnest appeared more cheerful than he had ever appeared before, laughing and smiling throughout the session. During the past two weeks there had not been any calls from school. Maribel reported that the children were minding her. She did not have to repeat herself in asking them to complete required chores. Since this improvement was clearly a freak occurrence, and since the children were talking while being together, it was agreed that the time together would be shortened if they talked and that they would be together three times a week for a duration of ten minutes. The family returned two weeks later to report that again, there had not been any calls from the school, the children were taking responsibility for chores without reminders from the mother, and the whole family seemed to get along better. Still not convinced that there had been any serious change, the therapist suggested that instead of two weeks the next session would take place in four weeks. Earnest objected to this suggestion and indicated his desire to come back in two weeks.

During this visit (which lasted fifteen minutes), Earnest was relaxed and quite ebullient. Both Maribel and the children reported gleefully that they had not practiced the task, because, as the mother explained, "I am now very affectionate toward them all the time. . . . We do not need the task because I changed . . . I understand that they need affection as much as I do." Both older children agreed with the mother. The mother reported that she did not receive any calls from school, while in the past, she confirmed, she would receive "three to four calls a week." We agreed to follow up in a month to see whether this was a fluke (without reaction from Earnest) and in subsequent months. When the family expressed concern about being dropped from treatment, they were reassured about the continued interest of the therapist and that they would be followed up until one year had elapsed from the beginning of treatment (i.e., administration of the task). They seemed happy to receive this reassurance.

A follow-up telephone call a year later found the whole family functioning well, as far as their verbal report went. Earnest was now getting along better in school, without any phone calls from teachers, and making good grades (mostly As and Bs).

Contraindications for Use

Clearly, this prescription should not be used in cases of incest or sexual or verbal abuse, unless these conditions have already been treated successfully. It seems also contraindicated for enmeshed or extremely rigid families, whose boundaries are either too permeable or too impermeable. Consequently, if difficult or impossible to prescribe toward the beginning of therapy, this task could be assigned toward the end of therapy, before terminating it, as a diagnostic tool to determine at what level a couple or family is functioning.

Hence, it could be that 3HC could be more successfully prescribed with couples and families with internalizing disorders. Its administration to severely dysfunctional couples and families, if any, should take place under very controlled conditions. Additional scripts and treatment plans for a variety of individuals (children, adolescents, adults), couples, and families can be found on the Internet (L'Abate, 1996). These plans can be used as structured interviews as well as workbooks. They are classified by test score or test profile and by referral question. Symptoms or problems by referral question are further subdivided by internalizing (anxiety, depression, fears), externalizing (anger, hostility, aggression, and impulsivity), and psychopathological, thought or behavior disorders.

Conclusion

3HC is so simple that one must wonder why it has not already been administered as standard operating procedures in couple and family therapy. One reason for such neglect could lie in the very medium used by many therapists, that is, words rather than activities or systematic, written homework assignments (L'Abate, 1999, 2000a). Another more insidious reason for the relative neglect of this prescription may lie in the personal experience of therapists ourselves. If we have not experienced 3HC in our developmental histories and as adults, how can we ever prescribe it?

References

Anderson, E. M., & Murray, L. (1999). Concerns about allegations of child sexual abuse against teachers and the teaching environment. *Child Abuse and Neglect, 23,* 833-843.

Coverdale, J., Bayer, T., Chiang, E., & Moore, C. (1996). Medical students' attitudes on specialist physicians' social and sexual contact with patients. *Academic Psychiatry, 20,* 35-42.

Felmlee, D. H. (1999). Social norms in same- and cross-gender friendships. *Social Psychology Quarterly, 62,* 53-67.

Field, T., Harding, J., Soliday, B., & Lasko, D. (1994). Touching in infant, toddler, and preschool nurseries. *Early Child Development and Care, 98,* 113-120.

Gupta, M. A., & Schork, N. J. (1995). Touch deprivation has an adverse effect on body image: Some preliminary observations. *International Journal of Eating Disorders, 17,* 185-189.

Gurman, A. S., & Kniskern, D. P. (Eds.). (1981). *Handbook of family therapy.* New York: Brunner/Mazel.

Gurman, A. S., & Kniskern, D. P. (Eds.). (1991). *Handbook of family therapy: Volume II.* New York: Brunner/Mazel.

L'Abate, L. (1986). *Systematic family therapy.* New York: Brunner/Mazel.

L'Abate, L. (1994). *A theory of personality development.* New York: Wiley.

L'Abate, L. (1996). *Workbooks for better living.* http://www.mentalhealthhelp.com.

L'Abate, L. (1997). *The self in the family: A classification of personality, criminality and psychopathology.* New York: Wiley.

L'Abate, L. (1999). Taking the bull by the horns: Beyond talk in psychological interventions. *Family Journal: Therapy and Counseling with Couples and Families, 7,* 206-220.

L'Abate, L. (Ed.). (2000a). *Distance writing and computer-assisted interventions in psychiatry and mental health.* Stamford, CT: Ablex.

L'Abate, L. (2000b). *Hugging, holding, huddling, and cuddling: A theory-derived prescription for couples and families.* Manuscript submitted for publication.

L'Abate, L., Johnson, J., & Weeks, G. R. (1979). Forced holding: A technique for treating parentified children. *Family Therapy, 6,* 124-132.

Linderman, T. M., & Stewart, K. B. (1999). Sensory integrative-based occupational therapy and functional outcomes in young children with pervasive developmental disorders: A single-subject study. *American Journal of Occupational Therapy, 53,* 207-213.

Mikesell, R. H., Lusterman, D., & McDaniel, S. H. (Eds.). (1995). *Integrating family therapy: Handbook of family psychology and systems theory.* Washington, DC: American Psychological Association.

Warren, C. S., & Messer, S. B. (1999). Brief psychodynamic therapy with anxious children. In S. W. Russ & T. H. Ollendick (Eds.), *Handbook of psychotherapies with children and families: Issues in clinical child psychology* (pp. 219-237). New York: Plenum.

Weeks, G. R. & L'Abate, L. (1982). *Paradoxical psychotherapy: Theory and practice with individuals, couples, and families.* New York: Brunner/Mazel.

Professional Readings and Resources

Jordan, K. B., & L'Abate, L. (1999). The tape of the mind workbook: A single case study. *Journal of Family Psychotherapy, 10,* 13-25.

L'Abate, L. (1999). Decisions we (mental health professionals) need to make (whether we like them or not): A reply to Cummings and Hoyt. *Family Journal: Therapy and Counseling for Couples and Families, 7,* 227-230.

L'Abate, L. (1999). Programmed distance writing in therapy with acting-out adolescents. In C. Schaefer (Ed.), *Innovative psychotherapy techniques in child and adolescent therapy* (pp. 108-157). New York: Wiley.

L'Abate, L. (1999). Structured enrichment and distance writing for couples. In R. Berger & T. Hannah (Eds.), *Preventive approaches in couples therapy* (pp. 106-124). Philadelphia: Taylor & Francis.

L'Abate, L. (2000). Psychoeducational strategies. In J. Carlson & L. Sperry (Eds.), *Brief therapy strategies with individuals and couples* (pp. 396-436). Phoenix, AZ: Zeig/Tucker.

L'Abate, L., De Giacomo, P., McCarty, F., Verrastro, G., & De Giacomo, A. (2000). Testing three models of intimate behavior. *Contemporary Family Therapy: An International Journal, 22,* 103-122.

L'Abate, L., Esterling, B. A., Murray, E., & Pennebaker, J. M. (1999). Empirical foundations for writing in prevention and psychotherapy: Mental and physical outcomes. *Clinical Psychology Review, 19,* 79-96.

HANDOUT 6.1. 3HC WITH COUPLES AND FAMILIES

Even though this task seems very simple, it is not as simple as it may seem at first blush. You are being asked to hug and hold each other, huddling and cuddling with each other by appointment only at the beginning and at will later, if you enjoy doing it for longer than just a few minutes. When you have learned this task well, you may want to do it on your own as often as you like.

Step 1. Make an appointment at least twenty-four hours before the task is to be performed. Make sure that everybody agrees about how important it might be for couples and families to hug and hold each other, huddling and cuddling in ways that are not usually done in our fast-moving culture and our busy schedules. Unless everybody understands the importance of this task, you may need to hold a couple or family conference to make sure that everybody in the family agrees about how important this task might be for the couple or whole family's well-being. Determine beforehand how long this task will last (anywhere from ten to fifteen minutes depending upon how often you perform it (every day, every other day, twice a week, once a week).

Step 2. Before starting this task, make sure that there will not be interruptions while you are doing it. Take the phone off the hook if you do not have an answering machine, cut out all the lights, including the natural light from windows, and, if necessary put a Please Do Not Disturb sign outside your residence door.

Step 3. Find a place in the house that is comfortable for everybody and that will contain all the family members. If a sofa is not roomy enough to hold everybody in the family, use a large bed, or if you have a very comfortable rug, use that.

Step 4. Before starting this task, make sure that you set an alarm or timer for the time agreed upon by everybody.

Step 5. Form a huddle by making sure that everybody is hugging and holding everybody else as much as possible. Allow yourselves to feel whether you are enjoying cuddling and being cuddled.

Step 6. While you are cuddling, it is important to have no talk. Everybody needs to be silent in order to concentrate on being together without any talk or interruptions of any kind. Talking or nonrequired movements would interfere with the concentration needed to perform and complete this task successfully.

Step 7. Once the alarm or timer goes off, break the huddle and remind each other about the next time you are going to do it again. Partners or caretakers should take down in writing any comments offered freely by any family member. If you do write these comments down and are presently under the care of a mental health professional, bring these notes to your next session.

We hope that you have enjoyed this task and that you will make it an important routine in your marriage and family life.

L'Abate, L. (2007). Hugging, holding, huddling, and cuddling (3HC): A task prescription in couple and family therapy. In L. L. Hecker, C. F. Sori, & Associates, *The therapist's notebook, volume 2: More homework, handouts, and activities for use in psychotherapy* (pp. 47-55). Binghamton, NY: The Haworth Press.

7

Bridging Game for Ill and Well Siblings

Catherine Ford Sori
Nancee M. Biank

Type of Contribution: *Handouts, Activity*

Objectives

When a child is seriously ill, sibling relationships are often adversely affected. The primary purpose of this activity is to open communication among siblings in order to help them better understand the impact of the illness on both the ill and well children. This will help to strengthen sibling relationships, reduce negative sibling exchanges, and promote more positive interactions among ill and well siblings. It may be played with up to four siblings.

Rationale for Use

Impact of Childhood Illness on a Family

Having a child with a serious or chronic illness impacts all individuals and relationships within a family. Parents often feel devastation and guilt when a child is diagnosed with a serious illness, believing they are supposed to be able to protect their child from harm. Much of their time and energy must be often redirected into the treatment and care of an ill child. In addition, they must earn a living, care for other children and their home, and sometimes also take care of other ill or older family members (Sori & Biank, 2006). These increased demands place an extra burden of stress on the parents as individuals and often affect their relationship as a couple as well. Unresolved marital issues and other family problems (such as child behavior issues) often get put on hold because the illness demands so much of the family's resources. In addition, researchers have reported high degrees of symptoms in the parents of children with cancer, including post-traumatic stress disorder, anxiety, depression, and sleep problems, and many of these symptoms last for several years (see Die-Trill & Stuber, 1998; Hill & Stuber, 1998).

As the family organizes around the illness, there can be little time or emotional energy to focus on the needs of individual family members. Often mothers devote much of their attention to the ill child, which can lead fathers and well children to feel isolated and excluded (Sori & Biank, 2006).

Impact of Illness on Child

A child who is diagnosed with a serious illness can have a wide range of emotional reactions, including depression, anxiety, and panic (Frager & Shapiro, 1998), as well as withdrawal from peer relationships, separation anxiety and attachment issues with parents (either in the form of

doi:10.1300/5550_07

clinging or distancing behaviors), and regression (Sori & Biank, 2006). Parents (especially mothers) may become overprotective, and children may rebel against this by refusing to comply with treatment or dietary restrictions (Sori & Biank, 2006). Children are often dismayed at the change in their appearance following surgery (e.g., amputations) or as the result of treatment (e.g., alopecia or significant weight gain). Some children's appearance may be so changed that they are mistaken for the opposite sex. This can interfere with the development of sexual identity as well as normal peer relationships. In addition, if a child has experienced repeated or prolonged hospitalizations, the removal from everyday family life can interfere with normal family relationships, especially among siblings. A child who is confined to the hospital or home for long periods of time often resents the normal life that his or her siblings continue to lead. Ill children may be forced to sit on the sidelines while their well siblings play sports, attend parties, and participate in extracurricular activities that may be off limits to a critically ill child.

Impact of Illness on Well Siblings

Studies have shown that well siblings are often impacted as much or more than an ill child in areas such as level of fear, having low self-esteem, and feeling socially isolated (Rait & Lederberg, 1990). Some studies have found healthy siblings of pediatric cancer patients to have symptoms of PTSD (see Hill & Stuber, 1998), while other research has found more positive outcomes for these children (e.g., Rait & Lederberg, 1990; Rolland, 1994).

Well siblings often experience a myriad of losses related to illness in a brother or sister. These include loss of parents' time, attention, and resources, which are often focused heavily on treatments, doctor appointments, and caring for the ill child. Families may be strapped financially and parents may not have the time to taxi well children to and from events, so well children may have to drop out of sports, music lessons, or other activities that they enjoyed and that were important to their identity. Above all, they experience the loss of being normal and feel different from children their age, and from other families.

Well siblings often experience a myriad of confusing and ambivalent feelings (Sori & Biank, 2006). They wonder not only if their sibling might die but also if they might die, and if their parents die, they worry about who will take care of them. Younger children who are egocentric may feel guilty, believing that they somehow caused their brother or sister to get sick, and may also experience guilt because they are still able to go to school and participate in everyday activities that are forbidden to their sick sibling. Simultaneously, they can feel jealous of all the time and attention the ill child receives from parents, extended family, and friends. Parents may not openly share information about the diagnosis or prognosis, which may leave well children anxious and fearing the worst. Sometimes siblings may be separated from family members for extended periods when a parent (often the mother) moves with the ill child to be closer to a treatment facility, either leaving a parent behind with the well children or farming out well children to relatives for the duration of treatment. Children are often left in the dark, worried and anxious, and longing for a return to normal family life.

Even when the family remains intact, children often sense the level of anxiety and stress their parents are experiencing. In an effort to spare parents any additional worries, well siblings may not question their parents about what is happening or share worries about their own lives. They may internalize their distress and try to compensate their parents by being as perfect as they can, striving for all As in school or being extra compliant and helpful, asking for little for themselves. Conversely, well children may develop behavior problems in reaction to the distress in the family, perhaps as an attempt to distract distraught parents from their worry about the ill child. In either scenario, well children's normal emotional and developmental needs are often overlooked as a family organizes their energies and attention around caring for an ill child, especially one with a life-threatening illness such as cancer, diabetes, or cystic fibrosis.

As a result, sibling relationships often suffer. Ill children may resent that well siblings are able to lead a normal life, attending school, going to movies and parties, and participating in extra-curricular activities. At the same time, they may feel guilty for taking up so much of the parents' time and the family resources, often at the expense of the other children in the family. Well children may resent the special status and attention given to the ill child, and yet worry about their ill sibling and parents, and experience guilt over their jealousy and the fact that their brother or sister is suffering. Both well and ill children experience losses related to their previous roles and functioning in the sibling subsystem.

The game described in this chapter is designed to bridge the gap that can occur when roles become polarized, in order to help both well and ill siblings begin to dialogue about how the illness experience has affected them individually, as siblings, and within their family as a whole.

Instructions

You will need one die, miniature figures or markers (such as small colored stones or markers from another board game), the game board, and game cards, which can be found in the handout at the end of this chapter.

The clinician may photocopy the playing board and laminate it for durability, if desired. There are three sets of question cards: one for ill children, one for either sick or well siblings, and one for well siblings. These cards may be printed on card stock, laminated, and cut. They should be divided into three piles.

Ill and well siblings play the game according to the instructions below. When a card is chosen, the clinician should help siblings to share their answers and expand to create conversations that help children better understand each other's experiences of being an ill or well sibling. The game is played as follows:

Each player gets ten points or chips to start the game. Players roll one die and move the amount of spaces requested. When landing on a space that indicates a card should be chosen, ill children may select a card from either the ill child cards, or the stack of cards for ill or well siblings. Likewise, well children have the option of choosing a card from either the well sibling stack or the ill or well sibling stack. If children answer the question or follow the activity, they earn one point or chip. If they choose not to answer a question or activity, they lose a point or chip. Players who decide to answer a question that was asked of someone else also get a point or chip; or if they choose not to answer it and another player does, the player who answers gets two points or chips.

The game is over when the last person lands on the finish line. Everyone counts up their points or chips. The winner is the person with the most points.

Brief Vignette

The Welty family consisted of Mary, the mother; Tom, the father; Sandra, a nine-year-old well child; and Susan, a six-year-old girl who had been sick with leukemia for approximately three years. Despite treatment, Susan had relapsed and her prognosis was uncertain. Susan had been out of school for more than a year. Although she was currently in a second remission, her mother was still quite worried about her. Even though the doctor had said Susan was now well enough to go back to school, Mary called the school each morning to talk to the nurse to check that no one was sick in Susan's class in case she might catch something that could harm her impaired immune system. If a rash of flu or colds occurred in the school, Mary would keep both children home.

Mr. and Mrs. Welty felt they were handling everything reasonably well but brought the children into their local cancer support center on the recommendation of the hospital's pediatric oncology social worker. After a few family sessions, the parents enrolled Sandra in a support group for children who had a close family member with cancer. Sandra was an extremely bright and hard working fourth grader. She was functioning well at school both academically and socially, played soccer, and loved to help her sister each night with homework.

Sandra seemed to enjoy coming to the groups at the cancer center, where she participated actively in both activities and discussions. In one group, the children were reflecting on changes in their families and in family relationships since the illness. After listening intently to the discussion, Sandra said in an animated voice that she didn't think it should be her responsibility to make sure that her sister learned to read, and that it wasn't fair that her Aunt Sally and Uncle Jim brought special presents to Susan and not to her. She also didn't think it was fair that her mom sometimes kept her home from school just because somebody in her class was sick, and Mom worried she'd bring some germ home to Susan, which could be quite serious because her immune system had been compromised due to the cancer treatment. When the children were asked to think about what changes had occurred in the sick person's life, Sandra remarked that she bet Susan missed being able to play outside and go to birthday parties.

In one family session, both parents were encouraged to talk with each other about all the changes that had occurred in the family during the course of Susan's illness, treatments, remission, relapse, and second remission. They also discussed the roller coaster of emotions that accompanied all these changes, as well as how roles and relationships had changed within the family. The parents were open to answering questions Sandra had about Susan's illness.

The Bridging Game for Siblings was chosen to provide Sandra and Susan with a playful activity to help them begin to share how the illness had impacted each of them and their relationship. The children were excited to play a game together, which strengthened the boundary around the sibling subsystem.

Sandra caught on quickly to the rules of the game, and offered to help Susan read her cards, which Susan appreciated, allowing the children to play with minimal help from the therapist. As they moved their markers around the board and answered questions on the cards, the children were able to share their illness experiences quite openly with each other. For example, Sandra told Susan that what she missed the most was that they couldn't ride their bicycles together anymore and that they didn't get to go on vacation again that year. What made her sad was when Susan had to be in the hospital for months, and when she knew that Susan had to get shots and chemotherapy that hurt and made her sick. Sandra confessed that she worried a lot about both Susan and her parents, but also felt it wasn't fair that she had to be the one to make sure Susan kept on track with her schoolwork. It just felt like too big a worry for her, and she wished Mom and Dad would help Susan more with her homework. Sandra said what wasn't fair was when she didn't get to go places because Mom was afraid she'd bring home a germ that Susan would catch. She confessed that even though she sometimes felt jealous of all the attention Susan got, she knew it was hard for Susan to have to be home all the time, so it was really okay. What made her happy was that there were still things they could do together, like playing Barbies and games, and having family video night. Sandra was very hopeful that Susan would get well and said she prayed for Susan every night.

Susan said what she missed the most was going to school or playing sports like Sandra did. She missed just being like the other kids. She also said that while she sometimes got presents from relatives, she didn't think it was fair that she never got to go to the movies or to birthday parties, like Sandra, and she missed playing with friends in the neighborhood. She said going to the doctor was okay, but she was embarrassed to go back to school wearing a hat because she had lost most of her hair from the chemotherapy. She worried that she'd never learn to read as well as Sandra, since schoolwork seemed really hard for her. She said she'd ask Mom to help her more with schoolwork so Sandra could play outside right after school. Sometimes she felt bad that she got more attention from Mom and Dad. But one good thing that came from being sick was that Sandra spent more time playing with her, and she was happy when Sandra read to her as well.

During the course of the game, Sandra told Susan it was okay if she got more attention at home, because Sandra got attention from whichever parent came to her games. Susan shared how much Sandra's cards and visits meant to her when she was in the hospital, and the girls came up with some games they might play together. In addition, Sandra promised to walk Susan to her class each morning until she wasn't embarrassed about her hat anymore. They also talked about the fun bike rides they would take in the summer, when Susan was stronger.

After the game, the children shared some of what they talked about with Mr. and Mrs. Welty. The parents listened in amazement at how frank and open the girls were with each other in sharing how cancer had affected their lives and relationship. In the family discussion that followed the game, Mr. and Mrs. Welty told Sandra that they had no idea she had been holding in so many feelings and that they were glad she had shared them. Mrs. Welty said she would try not to keep Sandra home unless there was a clear danger to Susan's health. They family talked about the possibility of taking a vacation at a cottage that a friend had offered to lend them. They had thought Sandra had liked helping her sister with homework but realized now that it was too much responsibility. After some discussion with the parents alone, Mr. and Mrs. Welty agreed to talk to the school about having Susan tested for any learning disabilities that could have resulted from her cancer treatment.

At the end of the session, the therapist complimented the girls on how well they played the game and asked what it was like for them. Sandra said she loved it and felt so much better. Susan asked if they could have a copy to take home so they could play it sometimes by themselves and even make up their own questions. The parents stated that they were very relieved, since so many thoughts and feelings had been openly discussed, and they looked forward to the therapist's suggestion that they start having regular date nights when they would focus on each other rather than on anything related to illness or problems. The family all agreed that they had many strengths and were confident that they could handle the future.

Suggestions for Follow-Up

Additional cards can be made to address any specific concerns that arise during the course of therapy. Cards may be created to address adolescent issues (such as sex and dating) or to include parents as well.

Contraindications

This game should not be used in situations in which the therapist believes there may be negative repercussions for children who share thoughts or feelings toward family members. As with all therapy involving children, therapists should set a ground rule that children not be punished for anything that they say in sessions. In addition, sometimes parents are very protective of their children, so this activity should be timed to use when parents are ready for more open communication about the illness and its effects on family members. Therapists may want to edit or eliminate some cards initially until the family is more open to discussing more sensitive topics, such as spirituality or death.

References

Die-Trill, M., & Stuber, M. L. (1998). Psychological problems of curative cancer treatment. In J. Holland (Ed.), *Psycho-oncology* (pp. 897-906). New York: Oxford University Press.

Frager, G., & Shapiro, B. (1998). Pediatric palliative care and pain management. In J. Holland (Ed.), *Psycho-oncology* (pp. 907-922). New York: Oxford University Press.

Hill, J. M., & Stuber, M. L. (1998). Long-term adaptation, psychiatric sequelae, and PTSD. In J. Holland (Ed.), *Psycho-oncology* (pp. 923-929). New York: Oxford University Press.

Rait, D., & Lederberg, M. (1990). The family of the cancer patient. In J. Holland & J. H. Rowland (Eds.), *Handbook of psycho-oncology: Psychological care of the patient with cancer* (p. 589). New York: Oxford University Press.

Rolland, J. S. (1994). *Families, illness, and disability: An integrative treatment model.* New York: Basic Books.

Sori, C. F., & Biank, N. M. (2006). Counseling children and families experiencing serious illness. In C. F. Sori (Ed.), *Engaging children in family therapy: Creative approaches for integrating theory and research in clinical practice* (pp. 223-244). New York: Routledge.

Professional Readings and Resources

Binger, C. M. (1984). Psychosocial intervention with the child cancer patient and family. *Psychosomatics, 25*(12), 899-902.

Holland, J. C. (Ed.). (1998). *Psycho-oncology.* New York: Oxford University Press.

Kazak, A. E. (1989). Families of chronically ill children: A systems and social-ecological model of adaptation and challenge. *Journal of Consulting and Clinical Psychology, 57*(1), 25-30.

Kellerman, J. (1980). *Psychological aspects of childhood cancer.* Springfield, IL: Charles C Thomas.

McDaniel, S. H., Hepworth, J., & Doherty, W. J. (1992). *Medical family therapy: A biopsychosocial approach to families with health problems.* New York: Basic Books.

McDaniel, S. H., Hepworth, J., & Doherty, W. J. (1993). A new prescription for family health care. *Family Therapy Networker, 17*(1), 19-29, 62-63.

Pearse, M. (1977). The child with cancer: Impact on the family. *Journal of School Health*, March, 174-179.

Rolland, J. S. (1994). *Families, illness, and disability: An integrative treatment model.* New York: Basic Books.

Sargent, J. (1983). The sick child: Family complications. *Developmental and Behavioral Pediatrics, 4*(1), 50-56.

Sori, C. F., & Biank, N. M. (2006). Counseling children and families experiencing serious illness. In C. F. Sori (Ed.), *Engaging children in family therapy: Creative approaches for integrating theory and research in clinical practice* (pp. 223-244). New York: Routledge.

Bibliotherapy Sources for Clients

Biank, N., & Sori, C. (2003). Tips for parents when there is illness in the family. In C. Sori & L. Hecker (Eds.), *The therapist's notebook for children and adolescents: Homework, handouts, and activities for use in psychotherapy* (pp. 150-156). New York: The Haworth Press. (Excellent handout for parents.)

Fromer, M. F. (1995). *Surviving childhood cancer: A guide for families.* Washington, DC: American Psychiatric Press. (Discusses emotional reactions of family members; how to explain a cancer diagnosis to children at different developmental stages; adapting and coping; school issues.)

Saltzman, D. (1995). *The jester has lost his jingle.* Palos Verdes Estates, CA: The Jester Co.

Woznick, L. A., & Goodheart, C. D. (2002). *Living with childhood cancer: A practical guide to help families cope.* Washington, DC: American Psychological Association.

QUESTION CARDS FOR ILL CHILDREN

What makes you the most angry about being sick?	How does it feel when you can't play with your friends?
What scares you?	What is it like to be sick so often?
What do you do to make yourself feel better when you are feeling stressed?	What is your favorite video game? (Ask this question to person on your left)
What makes Mom the most angry?	How is it to have to take medicine every day?
What makes Dad the most angry?	What is your biggest worry?
Tell something good that has come from being sick.	Do you think Mom and Dad play fair?
Are you ever embarrassed about being sick? If so, what embarrasses you?	What is it like to have to go to the doctor so often?
What do you think about not being able to go to school?	Who do you think gets more attention? Why?
What about your Dad makes you the most angry? What about your Mom makes you the most angry?	What can't you do together with your brother(s) or sister(s) that you miss?
Do you think about dying? When? What is that like?	What is your biggest gripe?
Do you believe in miracles?	Free Pass
What is the most fun you have ever had?	Free Pass
What do you miss the most?	If you could have one wish, what would it be?
What makes you laugh?	What makes you cry?
How has being ill changed you?	How are you still the same?
What things have you learned since being ill?	What things can you still do with your siblings that you really enjoy?
If you could ask God one question, what would it be?	Do you pray? If so, what and how do you pray?
Why do you think you got sick?	What's the hardest part of being ill?

Sori, C. F., & Biank, N. M. (2007). Bridging game for ill and well siblings. In L. L. Hecker, C. F. Sori, & Associates, *The therapist's notebook, volume 2: More homework, handouts, and activities for use in psychotherapy* (pp. 57-67). Binghamton, NY: The Haworth Press.

HANDOUT 7.2

GENERAL QUESTIONS FOR BOTH SICK AND WELL SIBLINGS

Why do you think people get sick?	Do you believe in heaven?
What has changed the most in your family since the illness?	What things are still the same?
What can't you do now that you used to do?	What things can you still do?
Who helps you feel better when you are feeling bad?	If you could ask your parents anything, what would it be?
If you could tell your parents anything, what would it be?	What questions would you like to ask the doctor about your (your sibling's) illness?
When are times that you forget about the illness?	What is it like to have pain or see your sibling in pain?
How do you and your sibling play?	What is different about your play now than before the illness?
What is the most unfair thing about being ill or having an ill sibling?	How do you think your sibling feels?
Who in your family is most affected by the illness?	Who in your family is least affected by the illness?
Free Pass	Free Pass
What helps you feel better when you are worried, sad, or anxious?	

Sori, C. F., & Biank, N. M. (2007). Bridging game for ill and well siblings. In L. L. Hecker, C. F. Sori, & Associates, *The therapist's notebook, volume 2: More homework, handouts, and activities for use in psychotherapy* (pp. 57-67). Binghamton, NY: The Haworth Press.

HANDOUT 7.3

QUESTION CARDS FOR WELL SIBLINGS

Who do you think gets more attention? Why?	(Ask this question to the person to the right) Do you ever feel left out? When? What do you do?
What can't you do together that you miss?	What is your favorite TV show? (Ask this to person on your right)
What makes you the most angry about having a sibling who is sick?	What is your biggest worry?
What about your mom makes you the most angry? What about your dad makes you the most angry?	What is it like for you when your sibling has so many doctor appointments?
Do you think Mom and Dad play fair?	Do you believe in miracles?
Can you name one good thing that has come from having a sick sibling?	Are you ever embarrassed about having a sick sibling?
What is it like for you when your sibling gets to stay home from school?	Do you think about your sibling dying? When?
Free Pass	Free Pass
What scares you?	What are your dreams for the future?
What do you do to make yourself feel better when you are feeling stressed?	What makes you saddest?
What makes you happiest?	What gives you hope?
What is it like to have a sister/brother who is so sick so often?	How is it to watch your sister/brother take medicine every day?
Free Pass	Free Pass

Sori, C. F., & Biank, N. M. (2007). Bridging game for ill and well siblings. In L. L. Hecker, C. F. Sori, & Associates, *The therapist's notebook, volume 2: More homework, handouts, and activities for use in psychotherapy* (pp. 57-67). Binghamton, NY: The Haworth Press.

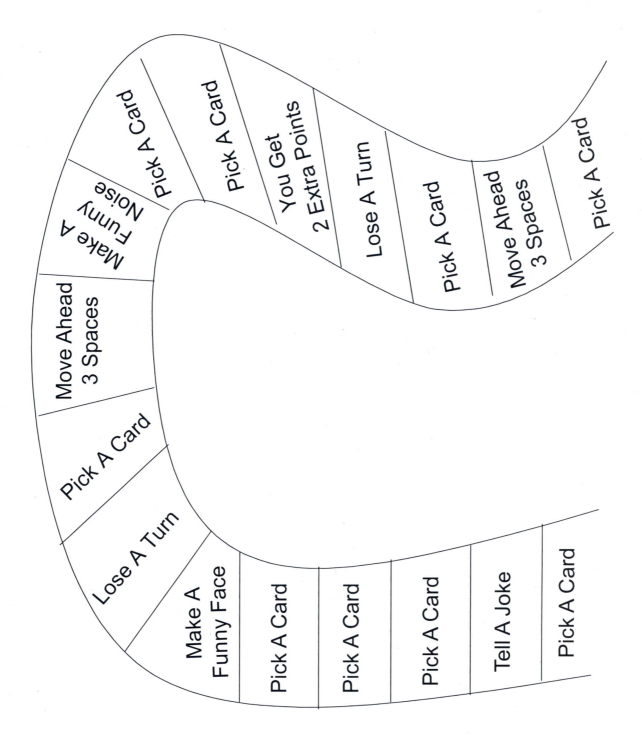

Sori, C. F., & Biank, N. M. (2007). Bridging game for ill and well siblings. In L. L. Hecker, C. F. Sori, & Associates, *The therapist's notebook, volume 2: More homework, handouts, and activities for use in psychotherapy* (pp. 57-67). Binghamton, NY: The Haworth Press.

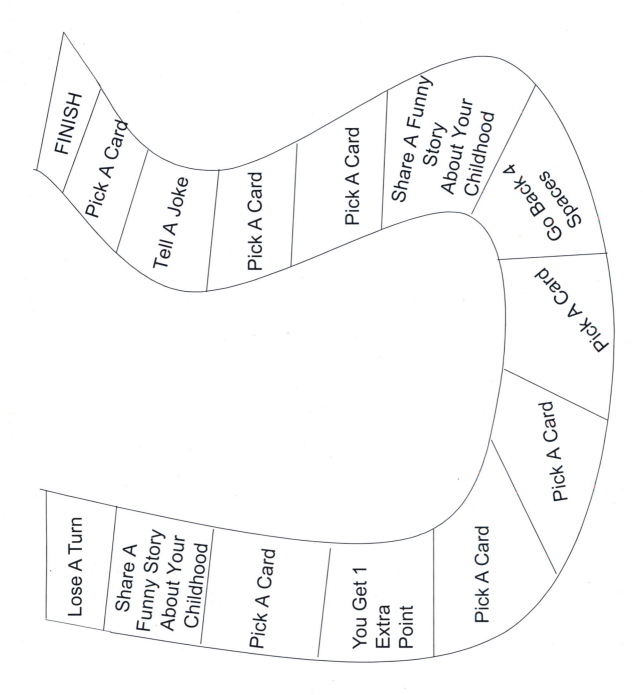

Sori, C. F., & Biank, N. M. (2007). Bridging game for ill and well siblings. In L. L. Hecker, C. F. Sori, & Associates, *The therapist's notebook, volume 2: More homework, handouts, and activities for use in psychotherapy* (pp. 57-67). Binghamton, NY: The Haworth Press.

8

Connecting Spaces:
Experiential Encounters for Families

Scott A. Edwards
Erica J. Weekes

Type of Contribution: *Activity, Handout*

Objectives

Connecting Spaces can be used in couples or family therapy contexts as both an assessment and intervention. This activity is effective in assessing relational and affective processes within various constellations of significant others: adult partners, parent-child, and siblings. During the creative, metaphorical activity, the therapist is able to observe various structural and affective processes of the relationship.

In addition, the encounter is effective as an intervention in facilitating change in communication patterns and relational postures. The therapist can use the metaphorical language and experience as a foundation for exploring and enhancing alternate ways of connecting. Although the activity is derived from an experiential perspective, it is congruent with various other therapy perspectives such as narrative therapy, strategic family therapy, solution-focused therapy, internal family systems, and structural family therapy.

Rationale for Use

Experiential activities have been used to facilitate change and highlight relational processes in numerous contexts, both inside and outside the therapy office. The fields of experiential education and adventure-based therapy provide numerous examples of such activities (Carns, Carns, & Holland, 2001; Ewert, McCormick, & Voight, 2001; Fletcher & Hinkle, 2002; Rohnke, 1977). In contrast to utilizing adventure-based experiences with clients in the outdoors (Glass & Benshoff, 2002; Walsh-Burke, 2002), we have modified an activity for use in the clinical context. Our Connecting Spaces activity is modified from an adventure-based ropes course element commonly known as the Wobbly Woozy or Tension Traverse (Rohnke, 1977).

Grounded in an experiential perspective (Napier & Whitaker, 1978; Satir, 1988; Whitaker & Bumberry, 1988), this activity provides opportunities for assessment and intervention in relational systems. From a symbolic-experiential lens, Roberto (1991) punctuated the organizational structure and affective processes within family systems. Connecting Spaces can be used for assessing relational boundaries, alliances, coalitions, communication patterns, and role expectations. In addition to the organizational structure of relationships, this activity is effective in assessing affective processes such as emotional safety, attachment, trust, intimacy, creativity, conflict resolution, and humor.

The Therapist's Notebook, Volume 2
doi:10.1300/5550_08

In addition to being a creative and lively assessment tool, this encounter can be a powerful intervention. The experiential exercise creates opportunities for increased cohesion within the relationship. Furthermore, the emerging physical and linguistic metaphors provide numerous opportunities to shift client postures, change communication patterns, and explore contextual meanings based on the clients' specific goals. In other words, rather than being directive with a prescribed manner of carrying out the activity, the therapist codirects the intervention based on the assessment from the initial phase, the client goals, and the generative experience.

Instructions

Prior to describing and facilitating the activity with clients, it is important for the therapist to prepare adequate space for the activity and identify potential safety hazards, such as toys, chairs, or tables on the ground. There is a chance clients may lose their balance. In general, a seven-foot by four-foot area of space free of objects is sufficient. This activity is most commonly used with relational dyads, such as couples, parent/child, and siblings.

During the initial phase of Connecting Spaces, basic instructions are provided. It is important to keep it simple and nonspecific, thus limiting constraints of what the end result ought to look like. The primary focus of this phase is on assessment of process and experience, whereas the clients may perceive it to be on completing the activity correctly if the instructions are too specific. Brief instructions also allow room for metaphors to emerge that resonate with the client system rather than the therapist imposing or suggesting metaphors.

The activity may start with the therapist asking clients if they might be interesting in engaging in a little experiment. The introduction might be something as simple as: "This is an activity to experience both closeness and distance in a relationship."

The instructions for the activity begin with safety (as is important in all relationships); inform the clients there is a chance they may lose their balance and if at any time they feel they may fall, they should stop the activity to maintain their safety. The therapist then asks the clients to (1) stand facing each other, (2) place their hands together palm to palm at shoulder height, and (3) take small steps backward, keeping their hands together. As they do this, their arms will extend and become straight. Depending on how far back they step, they may end up leaning forward, being balanced by the other person.

Following the instructions, the dyad experiences a physical opportunity for both distance and connectedness at the same time. Once the clients have stepped as far away from each other as they choose while maintaining contact with their hands, the therapist then processes the experience, both in regard to physical structure and affective processes. For example, the therapist may point out how only one partner is leaning on the other and then begin to explore feelings of trust, closeness, and the process of depending upon each other as partners. After this initial phase and processing, the therapist begins the intervention phase, where the clients are directed to engage in the activity again, given more prompting by the therapist.

The intervention phase of Connecting Spaces provides the clients an opportunity to experience each other differently based on the experience of the initial exercise. Following the client experience and dialogue, the therapist may challenge the clients to try the activity again while stepping back further, by leaning their weight on each other, thus both visually supporting and emotionally connecting with each other through trust. In addition, the therapist may be more directive in the questions as they relate to client goals, the creative metaphors just experienced, and theoretically based explorations. Examples of process and exploration questions are presented in both the vignette and handout at the end of this chapter.

The Connecting Spaces encounter can be used with various dyads, including couple, sibling, and parent-child pairs. The following clinical vignette highlights the use of this activity within a couple relationship.

Brief Vignette

Reed and Susi, a couple in their early forties with two children ages eight and five, presented for therapy with communication problems in their relationship. They both stated they had experienced a lack of intimacy in their relationship ever since their youngest child was born. They also reported feeling disconnected, especially when around their children. The therapist used the Connecting Spaces activity during the second session with the couple. The activity was presented as a helpful way for the therapist to assess their relationship and begin addressing their stated goals.

During the initial phase of the activity safety was discussed, and then Reed and Susi were asked to stand face to face in the middle of the office. They were then asked to touch their hands together and, when ready, to begin walking slowly backward while remaining connected.

The clients stepped backward as far as they could while remaining connected, yet without leaning on each other. They glanced at the therapist quite frequently during the encounter. The therapist asked some process questions:

- What is this experience like for each of you?
- I am curious to hear what you thought about how much you talked with each other.
- How was it to glance at me rather than look at each other?
- What in your everyday life pulls you apart?
- How were you able to remain connected?

Reed and Susi had some pertinent responses to the therapist's process questions. The couple reflected that they were silent during the experience and did not communicate with each other. Reed responded, "I was looking at [the therapist] for direction and I was wondering if I was doing this right." Susi discussed how differences around parenting pulled them apart. She added, "The more we moved our feet apart, the more our hands came apart. We kept our fingers touching by pushing a little."

The next phase of the activity began when the therapist asked them if they would like to do it again while challenging themselves to move farther apart. The couple communicated more effectively with each other, looked at each other without glancing at the therapist, and moved far enough away that they were leaning on each other quite significantly. Based on the client goals and the varied experiences of the two encounters, the therapist asked the following questions:

- What felt different this time?
- What was it like to lean on each other? How were you able to do so?
- Describe what you experienced as you felt the other's support.
- How were you able to look at each other this time?
- What other glancing do you do that prevents you from remaining connected?

Susi responded, "The farther apart we moved this time, the more our hands actually touched each other's." Reed commented that they were both balancing and adjusting to each other's weight naturally. "We even laughed a little bit together while we were balancing on each other. I felt just as much support from you as I was leaning on you. The more I leaned, the more support I felt."

As Susi and Reed explored their experiential encounter, they reflected that the amount of support they felt was directly related to the amount of trust and vulnerability they had for each other—and that it was balanced. They remained leaning on each other during the reflection. The therapist was directive in exploring the increased connection and cohesion, balance in the relationship, more effective communication, and strength of supporting each other. They were able to identify other topics in addition to their children that prevented them from connecting with each other. In a follow-up session, Reed and Susi each reported a shift in their relationship, an increase of emotional connection and support, with a spillover effect to increased effectiveness in their parenting roles.

Suggestions for Follow-Up

The therapist may continue to explore and expand the activity while empowering and challenging the clients in various ways. For example, the therapist may ask one or both of the clients to remain silent and repeat the exercise. Or the therapist may ask the clients to close their eyes during the encounter, providing yet another perspective and opportunity for relational and affective exploration. In addition, the therapist may ask clients in what way they could do the activity that would be more meaningful for them. Furthermore, therapists could work with client constellations of more than just dyads. Connecting Spaces has been used with relational units of three or more individuals. This provides even more complex variations for metaphors of connectedness and distance within family encounters.

The use of metaphorical experiences will highlight the client-specific nature of the activity, making it useful with almost any client. Based on the client goals, the theoretical hypotheses, the treatment plan, and the initial encounter, some additional follow-up, metaphorical process, and exploration questions are found on the handout, Connecting Spaces: Useful Process Questions.

Contraindications

Trust is the most necessary element between clients engaging in this exercise. A primary concern when using this intervention is whether one or more clients have previously been abused in some manner and have not healed from that abuse. The therapist should also take note of any physical disabilities as this exercise may be contraindicated for clients with balance problems or neurological disorders. Connecting Spaces has been effective and helpful with individuals with disabilities when additional attention is given to safety.

References

Carns, A. W., Carns, M. R., & Holland, J. (2001). Learning the ropes: Challenges for change. *TCA Journal, 29*(1), 66-71.

Ewert, A. W., McCormick, B. P., & Voight, A. E. (2001). Outdoor experiential therapies: Implications for TR practice. *Therapeutic Recreation Journal, 35,* 107-122.

Fletcher, T. B., & Hinkle, J. S. (2002). Adventure based counseling: An innovation in counseling. *Journal of Counseling and Development, 80,* 277-285.

Glass, J. S., & Benshoff, J. M. (2002). Facilitating group cohesion among adolescents through challenge course experiences. *Journal of Experiential Education, 25,* 268-277.

Napier, A. Y., & Whitaker, C. A. (1978). *The family crucible.* New York: Harper & Row.

Roberto, L. G. (1991). Symbolic-experiential family therapy. In A. S. Gurman and D. P. Kniskern (Eds.), *Handbook of family therapy* (Vol. 2, pp. 444-476). New York: Brunner/Mazel.

Rohnke, K. (1977). *Cowstails and cobras : A guide to ropes courses, initiative games, and other adventure activities.* Hamilton, MA: Project Adventure.

Satir, V. (1988). *The new peoplemaking.* Palo Alto, CA: Science and Behavior Books.

Walsh-Burke, K. (2002). Experiential education and oncology: Applications for professionals and clients. *Illness, Crisis and Loss, 10*(1), 51-61.

Whitaker, C. A., & Bumberry, W. M. (1988). *Dancing with the family: A symbolic-experiential approach*. New York: Brunner/Mazel.

Professional Readings and Resources

Rohnke, K. (1977). *Cowstails and cobras: A guide to ropes courses, initiative games, and other adventure activities*. Hamilton, MA: Project Adventure.

Rohnke, K. (1984). *Silver bullets: A guide to initiative problems, adventure games and trust activities*. Hamilton, MA: Project Adventure.

Satir, V. (1988). *The new peoplemaking*. Palo Alto, CA: Science and Behavior Books.

Schoel, J., Prouty, D., & Radcliffe, P. (1989). *Islands of healing: A guide to adventure based counseling*. Hamilton, MA: Project Adventure.

Whitaker, C. A., & Bumberry, W. M. (1988). *Dancing with the family: A symbolic-experiential approach*. New York: Brunner/Mazel.

Bibliotherapy Sources for Clients

Napier, A. Y., & Whitaker, C. (1988). *The family crucible: The intense experience of family therapy*. New York: Harper & Row.

Richardson, R. W. (1999). *Family ties that bind: A self-help guide to change through family of origin therapy*. Bellingham, WA: Self-Counsel Press.

Rohnke, K. (1977). *Cowstails and cobras: A guide to ropes courses, initiative games, and other adventure activities*. Hamilton, MA: Project Adventure.

Rohnke, K. (1984). *Silver bullets: A guide to initiative problems, adventure games and trust activities*. Hamilton, MA: Project Adventure.

Satir, V. (1988). *The new peoplemaking*. Palo Alto, CA: Science and Behavior Books.

HANDOUT 8.1

CONNECTING SPACES: USEFUL PROCESS QUESTIONS

1. What pulls you apart in your everyday life?
2. How do you continue to stay connected in this space?
3. How are you able to lean on each other?
4. How would it be different if you were/were not leaning on each other?
5. Describe a time in your relationship when you leaned on each other more? Less?
6. What is required to lean? (e.g., trust, vulnerability)
7. How are you able to stay together when forces in life pull you apart?
8. How are you able to move closer when forces in life pull you apart?
9. What supported you in constructing your support?
10. What resources do you use for balance?
11. How do you not fall flat on your faces?
12. What space does your bridge cross?
13. How long did it take to build the bridge?
14. What differences does your bridge connect together?
15. What is your bridge made of? What would you like it to be?
16. How do you maintain balance in your relationship? In your family?
17. In what ways does this stretch you? How are you stretched every day?
18. How would this be with other family members?

Edwards, S. A., & Weekes, E. J. (2007). Connecting spaces: Experiential encounters for families. In L. L. Hecker, C. F. Sori, & Associates, *The therapist's notebook, volume 2: More homework, handouts, and activities for use in psychotherapy* (pp. 69-74). Binghamton, NY: The Haworth Press.

9

The Feeling Head

Adam Zagelbaum

Type of Contribution: *Activity*

Objectives

The objective of this activity is to help children or adolescents identify, understand, and express their feelings. In addition, it will enable them to distinguish between thoughts and feelings. This activity also allows children to communicate more effectively to others about their feelings. Last, it empowers children to examine and understand how their feelings and actions interact. The activity can be used in a school, community mental health center, and other counseling settings such as alternative schools or correctional facilities. It is best when conducted in an individual or family session, and it can also be used in one session, or over a course of sessions.

Rationale for Use

Children and adolescents often have a difficult time talking about the abstract world of feelings. However, the nature of therapy often involves defining and describing feeling words (Carkhuff & Anthony, 1979). The Feeling Head activity provides a three-dimensional visualization to clients of their feelings. It allows a better understanding of how feelings are processed within the mind, and of what it means to have feelings intermingled with thoughts.

This specific activity was developed out of client sessions with adolescent and preadolescent schoolchildren and their parents as a way of illustrating their feelings so that a visual, cognitive, and interpersonal link can be made between people's thoughts, feelings, and behaviors. It follows the approach of feeling charts and drawings that help clients uncover and identify their feelings.

The Feeling Head also combines well with storytelling techniques designed to help children better understand feelings and emotions that are often difficult for them to express through direct interviewing (Gil, 1994). Children are not always comfortable speaking directly about themselves, but stories that contain a main character, or hero, that is facing a difficult issue can allow children to safely speak about the themes or patterns that are relevant to their personal lives via this technique (Berg & Steiner, 2003).

Instructions

The therapist should establish good rapport with the client and have an overall sense of the client's situation. This enables the therapist to create a therapeutic story that parallels the client's experience. The process of constructing a story is based on the premise that in order to address a

doi:10.1300/5550_09

problem, some action or insight must be gained by the main character. This premise is true of virtually all children's and adult stories.

Based on the work of Berg and Steiner (2003), the elements of a story are thus:

1. The stage is set for the story. The background is set and the main character is described. The main character or hero's positive qualities and strengths are described.
2. The main character or hero in the story must encounter some sort of difficulty or danger.
3. The main character or hero must overcome the obstacles or dangers (this can be an obstacle or evil character), and the main character may utilize the help of other characters, tools, or magic powers. Be sure to set the stage for the story, describe the main character or hero, and describe the danger or difficulty encountered.
4. The main character or hero often experiences several roadblocks before he or she is successful in the quest; but the hero inevitably succeeds.
5. A celebration or ritual follows the successful quest.

This storytelling process, when combined with the Feeling Head technique, allows clients to express themselves verbally and nonverbally. It is a visual and tactile way of tapping into the otherwise abstract quality of feelings and to expand clients' possibilities for change.

For this activity, you will need the following materials:

1. One round, transparent container (preferably clear glass or plastic) that is round like a human head. A clear, round bowl or vase can be purchased to meet this criterion. However, plastic containers or cups may be substituted as well, so long as they are transparent.
2. Markers or materials that can be attached to or drawn on the face of the container (such as paper ears, eyes and a mouth, or, if preferred, drawn-on versions of ears, eyes, and a mouth).
3. A list of feeling cards (of business card size or less) with feeling words printed on each of them.

Since clients are the experts in identifying goals and interests (Walter & Peller, 1992), it is important to recognize that there are no correct or perfect responses associated with this activity. It is also helpful to use the language of the client as much as possible; this not only ensures genuineness on the part of the facilitator (Yalom, 1995) but also allows the student to gain a sense of interest in the overall activity (Petty & Cacioppo, 1984; Pintrich & Schunk, 2002). Thus, clients understand that they have control of their feelings and can share these feelings with others more effectively because of the visual clarity and tactile stimulation of the Feeling Head.

1. Place a transparent container (or Feeling Head) between therapist and client.
2. Lay out several small cards in front of the client containing feeling words (e.g., Creative Therapy Associates, 1996).
3. Tell a therapeutic story in which feelings can be readily described and identified. This story should be a metaphor or somehow illustrate a situation or problem similar to that of the client, as discussed above (see the brief vignette that follows for an example).
4. The therapist should place one feeling card in the container (or head) demonstrating to the client a feeling had by the character in the story, and which illustrates how the feeling is contained in one's head.
5. Ask the client to select a feeling card that the character in the story might have experienced, and place it in the head, following the lead of the therapist. Repeat the process until the client has identified several emotions that the hero in the story might have experienced during

the course of the story. The counselor can further engage in the storytelling process in order to help the client identify multiple feelings.

6. Ask the client if he or she ever has any reactions similar to those of the hero in the story. The client may identify cards already placed in the Feeling Head, or may select additional feeling cards to place in the head. Process these feelings with the client.

7. Call the client's attention to the fact that feelings remain in the head as long as someone is willing to let them stay there. Feelings can take up so much room that there is little space left for thinking about other things. This way, clients can see how, if feelings are left in one's head, metaphorically, it can distract or disrupt other things that are going on inside their head, such as thoughts about needing to focus on doing homework or reminders about how to calm down when a situation is becoming particularly stressful.

8. As a consequence of seeing the feeling cards contained in the head, the client has a visual image that depicts how sometimes people can tell how someone is feeling because they can read his or her face (head), and that feelings are not bad things to share with someone that we trust.

Brief Vignette

Tony, a twelve-year-old client, came from a middle-class household and had been labeled by his peers as strange. Tony was not able to talk with them about things in a manner that seemed real to them. Tony was a class clown, who appeared to be interested only in making jokes and getting people to laugh at him. He believed this was the best way to get attention. Although he had real feelings and things to say to his peers, he associated these ideas with being weak or stupid. His grandmother had recently died, and he was afraid of letting people know that he was struggling with this loss.

Tony came to the school counselor and privately admitted that he did not understand what was so important about having feelings, and he did not understand the benefits of talking about them. It was clear Tony was in pain but was at a loss for how to talk about it. The counselor asked if Tony wouldn't mind learning a bit more about his feelings as the counselor told a story. Tony agreed.

The counselor began telling Tony a story about a child whose pet dog died. The story went like this:

> In this family, there was a boy and a dog. The dog had grown old, but the boy had thought that somehow the dog was going to live forever, as though the dog was Superdog. Superdog and the boy spent so much time together. They played games, they played in the creek, and they went on long walks together. Superdog would lie at the foot of the boy's bed every night. The boy would pat Superdog's head, and Superdog would always respond with a knowing Superdog tail wag. You could always count on Superdog's tail wag, every time. Even when the boy grew older and got busier, Superdog was still there at the foot of his bed, every night. But then, one day, while the boy was away at school, Superdog died. For a few days the boy stayed in his room and didn't talk much to anyone about Superdog. But then one night, his dad pulled out some pictures of Superdog, and they started sharing funny stories about things Superdog did when he was a puppy. These stories made the boy and his dad both laugh and cry.
>
> Afterward the boy noticed that it helped to share memories of Superdog with Dad.

After telling the story, the counselor then took out several small cards with feeling words printed on them and also took out the Feeling Head container. The counselor then picked up one card with the word *shocked* printed on it, and placed it in the head. "I think one thing running through this boy's head was that he was shocked about how his dog was suddenly not around anymore," said the counselor. She then asked Tony to identify another feeling that might also be running through the main character's mind. Tony picked the word *sad* and placed the corresponding card in the head as well. This process of selecting and discussing feelings went on for a few minutes, and then Tony was asked what he noticed about the head filled with feelings. He responded that they looked kind of messy and that there were a lot of bad feelings.

The counselor used this information as a way to start a dialogue about how feelings can be things that swim around in our heads and don't always have the chance to be seen. She explained to Tony that sometimes people can tell how someone is feeling because their face shows what is swimming around inside their head. The visual display of the Feeling Head served as a good model with which Tony could follow the counselor's train of thought. He now saw why feelings are important things to talk about because they are real concepts that can become "messy and clouded" within one's head unless they are let out through discussion.

When the counselor asked Tony to think about what feelings were typically swimming around in his head that might be similar to those of the boy in the story, Tony had no problem identifying some of these feelings. He also identified some positive memories and feelings about his grandmother before she passed away. He placed those feeling cards in the head, and recognized while doing so that he had the power to put them in the head, but also to take them out and share them with others. The counselor pointed out that there are feelings swimming around in our heads all the time. Some feelings are positive, and some are negative. The point is that we have the power to let out some of the feelings that may otherwise cloud our heads and get in the way of being real and comfortable with other people. When we look at feelings in this controllable and important way, it shows that we are able to get help when we know things are messy and recognize that underneath the messiness are some real and positive feelings that can also come out. Tony left the session with a better understanding about why feelings are important to have, how people can sometimes tell that they exist, and how they can be shared with others.

After a few days, the school counselor did some following up with Tony. He reported his feelings, mentioned that he felt better, and that he had been able to get a little closer to some of his peers who previously thought he was fake and weird. It appeared that Tony was simply misunderstood by these individuals; once he began talking about his feelings with a few of his classmates whom he trusted, they recognized that Tony had many of the same thoughts and feelings that they shared about particular topics. Once he understood how to communicate feelings, it became easier for Tony to do so. It no longer seemed bad or weak to share these things with his classmates, because they had been holding some of the same feelings inside their heads. Many of his classmates also had family members who had passed away, and they might never have shared these things with Tony under different circumstances. Tony was able to communicate in a language that is not always understood by young people like him: the language of feelings.

Suggestions for Follow-Up

There are several variations to this activity. Although clients are initially asked to identify the emotions of the main character of the story while the hero is struggling with an issue, clients can also be asked to select cards to represent the feelings of the hero at the end of the story—when the main character has succeeded in reaching the goal or overcoming an obstacle or problem. Clients could also be asked to identify positive memories (as in the case of the loss of a loved one) or to generate possible solutions to the hero's problem (which is a metaphor for the client's situation), and to write these thoughts down on a card and place them in the head. Those thoughts and memories can then be taken out if the client wishes to share them with others, including family members.

The Feeling Head can be brought out at any time in any session. A client can use it as a visual aid to describe how he or she is feeling in the here and now (Yalom, 1995), or as a pre–post measure. For example, clients can compare a Feeling Head that they create in a current session to one that they made in a previous session. By looking at the amount of happy and positive feelings and whether they have increased or decreased since the last exercise, the client and counselor can see if there have been any improvements. It is up to the client and counselor to decide when and how often the exercise needs to be done. It is expected that as the client becomes more aware of how to communicate his or her feelings, there will be a less specific need to actually use the Feeling Head materials.

Contraindications

None noted.

References

Berg, I., & Steiner, T. (2003). *Children's solution work.* New York: Norton.

Carkhuff, R., & Anthony, W. (1979). *The skills of helping.* New York: Human Resource Development Press.

Creative Therapy Associates. (1996). *How are you feeling today? Cards and feeling chart.* Cincinnati, OH: Author.

Gil, E. (1994). *Play in family therapy.* New York: Guilford.

Petty, R., & Cacioppo, J. (1984). *Attitudes and persuasion: Classic and contemporary approaches.* Dubuque, IA: W. C. Brown.

Pintrich, P., & Schunk, D. (2002). *Motivation in education: Theory, research and applications.* Upper Saddle River, NJ: Pearson Education.

Walter, J. L., & Peller, J. E. (1992). *Becoming solution-focused in brief therapy.* New York: Brunner/Mazel.

Yalom, I. (1995). *The theory and practice of group psychotherapy* (4th ed.). New York: Basic Books.

Professional Readings and Resources

Carkhuff, R. R. (1969). *Helping and human relations: Volumes 1 and 2.* New York: Holt, Rinehart & Winston.

Carkhuff, R., & Anthony, W. (1979). *The skills of helping.* New York: Human Resource Development Press.

Cormier, S., & Cormier, W. (1997). *Interviewing strategies for helpers* (4th ed.). New York: Brooks/Cole.

Creative Therapy Associates. (1996). *How are you feeling today? Cards and feeling chart.* Cincinnati, OH: Author.

Geiselman, R., & Glenny, J. (1977). Effects of imagining speakers' voices on the retention of words presented visually. *Memory and Cognition, 5,* 499-504.

Pintrich, P., & Schunk, D. (2002). *Motivation in education: Theory, research and applications.* Upper Saddle River, NJ: Pearson Education.

Yalom, I. (1995). *The theory and practice of group psychotherapy* (4th ed.). New York: Basic Books.

Bibliotherapy Sources for Clients

Cain, J. (1999). *The way I feel.* Seattle, WA: Parenting Press.

Krueger, D. (1999). *What is a feeling?* Seattle, WA: Parenting Press.

10

The Gingerbread Figure Activity

George W. Bitar
Faith Drew

Type of Contribution: *Activity, Handout*

Objectives

The purpose of this activity and handout is to facilitate the externalizing process as family members access, explore, and support each member's emotional experience as it relates to the problem. In an expressive art activity, feelings can be accessed at deeper levels in ways that may not be possible through talk alone, as emotions are projected onto the gingerbread figure. This activity also helps family members practice and expand on language that more directly reflects each member's emotional experience.

Rationale for Use

Narrative therapy, developed by Michael White and David Epston, focuses on how lived experiences, or narratives, are overshadowed by problem-saturated stories. Narrative therapy, therefore, "emphasizes empowering client families to develop their own unique and alternative stories about themselves in the hope that they will come up with new options and strategies for living" (Gladding, 2002, p. 252). The process of externalizing problems is central to the development of alternative stories (White & Epston, 1990). The externalization process is "supported by the belief that a problem is something operating or impacting on or pervading a person's life, something separate and different from the person" (Freedman & Combs, 1996, p. 47). According to White and Epston (1990), the externalization process: (1) decreases conflict and arguments over who is to blame for the problem; (2) instills hope as the problem is conceptualized in a new and more productive manner; (3) invites a spirit of cooperation as people can unite to struggle for a solution to the problem; (4) creates new possibilities for people to take action to reclaim their lives from the influences of the problem; (5) encourages a lighter and less overwhelmed stance in dealing with a problem that may initially be perceived as extremely serious; and (6) increases space for productive dialogue, rather than monologue, to occur around the problem.

The first step in the externalization process "is simply taking the language the person uses to describe the problem, modifying it so that the problem is objectified, and asking the person questions about it" (Freedman & Combs, 1996, pp. 58-59). For example, if a person explains that she has a fear of public speaking, the therapist might ask, "How has the fear influenced you?" or "How have you influenced the fear so that it has not become more powerful?" Once a problem is externalized, unique outcomes can be identified which can provide the foundation for a dominant story that is liberated from the old, constraining narrative (Parry & Doan, 1994).

doi:10.1300/5550_10

Instructions

Step 1: The therapist and family collaborate to externalize the problem.

Step 2: Each family member is given the gingerbread figure handout and asked to write the name of the externalized problem at the bottom of the page. A bin of crayons consisting of a wide range of colors is then given to the family to share. The therapist explains that each color represents a different feeling and the bin, therefore, is like a big container of feelings. The therapist should also adapt the handout for each family member. For example, for an eight-year-old girl, the therapist might describe the figure as a "gingerbread girl."

Step 3: The therapist then instructs the family to select the crayons that are most like the feelings that they have about the problem. They are then instructed to draw the feelings on the gingerbread figure handout.

Step 4: The following guidelines are communicated to the family. Family members must keep their eyes on their own paper. A key should be drawn at the bottom of each page to identify the feeling that each color represents for the individual member. The family members are assured that ample time will be given for the activity so that there is no need to rush.

Step 5: Once everyone's drawing is complete, the therapist and the family form a circle in order to begin the sharing process. The therapist then asks for a volunteer to begin the process. Prior to sharing, the family members are asked to place their drawings on the floor and to remain attentive as each person shares.

Step 6: Each family member is then given the opportunity to share his or her drawing. Depending on the family's tolerance for vulnerability, the therapist can encourage members to share emotions directly with one another, or the process can be filtered more indirectly through the therapist. In either case, all members of the group should be encouraged to listen in an active and respectful manner. This is often an excellent time for the therapist to model reflective listening for the rest of the family.

Step 7: Once the sharing is complete, unique outcomes (i.e., specific instances where the family members were able to respond to the problem in a preferred manner) are identified. As an example of how unique outcomes may be identified, the therapist can ask the family to describe instances during the previous week when the problem was not as powerful or not present at all. The family members can then be asked to color how they feel on the gingerbread figure handout during unique outcomes. This connects the unique outcomes with their emotional experiences, reinforcing exceptions to the problem. A variation on this step involves having the family draw how they would like to feel in the future followed by a discussion of the steps required to move from current to ideal drawings.

Step 8: Each family member is asked to explain what the therapist and members of the family did to make the sharing easier and what was done that made the sharing more challenging.

Brief Vignette

A family composed of a mother (age thirty-five), a daughter (age ten), and a son (age eight) entered therapy. The parents were engaged in an ongoing divorce. When asked what prompted her to initiate therapy, the mother stated, "I am concerned with my son since he blows up at any little thing now that his father has moved out." The father was still involved in the children's lives, although he refused to attend therapy sessions.

During the first two sessions, the therapist worked with the family to externalize and join around a common problem. Although the son's anger was the central component of the initial complaint, it soon became clear to the family that they were all experiencing strong emotions regarding what they collectively called "the dark divorce." Once the family seemed to adopt externalizing language, the therapist decided to have the family engage in the Gingerbread Figure Activity. After they all completed the handout, the therapist began processing the activity.

THERAPIST: Who would like to begin?

SON: Me. I drew red in the middle of the gingerbread boy. He is angry a lot.

[Son showed the family his drawing that had red scribbled from the gingerbread figure's legs to the figure's neck. The figure's head was not completely colored in but had facial features drawn. The son had drawn a frown on the figure.]

THERAPIST: Yes. I can tell. He has a lot to be angry about. What do you think that anger is about?

SON: He is angry because the dark divorce made Dad move out of the house.

THERAPIST: So he is angry because the dark divorce made Dad move away? How do you think the gingerbread boy is feeling when he is frowning?

SON: Sad.

THERAPIST: So the dark divorce makes the gingerbread boy feel sad and angry? Is that right?

SON: Yes.

THERAPIST: How else does the dark divorce influence the gingerbread boy?

The session continued as the influence of the dark divorce was further explored. After the son finished sharing, the mother expressed feelings of frustration and sadness as she discussed her gingerbread figure. The daughter expressed feelings of sadness, anger, and depression. The therapist was very active at this point, since the family had not explored their feelings in this depth about the divorce before, and since this was the family's first time to engage in the activity. The therapist would return to this activity in future sessions, becoming less active until the family could discuss their feelings on their own. Since everyone had shared, unique outcomes were explored to begin deconstructing the problem-saturated story.

THERAPIST: Have you, as a family or individually, had times when you were able to stand up to the dark divorce and not let it take control?

MOTHER: I notice that during the weekends, when we all get to spend more time together as a family, the children and I seem happier.

THERAPIST: [Looks at the children] What do you both think about what your mom said?

DAUGHTER: I like the weekends too because we go to the park and do fun stuff.

The family members were each presented with another gingerbread figure and were asked to color in their feelings when the dark divorce was weak. The family members once again shared their drawings. This is a way to connect unique outcomes to emotional experiences more directly, making them seem more prominent in the new story that is being created.

The final step involved the family members processing what the other members did to make the sharing more comfortable.

THERAPIST: What did your family do or say to make the sharing easier?

DAUGHTER: They listened.

THERAPIST: How could you tell that they were listening?

DAUGHTER: Well, they were quiet and looked at me when I was talking.

THERAPIST: What else?

DAUGHTER: They care about what I'm saying.

The daughter continued, providing valuable information for the therapist and the rest of her family as she shared what she perceived as validating behaviors. Each family member completed this step.

Suggestions for Follow-Up

This activity can be repeated over the course of therapy, with the therapist becoming less active and the family members becoming more so each time the activity is repeated. A family can also be given a creative version of this activity for homework as they are asked to actually make gingerbread cookies and have different toppings represent different feelings related to the problem. They can then bring the cookies to the next session.

Contraindications

This activity should not be used in any case in which the vulnerability expressed could lead to any negative repercussions for the family members. It is also important that a basic feeling of safety and trust exist within the family and the therapeutic relationship before beginning the activity.

References

Freedman, J., & Combs, G. (1996). *Narrative therapy: The social construction of preferred realities*. New York: Norton.

Gladding, S. (2002). *Family therapy: History, theory, and practice*. Columbus, OH: Merrill Prentice Hall.

Parry, D., & Doan, R. (1994). *Story re-visions: Narrative therapy in the postmodern world*. New York: Guilford.

White, M., & Epston, D. (1990). *Narrative means to therapeutic ends*. New York: Norton.

Professional Readings and Resources

Freedman, J., & Combs, G. (1996). *Narrative therapy: The social construction of preferred realities*. New York: Norton.

Parry, D., & Doan, R. (1994). *Story re-visions: Narrative therapy in the postmodern world*. New York: Guilford.

Riley, S., & Malchiodi, C. (2003). Solution-focused and narrative approaches. In C. Malchiodi (Ed.), *Handbook of art therapy* (pp. 82-92). New York: Guilford.

White, M., & Epston, D. (1990). *Narrative means to therapeutic ends*. New York: Norton.

Bibliotherapy Sources for Clients

Brown, M. T., & Brown, L. K. (1988). *Dinosaurs divorce: A guide for changing families*. Boston, MA: Little, Brown.

Cain, B. S. (1990). *Double-dip feelings: Stories to help children understand emotions*. New York: Magination Press.

Emery, R. E. (2004). *The truth about divorce: Dealing with your emotions so your children can thrive*. New York: Penguin.

Lansky, V., & Prince, J. (1998). *It's not your fault Koko bear: A read-together book for parents and young children during divorce*. Deephaven, MN: Book Peddlers.

Long, N., & Forehand, R. L. (2002). *Making divorce easier on your child: 50 effective ways to help children adjust*. New York: McGraw Hill.

Monroe, R. P., & Melton, D. (2000). *Don't fall apart on Saturdays! The children's divorce survival book*. Kansas City, MO: Landmark Editions.

Spelman, C. M., & Parkinson, K. (2001). *Mama and daddy bear's divorce*. Chicago: Albert Whitman.

HANDOUT 10.1

THE EXTERNALIZING GINGERBREAD FIGURE

Name of Problem:

Color Key:

Bitar, G. W., & Drew, F. (2007). The gingerbread figure activity. In L. L. Hecker, C. F. Sori, & Associates, *The therapist's notebook, volume 2: More homework, handouts, and activities for use in psychotherapy* (pp. 81-86). Binghamton, NY: The Haworth Press.

11

The Creative Career Constellation

Adam Zagelbaum

Type of Contribution: *Activity*

Objectives

The Creative Career Constellation is an activity that helps provide tangible links between educational and career resources when developing career goals. It is designed to demonstrate the linkage between interests, hobbies, and pursuits that clients may have along with the training and choices involved with turning interests into careers. This activity has been adapted from a worksheet used within the school system of Trinidad and Tobago to help students understand course sequences they are expected to take during their school matriculation (Trinidad and Tobago Schools, 2006). It is expected that, upon completion of the activity, clients (and possibly their parents) will be able to:

1. Identify interests, values, and tasks that can be harnessed into a possible career
2. Identify educational coursework and guidelines that should be followed in order to work toward career goals
3. Make salient connections between coursework, personal interests, and career goals

Rationale for Use

Exploring career options can be especially challenging for adolescent and preadolescent populations. The pressures faced during middle school and high school regarding academic achievement and coursework can be quite trying, resulting in dissonance toward school and career connections (Bachay & Rigby, 1997). Adolescents can lack career objectives, have uncertain degree expectations, and possess general anxiety toward career or college options (Singaravelu & Bringaze, 2003). Even in cases in which clients enroll in college, the dissonance and anxiety associated with having an undecided major is significantly linked to attrition rates (Gordon, 1998). This activity can be used by school counselors in individual or group sessions, or by therapists who work with adolescents in an agency setting. It can also be used as an adjunct to family therapy.

Clients are seen as the experts in identifying their own goals and interests (Walter & Peller, 1992). Therefore, it is important to recognize that information gathered during this activity relates to the personal interests of the client constructing the constellation. It is also important to use the language of the client as much as possible; this not only ensures genuineness on the part of the clinician (Yalom, 1995) but also allows the client to gain interest in the overall activity (Pintrich & Schunk, 2002). As clinicians and clients interactively work through the steps associated with the creative career constellation, clients' sense of agency (Walter & Peller, 1992) is in-

The Therapist's Notebook, Volume 2
© 2007 by The Haworth Press, Inc. All rights reserved.
doi:10.1300/5550_11

creased because they are creating a specific constellation of their own ideas and integrating them into existing resources of their family, school, and community. Thus, clients have a sense of control over their own career and educational options and can share these ideas with others more effectively. When clients can recognize the tangible nature of the constellated goals, they gain a renewed sense of clarity of the otherwise abstract connections between school-to-work and school-to-college transitions (Buzan, 2002; Lent, 2005).

Instructions

The steps below should be used to help clients contruct a career constellation (see Figure 11.1 for an example).

First the therapist should explain to clients that many career options are available, but it can be hard to recognize all the options unless they are mapped out. Clients are then given a career constellation sheet, which has one circle drawn in the center of the page. Next clients are instructed to name an activity that they like to do for fun or in their spare time, and write the name of this activity within this circle on the page.

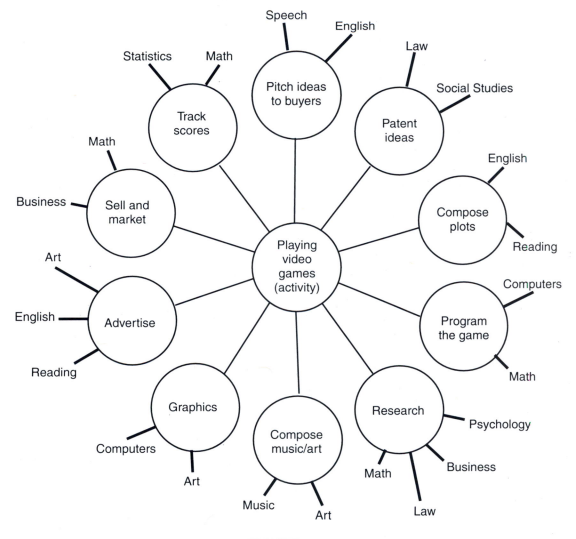

FIGURE 11.1

The therapist asks the client to name activities or services that people perform in association with that activity, which elicits ideas for related careers. For example, if the activity written in the center of the circle is "cook," the therapist would ask the client, "What are some things that people do to help cooks do their job well, or help cooks make money?" The therapist draws lines that extend out from the center circle, and then lists the client's responses and draws circles around them. For example, if a client responds to the question above about cooks with answers such as, "People teach them how to cook," and "people sell their food," the key words (such as "teach cooking" and "sell food") are encased in new circles radiating from the center circle.

The therapist asks the client to try to generate as many different activities as possible. The therapist can offer suggestions as needed, until a list of at least four responses is created. Clinicians should take a less active role in order to let the client generate as many activities as possible.

After all the possible careers have been drawn in circles radiating from the center circle, the client is asked to look at each possible career one at a time and name classes that are associated with that occupation. For example, the therapist would start with the "teach cooking" circle, and ask, "What classes would someone need to take in order to be good at teaching cooking?" This procedure is repeated for each job that is represented in the outer circles.

Clients list as many classes as they can think of that might relate to each occupation, and write the names of these classes on lines stemming from the job being discussed. For example, classes that are needed for people to become good at teaching people how to cook include food science, home economics, and education. Each of these classes is listed on lines stemming from the "teach cooking" circle. This process is repeated for each circle, with a list of classes being generated for each career.

The clinician asks clients to study the career constellation and think about which occupations related to their original area of interest they would most like to consider as possible career options. Clients may take the career constellation home to ponder this question, which can then be addressed in a subsequent session. Client may also discuss these options with parents or guardians, and the career constellation can be reviewed in family sessions.

Clients also can take the career constellation to teachers and discuss career options with them. Teachers may offer feedback about other classes or activities that would help students pursue the possible careers listed in the constellation. This information can be shared with the therapist and discussed in subsequent sessions.

The career constellation activity may be repeated several times to help clients generate other possible career options. The therapist may also encourage clients to research some of the careers generated within the constellated circles by using materials such as the *Occupational Outlook Handbook* (Bureau of Labor Statistics, 2004-2005). This information can help the client understand how much training is involved with each career, as well as how much the average salary would be for such careers.

If this is done as a group activity, the creative career constellation can be drawn on a chalkboard and worked on collectively using a single example, where all group members are encouraged to contribute ideas. Afterward, individuals may want to create their own career constellation and present it to the group for input and feedback.

Brief Vignette

This vignette is an example of using this activity in a school setting. Darrell approached the school counselor and privately admitted that he did not understand what to do regarding college majors, applications, and job pursuits. Darrell's counselor asked if he could create a map of the ideas floating around in his mind regarding school and career options, and said that she would be able to help him construct it on paper. Darrell agreed it was worth a try.

After presenting Darrell with an initial sheet of paper containing the center circle of the creative career constellation, the school counselor said that a good way to identify possible careers was to start with an idea of what he liked to do when he had spare time. Darrell stated that he enjoyed playing video games. His school counselor wrote "video games" within the center of the constellation circle. Then Darrell was asked about what types of things are done to create and distribute video games, and what types of people work to create and distribute video games. He began to form a list of ideas. "People sell video games," he said. His counselor drew a line from the center circle and wrote "sell video games," circling this phrase. She asked, "What are some other things that happen with video games?" Darrell came up with other ideas for jobs related to playing video games, such as designing, programing, and testing video games, asking people questions about what types of games they like, and finding ways of making video games more fun. All of these items were subsequently placed in other circles that radiated from the central circle.

Next the counselor asked Darrell to identify courses that might be related to each of the jobs listed in the outer circles. For example, the counselor asked Darrell, "What things must people learn in order to get a job selling video games?" He replied, "Well, you have to know math." The counselor wrote "math" on a short line extending from the circle containing the job "sell video games." She then asked, "Can you think of other classes?" They went through each of the possible career circles in this manner, listing the classes that relate to each occupation.

The more ideas that Darrell began to generate on his own, the more curious and energized he became. He finally saw an organized way of linking his interests to school courses and career paths. His career constellation is contained in Figure 11.1. The counselor offered Darrell other constellation sheets to take home to fill out for other activities that were of interest to him. His parents were impressed with his ability to clearly link his interests to possible occupations and educational goals.

The school counselor asked Darrell to consider which occupations were of particular interest to him. He was encouraged to speak to some of his teachers who taught the classes related to those occupations to learn more about how those or other classes could help him meet these career goals. The school counselor also suggested that he discuss with teachers and his parents which careers might be a good match for him.

Darrell was then introduced to the *Occupational Outlook Handbook* and the Internet to research programs related to the careers he was most interested in. He looked up various colleges, universities, technical institutes, apprenticeships, or direct jobs that were available upon completion of high school. Darrell now had a direct connection with his interests, schoolwork, and career options. He also had a salient and organized way of presenting his ideas to others, which gave him more confidence and self-efficacy in applying himself toward the realization of these goals.

Suggestions for Follow-Up

This activity can be reviewed from time to time, especially if used as a homework assignment. By guiding clients to look up resources within the the *Occupational Outlook Handbook, Dictionary of Occupational Titles* (U.S. Department of Labor, n.d.) and Internet resources regarding apprenticeships, college-level programs, and job searches, clients are able to perform their own follow-up procedures to ensure that the constellation is in line with their targeted goals. If presented in a group format, clients are encouraged to make a follow-up appointment with their school counselors or teachers so that individualized time can be allotted to the specific constellation and subsequent steps to be taken in pursuing any of the constellated goals.

Contraindications for Use

Some clients may need help with Internet research due to lack of either training or resources of computer and World Wide Web access. A clinician may need to take a more directive mode when engaging clients who may not be able to constellate activities as easily from experience. Also, when engaging parents in this informational activity, it is important for clinicians to look for linkages between the client's perceptions of career directions and parents' perceptions. For example, a client may define singing professionally as a possible career option, while his or her parents would prefer a career path along the lines of business or law. These two fields overlap in the areas of entertainment law, entertainment management, and promotional advertisement. In other words, a compromise can be made to find a career that covers both areas of interest, because they can be connected between multiple constellations.

References

Bachay, J. B., & Rigby, E. T. (1997). Welcome to our school community: A career development intervention for the newcomer. *Professional School Counseling, 1,* 13-15.

Bureau of Labor Statistics. (2004-2005). *Occupational outlook handbook.* Washington, DC: U.S. Department of Labor.

Buzan, T. (2002). *How to mind map.* New York: HarperCollins.

Gordon, V. (1998). *The undecided college client.* Springfield, IL: Charles C Thomas.

Lent, R. W. (2005). A social-cognitive view of career development and counseling. In S. D. Brown & R. W. Lent (Eds.), *Career development and counseling: Putting theory and research to work* (pp. 101-131). Hoboken, NJ: John Wiley and Sons.

Pintrich, P., & Schunk, D. (2002). *Motivation in education: Theory, research and applications.* Upper Saddle River, NJ: Pearson Education.

Singaravelu, H. D., & Bringaze, T. B. (2003). Parental involvement in an adolescent's career decision process. In C. Ford Sori, L. L. Hecker, & Associates, *The therapist's notebook for children and adolescents: Homework, handouts, and activities for use in psychotherapy* (pp. 204-208). Binghamton, NY: The Haworth Press.

Trinidad and Tobago Schools. (2006). *Form I and Form II classes.* Trinidad and Tobago: Author.

U.S. Department of Labor. (n.d.). *Dictionary of occupational titles.* Retrieved November 6, 2005, from http://www.occupationalinfo.org/contents.html

Walter, J. L., & Peller, J. E. (1992). *Becoming solution-focused in brief therapy.* New York: Brunner/Mazel.

Yalom, I. (1995). *The theory and practice of group psychotherapy* (4th ed.). New York: Basic Books.

Professional Readings and Resources

Bachay, J. B., & Rigby, E. T. (1997). Welcome to our school community: A career development intervention for the newcomer. *Professional School Counseling, 1,* 13-15.

Stewart, J. C. (1976). *Games and activities for career education.* Knoxville, TN: Knox County Schools.

U.S. Department of Labor (n.d.). *Dictionary of occupational titles.* Retrieved November 6, 2005, from http://www.occupationalinfo.org/contents.html

U.S. Department of Labor, Bureau of Labor Statistics (2005). *Occupational outlook handbook.* Retrieved November 6, 2005, from http://www.bls.gov/oco

Bibliotherapy for Clients

Buzan, T. (2002). *How to mind map.* New York: HarperCollins.

Military Entrance Processing Command. *Exploring careers: The ASVAB workbook.* North Chicago, IL: Corporate Text.

U.S. Department of Labor. (n.d.). *Dictionary of occupational titles.* Retrieved November 6, 2005, from http://www.occupationalinfo.org/contents.html

U.S. Department of Labor, Bureau of Labor Statistics. (2005). *Occupational outlook handbook.* Retrieved November 6, 2005, from http://www.bls.gov/oco

12

Props: Therapeutic Use of Common Objects

Joe M. Utay

Type of Contribution: *Activity, Handout*

Objectives

Counselors can enhance the effects of counseling via creative therapeutic use of common objects within any phase of the counseling process, regardless of population or theoretical orientation. Used judiciously, props can be useful and fun additions to a counselor's repertoire of techniques for helping clients move toward their short-term and lifelong social, emotional, behavioral, and spiritual goals.

Rationale for Use

Mental health and school professionals often recognize the need to use creativity to augment traditional approaches to maximize clients' hope, resiliency, and success. With clients of all ages, utilizing a nearby prop (e.g., cup, tape, chair) therapeutically can act as a metaphor for the client's counseling-related issue. In the psychodynamic model, for example, a client can project an aspect of the inner self onto an external object, thus offering an opportunity to consciously increase awareness of its character and influence. From a humanistic perspective, regardless of therapeutic goal or whether it is met, an attempt to use common objects in the counseling process at a minimum models creativity, responsible spontaneity, and the courage to experiment. Prop use similarly fits with many other theoretical orientations as well.

Props can be used at any point in a counseling relationship. When beginning a therapeutic relationship, props can be used in building rapport, gathering information, defining the problem, or gauging hope and commitment. In the working stage, props can be helpful starting, getting beyond an impasse, integrating learning, exposing clients to various perspectives, or to explore an old issue in a new way. For termination stage goals, props can be used for summarizing, exploring plans for future use of what was learned or gained, or expressing good-bye. Examples are described in the brief vignette.

Instructions

Because research has not progressed to the point of recommending one best practice, and due to the individualized and creative aspects of prop use, one set procedure may not be warranted. The following are the basic steps found by the author to be useful:

1. Introduce the idea of using a prop.
2. Check for willingness and commitment to experiment.

The Therapist's Notebook, Volume 2
© 2007 by The Haworth Press, Inc. All rights reserved.
doi:10.1300/5550_12

3. Show and describe the prop.
4. Explain what the client is to do with the prop.
5. Respond to the client's use of the prop according to your theoretical base.
6. Evaluate how well the process met the goal for this client at this time.
7. Plan for the prop's future use (a) keep the prop handy for use with this or other clients, (b) do not use this prop again, or (c) use the prop again with modifications such as changing timing, the introduction or use of the prop, or a physical aspect of the prop itself.

After some experience, these steps can be shortened or otherwise modified as needed. The entire process can be summarized and easily remembered as *introduce, do,* and *review.*

The Process of Using a Therapeutic Prop

1. *Introduce:* First the therapist should introduce the idea of using a prop and check for willingness and commitment to experiment. Then, show and describe the prop and explain what you want the client to do with or tell about the prop.

2. *Do:* Next, allow time for the response and modify as needed during the process. Respond according to your theoretical orientation.

3. *Review:* Evaluate how well the process met the goal for this counselee at this time and plan for the prop's possible future use.

Creating therapeutic use of ordinary objects comes naturally to some and is quite foreign to others. To help structure the process of attaching therapeutic relevance to things, the following four steps can be used, each involving the counselor answering a question about an object.

1. What is its *function* or how is it used?
2. What *information* do I have about it or how would I describe its characteristics?
3. What are its *limitations?*
4. How might it be *modified* or what are its possibilities?

A simplified way of remembering these is the acronym FILM (itself a potential prop).

Counselors can practice creating props just about wherever they are. They can look around their environment, remove an object from their purse or pocket, imagine their desk, or think about what is available in nearby rooms or outside. After choosing a common object, they can then ask themselves the FILM questions with special focus on potential therapeutic relevance. For example, a highlighting marker can be described by its color or chemical composition (probably not therapeutically relevant), or as something very useful in focusing a reader's attention only if what is under the cap is briefly uncovered and used (potentially therapeutically relevant when encouraging a client to consider being more open-minded).

In the vignette that follows, selected counselor questions and comments are listed for each stage of counseling. These are necessarily brief, certainly out of context, and do not include the full counseling process. The intent is to offer examples of the potential therapeutic use of common objects. Exact wording will vary according to age, culture, intellectual abilities, and many other factors.

Brief Vignette

This vignette describes the therapeutic use of several common objects applied in several stages of treatment with an adolescent boy. The boy felt pressure from his peers to engage in risky, sometimes illegal, activities. He did not want to join them yet did not want to risk losing their friendship. What follows are examples of how props were used at each stage in the therapeutic process, and the boy's response to the use of the props.

Beginning Stage

Building Rapport

COUNSELOR: [introducing a ring] My wedding ring here is very important to me. One thing it means to me is a commitment I made to be loyal to my wife. You seem to feel very loyal to your friends.

CLIENT: That's right.

This was said in a somewhat defiant, but not closed or angry, tone.

Gathering Information

COUNSELOR: [introducing coins] Pretend these coins are you and your friends and anyone else you want to include. How can you put them out on this table in such a way as to show me how your friends relate to each other?

The client put one coin on one corner far from the others, which were grouped in a tight circle. From this and the discussion that followed it was quite clear that he often felt set aside from his friends. This awareness was the beginning of shifting responsibility from his friends to himself in terms of who really controls distance in these relationships.

Problem Definition

COUNSELOR: [introducing a clock]: See that clock? If 1:00 means stay with your friends no matter what they do, and 12:00 means drop them as your friends, and 6:00 is right in the middle of those, where would you say you are at this time?

CLIENT: Between 5:00 and 7:00. Well, sometimes 1:00 and sometimes 12:00. It depends. But, mostly, around 6:00.

Gauging Hope and Commitment

COUNSELOR: [introducing shoes] I'm wearing these shoes because they're comfortable and fairly professional-looking. If you think of working on this as a kind of journey through a jungle, what kind of shoes would you wear? For example, sandals would be comfortable but show that you really don't plan to stay with the journey too long. I'm trying to get a sense of your commitment and hope.

CLIENT: In a jungle I'd wear running shoes in case I came across a lion or something.

This led to a discussion of risks involved with working on his personal issues and dealing with his potentially scary, or at least strong, feelings.

Working Stage

Starting

COUNSELOR: [introducing a driver's license] This license gives me the right to drive, as long as I don't abuse that privilege. If you had a "friendship license," what information might it include? What would be fair grounds for revoking it?

CLIENT: I don't need a license to be a friend. I don't need someone else to tell me I can or can't be someone's friend. That's up to me and the friend.

This was a great entrance to a discussion about what he found valuable in a friendship. He then described what it would take to end a friendship, such as, "betraying me, embarrassing me, or not watching my back."

Getting Beyond an Impasse

COUNSELOR: [introducing paper currency] You have five friends in this group and I have five one-dollar bills here. How are these like and unlike your friends? I also have another one-dollar bill and also a five-dollar bill. How do they fit in, or do they?

CLIENT: It's like I keep saying—they're all the same, like these (one-dollar bills) and sometimes I feel really different, like this five. [Studying the one-dollar bills] Well, they're not exactly the same. Some are the newer kind with different things on them or in the ink or something, so they're all ones, but they're also different.

This was important in that it led him to talking about how each person in the group was both an individual in many unique ways as well as a member of the group.

Integrating

COUNSELOR: [introducing shirt] How is your shirt (the buttons, pattern, or material) like the changes or realizations you've made so far? What's left?

CLIENT: This part of the picture is wild and crazy like I used to be. Well, I still am, but now I feel more comfortable sometimes being like this part over here where the dragon is just hanging out off to the side of the action. Next, I want that resting dragon to be even more away from the crazy stuff, sometimes.

Perspective Taking

COUNSELOR: [introducing hats] You're guessing how those other kids might feel about you hanging around with them. Trade hats with me. You wear mine and I'll wear yours. [After trading] Do you now know how I feel when I wear my hat? How might you find out for sure?

CLIENT: Ask. Or I can guess and look for proof that I'm right.

Either way meant not blindly reacting to assumptions of how they felt.

Old Issues/New Views

COUNSELOR: [introducing a blank CD] What would you have thought about this CD if someone handed it to you when you were two years old? What about eight years old? What about now? [After responses] So, your thinking changed the more you grew and learned about CDs. How has your thinking changed about friendships?

CLIENT: I used to think friends were like toys. They were there for me to play with the way I wanted. Now I know they have their own expectations of me too.

Ending Stage

Summarizing

COUNSELOR: [introducing keys] Keys are special tools to help get into places that otherwise would be difficult or even impossible to get into. If each of these keys is a change you've made, what would they be?

CLIENT: This car key is the lesson that says I can leave or not even show up for their craziness if I don't want to. This key stands for me being friends with at least some of them without the rest of them sometimes, and having fun with them alone like that.

Encouraging a Positive Future

COUNSELOR: [introducing a checkbook] Here is a blank check, not for money but for a reaction you'll make to your friends. You can cash it anytime you need it. What reaction—thoughts, feelings, and behavior—do you want to have ready and waiting? You've decided how to react to two of your old friends and you've done it too, but that may sometimes be difficult to keep up. So, when might you want to cash this check—to react to your friends the way you plan?

CLIENT: I need to be ready to think, "It's not a horrible thing if I don't join their crazy times," to feel confident and strong about deciding to stay away sometimes, and I need to be ready to really do it—to leave then join them later for my kind of fun.

Expressing Good-Bye

COUNSELOR: [introducing a wallet/pocketbook/purse] I've had this wallet for a while. There was a time when I didn't use it and put all my stuff in a notebook. I was glad I kept it though because later I decided to use it again. How many wallets have you had? I lost a wallet once that I liked a lot. I was really sad. Angry too. And afraid. I thought someone might find it and use my credit cards. I had all kinds of feelings for a while. How do you feel about this being our last meeting?

CLIENT: I feel good since I can see I've come a long way since we started. But I feel kind of sad too. I liked kicking around ideas with you and then trying things and telling you how it went.

I followed this with sharing my own feelings of pride and sadness as well as hope and confidence that he would continue to use both "inside and outside" resources to keep up his clearly valuable changes.

Suggestions for Follow-Up

As with any counseling approach, follow-up is vital for maximizing maintenance of progress as well as encouraging further development. Counselors can use new common objects to measure progress over time or return to update a previously used object. For example, if previously a clock was used to help define the problem and the client stated, "If 1:00 means I stay with my friends no matter what they do, and 12:00 means I should drop them as my friends, I would say I'm about at 1:20," the counselor can return to this same metaphor during a later follow-up process, for example: "If 1:00 means you've stayed with your friends no matter what they did, and 12:00 means you've dropped them as your friends, where are you now?"

The client is also free to create another option, such as when one adolescent client responded upon follow-up, "Sometimes it's like I'm in another time zone and the clock isn't right, at least for now." Working with metaphors, it is not uncommon for counselors to be more confused than the client, as was the case following that client's response. The client's explanation helped clarify his position: "I mean sometimes I don't go with them to do something stupid, but they're still my friends and we do other stuff together."

Contraindications

None noted.

Professional Readings & Resources

Bauer, P. J., Van Abbema, D. L., Wiebe, S. A., Cary, M. S., Phill, C., & Burch, M. M. (2004). Props, not pictures, are worth a thousand words. *Applied Cognitive Psychology, 18*(4), 373-392.

Constas, M. A. (1989). Empirical research of creativity: Possible heuristics for studying a complex phenomenon. *Contemporary Educational Psychology, 14*(3), 275-279.

Gladding, S. T. (2004). *Counseling as an art: The creative arts in counseling* (3rd ed.). Alexandria, VA: American Counseling Association.

Gordon, D. (1978). *Therapeutic metaphors.* Cupertino, CA: Meta Publications.

Grotstien, J. S. (1992). The enigmatic relationship of creativity to mental health and psychotherapy. *American Journal of Psychotherapy, 46*(3), 405-408.

Guttman, H. A. (1989). The augmentation of creativity: Epistemological concerns and the excitement of innovation in family therapy. *Journal of Family Psychology, 2*(4), 473-477.

Harvill, R., Jacobs, E. E., & Masson, R. L. (1984). Using "props" to enhance your counseling. The *Personnel and Guidance Journal, 62*(5), 273-276.

Jacobs, E. E. (1992). *Creative counseling techniques: An illustrated guide.* Odessa, FL: Psychological Assessment Resources.

Landreth, G. L. (2002). *Play therapy: The art of the relationship* (2nd ed.). NY: Brunner Routledge.

Nicholson, J. A. (1983). *The creative counselor.* New York: McGraw-Hill.

Sternberg, R. J., & Lubart, T. I. (1992). Creativity: Its nature and assessment. *School Psychology International, 13*(3), 243-247.

Utay, J., & Lampe, R. (1996). A cognitive-behavioral group play therapy approach to social skills training for children with learning disabilities. *Journal for Specialists in Group Work, 20*(2), 114-120.

HANDOUT 12.1

100 IDEAS FOR POTENTIAL THERAPEUTIC PROPS

Sixty Common Office Objects Potentially Transformed into Therapeutic Props

1. Air vent (intake, outflow)
2. Answering machine
3. Art (poster, picture, sculpture)
4. Book (various types)
5. Bookends
6. Calculator
7. Calendar (desk, wall, portable)
8. Chair
9. Clock
10. Coat/hat rack
11. Computer
12. Computer disk
13. Computer paper
14. Cup (plastic, paper, styrofoam)
15. Curtain
16. Desk
17. Door
18. Electric cord
19. Electric outlet
20. Fan
21. File cabinet
22. File folder
23. File folder label
24. Floor (rug, carpet, wood, tile, etc.)
25. Framed items (certificate, degree, license, etc.)
26. Highlighter
27. Index Card
28. Kleenex
29. Lamp
30. Light (ceiling)

Utay, J. M. (2007). Props: Therapeutic use of common objects. In L. L. Hecker, C. F. Sori, & Associates, *The therapist's notebook, volume 2: More homework, handouts, and activities for use in psychotherapy* (pp. 93-102). Binghamton, NY: The Haworth Press.

31. Light switch

32. Liquid paper

33. Marker (permanent, water-based)

34. Mug

35. Pen

36. Pencil

37. Pencil sharpener

38. Plant

39. Post-Its

40. Printer

41. Printer paper

42. Radio

43. Recording material (audio, video tapes)

44. Rubber band

45. Ruler

46. Scissors

47. Scratch paper

48. Shelf and/or bookcase

49. Snacks

50. Staple remover

51. Stapler

52. Stationary

53. Table

54. Tape

55. Telephone

56. Thermostat

57. Trash can (with or without liner or lid)

58. Various business cards (old, new)

59. Window

60. Writing paper

A Dozen Potentially Therapeutic Props Counselors Usually Have with Them

61. Check/checkbook

62. Coins

63. Driver's license

Utay, J. M. (2007). Props: Therapeutic use of common objects. In L. L. Hecker, C. F. Sori, & Associates, *The therapist's notebook, volume 2: More homework, handouts, and activities for use in psychotherapy* (pp. 93-102). Binghamton, NY: The Haworth Press.

64. Keys

65. Pants, skirt, or dress

66. Paper currency

67. Ring

68. Shirt

69. Shoes

70. Socks

71. Wallet/pocketbook

72. Watch

A Dozen Potentially Therapeutic Props Usually Found Outside

73. Tree (young, midsize, full grown)

74. Weather (rain, snow, clouds, etc.)

75. Driveway or parking lot

76. Signs (stop, ads, street name, etc.)

77. Creature (bird, animal, etc.)

78. Vehicle (car, truck, bike, etc.)

79. Dirt

80. water (River, Pond, Puddle, Faucet, etc.)

81. Rock

82. Roots

83. Telephone pole

84. Plants (grass, flower, etc.)

A Dozen Cheap Potentially Therapeutic Props

85. Juggling balls

86. Magic trick

87. Mirror

88. Pipe cleaner

89. Timer

90. Balloon

91. Magnet

92. Oversized eraser (for BIG mistakes)

93. Rope

94. Silly putty

Utay, J. M. (2007). Props: Therapeutic use of common objects. In L. L. Hecker, C. F. Sori, & Associates, *The therapist's notebook, volume 2: More homework, handouts, and activities for use in psychotherapy* (pp. 93-102). Binghamton, NY: The Haworth Press.

95. Board game
96. Deck of cards

Four Potentially Therapeutic Nonvisual Props

97. Sounds (nature, music, voice)
98. Movement
99. Smells
100. Tastes

Utay, J. M. (2007). Props: Therapeutic use of common objects. In L. L. Hecker, C. F. Sori, & Associates, *The therapist's notebook, volume 2: More homework, handouts, and activities for use in psychotherapy* (pp. 93-102). Binghamton, NY: The Haworth Press.

SECTION III:
ADULTS

13

Client Family-of-Origin Interviews with Parents: Questions That Support Discovery and Connection

Fred P. Piercy

Type of Contribution: *Homework*

Objectives

The therapist gives questions (included in this chapter) to adult clients who use them to interview their parents or primary caregivers.

About twenty-three years ago, several of my therapist colleagues interviewed their parents as part of their family-of-origin supervision group, led by Donald Williamson. I thought these interviews were a good idea and subsequently conducted individual interviews with my own mother and father. I asked them what they remembered about growing up, how they fit into their own families, what their relationships were like with their siblings, how they met, what each of them was like back then, challenges they faced, and so on. I also asked them what they remembered about me as a child, and my relationships with them and others.

I felt close to my parents during and after these interviews. I also learned a lot about them and me, and saw parallels that surprised me. For example, I saw a lot of me in my parents' optimism, humor, and support of one another. I also saw several of my less complimentary characteristics.

Recently, I played portions of the tapes of these interviews when I presented my genogram to a group of family therapy graduate students. I got goose bumps as my parents talked about each other and me. Although they died years earlier, my mother and father were clearly still with me. And, as the tape demonstrated, a lot of who I am comes from them.

Because of the insights and emotional connections from these interviews, I occasionally suggest that my clients interview their own parents. Sometimes they learn important things about themselves and their families, and occasionally they become reacquainted with this important source of support. In this chapter, I summarize the process of these interviews and provide the questions I give clients to help them conduct these interviews.

Rationale for Use

Bowen (1978), Framo (1982), Williamson (1981, 1991), and other intergenerational therapists conduct intergenerational therapy sessions or assign homework so that their clients can learn to differentiate from their families of origin, and consequently not be so reactive to them and others. Framo (1982) also talked about the need to see one's own current family without the ghosts of one's family of origin clouding that vision. For Framo, therapy sessions with clients and their parents decrease the parental introjects that clients project onto their present family members. In the process, contended Framo, clients begin to get to know their parents as real

The Therapist's Notebook, Volume 2
© 2007 by The Haworth Press, Inc. All rights reserved.
doi:10.1300/5550_13

people. Similarly, Williamson (1981, 1991) discussed the need for adult clients to develop less hierarchical, more peerlike relationships with their parents, and in so doing to claim their own personal authority.

The parent interviews I suggest to clients have many of the same goals. In addition:

- Sometimes clients can learn a lot about themselves from these interviews. They can learn, for example, that certain issues that they are dealing with in their own lives (e.g., the need to fit in, to be perfect, to be taken seriously) are also issues that their parents dealt with.
- Clients often learn that the dynamics that they are experiencing in their present relationships are the same dynamics that they learned long ago in their relationships with their parents or siblings.
- Through these interviews, clients are often reminded of the support system they have in their families of origin. They connect with their parents as people who want the best for them and are there to help them through difficult times.
- If the client tape records the interviews, he or she has a valuable record of the past—a family history—that he or she can play in future years.

Instructions

When I suggest that clients interview their parents, I say something like this:

I want to give you a homework assignment to interview your parents. A lot of who you are came from your relationship with them. They also have insights about you and how you related to others as a child that may be useful to us in therapy. Most people develop a style of relating as a child that they carry over to their adult lives. It would be particularly helpful for you to learn about how you fit in as a child to better understand how you fit in today.

I'd like you to interview your mother and father in separate interviews, without the other watching or listening. Plan at least an hour and a half with each. Be sure to tape record each interview so you have a record of it. I did similar interviews with my parents over twenty years ago. I learn something different about my own parents and me every time I listen to the tape recordings of these interviews.

Here is a list of questions you may want to ask your mother and father. Don't feel tied to these questions, however. You can skip some and add others of your own. . . .

The Questions

Below are the questions that I give adult clients to help them conduct their interviews with their parents. Some are adaptations of the Adlerian lifestyle interview questions I have used for years, and others I developed in the course of my practice.

1. What are some of the earliest memories of the family you grew up in?
2. Tell me about your own mother and father. What kind of relationship did you have with your mother? Your father?
3. What hopes did your mother and father have for you?
4. How would you describe each of your siblings? Tell me about your relationship with each of your siblings as you were growing up.
5. How would your mother describe you? How would your father describe you?
6. What kind of relationship did your parents have? How do you know?
7. In what way did you want your marriage to be different from that of your parents? In what ways did you want it to be the same?

8. What were some critical events you can remember from your childhood? How did each member of the family respond to these events?
9. What did you do for fun as a child?
10. If you could come up with a motto for the family you grew up in, what would it be?
11. What was good about the family you grew up in? Do you have any regrets about the family you grew up in? If you could change something about the family, what would it be?
12. In what ways are you similar to or different from each of your parents?
13. As a parent, what values have you tried to instill in your own children?
14. What do you value about your present family? Any regrets?
15. What wishes and dreams did you have for each of your children?
16. How have I made you proud? How have I disappointed you?
17. How would you describe each of your children when they were eight? Do you see any of the same characteristics in them today? Please explain.
18. What was the best thing about raising me? What was the hardest thing?
19. What memories of happiness and sadness do you have regarding your family?
20. If you could come up with a motto or theme that represents your present family, what would it be?
21. Was there anything that you had trouble talking to me about when I was a child? How about now?
22. As we get older, what would you like our relationship to be like?
23. How would you describe the way I relate to others? Do you think that I have any blind spots? What are they?
24. How do you see me handling conflict? What do you think I'm good at? Not so good at?
25. How would you describe me to others?
26. Who am I most like in our family? Who am I least like? Why?
27. What do you appreciate about our relationship? What I appreciate about our relationship is . . .

Brief Vignette

I gave this assignment to Mike and Beth, who were having marital troubles. In their interviews with their parents, each learned how issues from their families of origin were alive and well in their own stormy relationship. For example, Mike said that he understood for the first time why he felt so at sea when Beth got angry with him. "My parents didn't argue," said Mike. "So I have no model for how to disagree. The most my folks would say is, 'We can make this work.' That's what I always tell Beth, but I don't have a clue in the world how to do it. My parents would just shut up when they disagreed, and things would eventually blow over. When I try this, it drives Beth crazy."

Beth added, "My mom got unbelievably angry at my dad, just like I do with Mike. Since my dad was so goddamned logical and reasonable, Mom always ended up looking like it was her fault—just like I do. After a blowup, I also end up hating myself just the way Mom hated herself."

Mike and Beth made other discoveries, as well, all of which allowed us to see their concerns not as character flaws but as patterns each learned from their families of origin. When they realized that these patterns had a history older than they were, they mellowed a little and committed to break their negative family traditions. This became the focus of our therapy together.

Suggestions for Follow-Up

I usually ask my clients what they learned in their interviews and what patterns from their families they see in their lives today. Mostly, though, I just listen. I've learned that my clients get out of this activity what they need to learn at the time.

Contraindications

I would hesitate to suggest the parent interviews if abuse occurred in the family, or if the relationships between my clients and their parents were particularly conflictual.

References

Bowen, M. (1978). *Family therapy in clinical practice.* Northvale, NJ: Jason Aronson.

Framo, J. L. (1982). *Explorations in marital and family therapy: Selected papers of James L. Framo, PhD.* New York: Springer.

Williamson, D. (1981). Termination of the intergenerational hierarchical boundary between the first and second generation: A "new" stage in the family life cycle. *Journal of Marital and Family Therapy, 7,* 441-452.

Williamson, D. S. (1991). *The intimacy paradox: Personal authority in the family system.* New York: Guilford.

Readings and Resources for Psychotherapists and Clients

Lerner, H. (1985). *The dance of anger.* New York: Harper and Row.

Lerner, H. (1989). *The dance of intimacy.* New York: Harper and Row.

14

Externalizing Problems: It's in the Bag

Margaret L. Keeling

Type of Contribution: *Activity*

Objectives

This activity uses art to facilitate the process of externalization in narrative therapy. Although it is presented here in a narrative therapy context, the activity lends itself to multiple therapeutic approaches. The utility of art in narrative therapy has been established in the clinical and research literature (Bermudez & Bermudez, 2002; Carlson, 1997; Keeling & Bermudez, in press; Keeling & Nielson, 2005; Zimmerman & Shepherd, 1993). In addition to addressing a variety of presenting problems, this activity can be used with individuals, couples, families, and groups. It is designed to help clients externalize problems in a tangible way that helps them explore their relationships with their problems, encourages a systemic, nonblaming perspective, and increases clients' sense of agency to overcome their problems.

Rationale for Use

This externalization activity quite literally allows clients to face their problems. It may also hold special appeal for clients who think visually or who struggle with the abstract, complex nature of their presenting problems. Facing and interacting with a problem in this way tends to elicit strong experiencing and affect, and clarifies emotions, intentions, and desires. In addition, the use of art and humor can de-escalate negative interactions, induce positive affect, and engage family members of different ages in an enjoyable but meaningful shared creative experience.

Consistent with the narrative therapy approach, the way in which the relationship with the problem is conceptualized and the source of strength and solutions is the client system. Therefore, clients believe they are finding their own answers, so solutions fit for them (St. James O'Connor, Meakes, Pickering, & Schuman, 1997). Bringing client resources to light can facilitate client agency and empowerment (Freedman & Combs, 1996; White, 2000). In addition, because the resources for addressing problems are emanating from the clients, they may be more likely to maintain the skills and qualities they need to continue making progress after therapy is over.

Addressing problems as external entities helps clients explore their relationships with problems in a way that minimizes blame but emphasizes accountability. They are able to examine how they and others support and maintain their problems, while avoiding unproductive self-blame or scapegoating that come from confusing the problem with the person (White & Epston, 1990).

Finally, because clients are encouraged to view themselves in relation to their problems, they may be able to acknowledge their problems' previously hidden benefits or good intentions. They

doi:10.1300/5550_14

may also deal with especially stubborn problems or relapse in a more forgiving way, as they seek to fulfill their needs and preferences in preferred ways that involve embracing or balancing the problem rather than eradicating it.

Instructions

The following instructions assume that the therapist has spent adequate time with clients to hear their story and establish an empathic, trustworthy alliance.

1. Identify a simple term or name (noun form) for the problem, using the clients' language, or a word or phrase easily accepted by the clients.
2. Introduce the notion of the problem as an outside entity that is intruding into the clients' relationship. Explain this as another way of looking at the situation that might seem odd at first, but which may be helpful.
3. Elicit clients' cooperation for a playful but meaningful activity. If the client system includes children, it is easy to explain the activity in terms of engaging the children. If not, it can be introduced as a way of lightening things up, which is often welcome.
4. Explain that it can be helpful to have something concrete to represent the problem (I often explain this as something that is helpful to me, or something that other clients have found helpful).
5. Bring out the bag, markers, and any other materials you want to make available (colored paper, scissors, glue sticks, yarn, pipe cleaners). Engage the clients in a conversation about the "personality" of the problem (use the problem's name consistently). Is it angry? Sad? Stressed? Panicked? Is it like a monster, an animal, a person, a demon? Encourage clients to use the art supplies to personalize the bag so its personality shows. The bag needs to be left open at the top but otherwise can be squashed, wrinkled, twisted, or shaped to suit its personality. See Figure 14.1 for illustrations of different types of problems.
6. Place the finished bag between the clients and encourage them to reflect on its effects on their relationship, feelings, view of self and other, behaviors, well-being, and quality of life (relative influence questions).
7. Allow clients to express their feelings toward the problem (bag), as well as what they would like to see happen (or what they would like to do) to the problem.
8. Provide clients with a small stack of colored sticky notes, with a different color provided for each client. Encourage each client to jot down ways that he or she feeds the problem (contributes to it) to keep it alive, even inadvertently. Help young children write their responses. Ask clients to take turns reading their contributions, feeding each one into the problem bag after it is read.
9. Explain that, now that you and the clients know what feeds the problem and keeps it alive, you are going to explore the strengths the clients have that might starve, weaken, or even eliminate the problem. Place the problem bag in the middle of a large (11" × 17" or larger) blank sheet of paper, and allow the clients to write or draw the strengths they bring as individuals and as a family.
10. Using these strengths as a foundation, the clients can then explore for unique outcomes—times when their strengths were nurtured and the problem was weakened or absent—and consider how their strengths and resources may be nurtured in the present and into the future to bring about their preferred ways of being. Even the ways the clients feed the problem may be pulled out of the bag and related to feelings and motives that are sources of power and empathy to overcome the problem.

FIGURE 14.1. Line drawings of different problems. From left to right, Conflict, Depression, and Time Stress.

Brief Vignette

Gil and Betty, a couple in their midforties, came to therapy with concerns about their sixteen-year-old daughter, Leah. They stated that in the past two years Leah had become increasingly defiant and argumentative, especially toward Gil. Leah had little to say initially, although she acknowledged that she and her dad argued frequently. In other respects, Leah was doing well. She consistently made good grades in school and did not show other conduct problems such as staying out late, or drug or alcohol use. Betty commented that she often felt stuck in the middle between Leah and Gil, as she tried to act as a buffer between them, and usually intervened in their arguments. She stated her belief that although Leah was quick to speak her mind, Gil was too harsh toward Leah and tended to provoke her. In private sessions with Gil and Betty, the couple revealed that they were also having serious marital problems and sometimes argued in front of Leah. Betty admitted to confiding in Leah and relying on her for emotional support. In an individual session, Leah was much more talkative. She portrayed her father as verbally abusive toward her and her mother and described her mother as emotionally fragile. She also said that both her parents had told her that if the family broke apart, they would hold Leah responsible because of her argumentative ways. In subsequent family sessions, the parents admitted this was true, and that although they were ashamed to have said it, they believed that the tension between Leah and Gil was contributing to the disintegration of the family.

The family seemed locked into a negative pattern of interaction characterized by blame, especially toward Leah. The therapist wanted to reduce blaming and defensiveness, while opening space for exploring the issues more thoroughly and contextually. The therapist also wanted to encourage personal accountability from each family member and see if they could pull together as a team to fight a common problem, rather than fighting each other. Using the family's language, the therapist introduced conflict as a problem that was affecting the whole family, in which each member played a role, and which the entire family desired to overcome. They readily agreed with these ideas.

Feeling that she had gained the trust of the family, the therapist asked them if they could play a little, noting that even though their problem was very serious, it might feel good to lighten things up a bit. They liked this idea as well. She asked them to think about conflict as if it were a separate entity (a person, a monster, a badly behaved pet, etc.). To help them visualize this, the therapist brought out a brown paper lunch bag and told the family that perhaps this could represent Conflict in some way. She asked them to think about what it should look like (facial expression and so on) and provided markers for them to transform the bag into the personification of Conflict. Leah seemed eager to do the drawing as Betty and Gil contributed ideas.

Then the open Conflict bag was placed in the center of the room, with the family sitting around it. The therapist asked them to comment on the effects of Conflict on their family, addressing it in person (e.g., "You keep us from feeling close") if they felt comfortable doing so. She then asked them to tell Conflict what they wanted to see happen, eliciting comments such as, "I wish you would go away and leave us alone," and "I'm sorry we ever let you in."

Each family member was handed a different-colored stack of sticky notes by the therapist, who asked them to write down how each of them personally had fed the problem to keep it alive. Gil wrote comments like, "I take out problems from work on my family," and "I feel like I need to control Leah to keep her out of trouble." Leah wrote, "Sometimes I just can't keep my mouth shut," and "I feel like I have to stand up to him [Gil] because no one else does." Betty wrote, "I jump in to keep them [Gil and Leah] from hurting each other."

Taking responsibility for how each family member contributed to the problem helped take Leah out of the position of blame. The family noticed similarities in the motives for their problem-sustaining behaviors, such as a desire to protect loved ones from harm. As the family increasingly became aware of their common desires for closeness, protection, and safety, they also grew more empathic toward one another's fears and insecurities. Hostility and defensiveness decreased.

Using their common desires as a starting point, the therapist suggested that the family think of the strengths they have to defeat or starve Conflict. The therapist placed a large sheet of blank paper on the floor, and put the Conflict bag in the middle. The family then drew and wrote on the paper, to surround Conflict with their strengths, which included such things as love, a desire to be close, and humor. These strengths laid the groundwork for subsequent discussions about factors that appeared to starve Conflict. Working from what they had noticed in the past (unique outcomes), they were able to bring Conflict-starving/family-nurturing behaviors into the present, such as talking honestly and calmly about feelings, acknowledging and apologizing for mistakes, and engaging in enjoyable family activities.

Over the subsequent weeks, Leah reported a marked decrease in conflict between herself and Gil, and on feeling less pressed by Betty to be a confidant and source of support. Betty and Gil, having become aware of contextual influences that fed the family conflict and their marital problems, sought out couple therapy.

Suggestions for Follow-Up

Clients may continue to interact with the problem bag through subsequent sessions in a variety of ways. They may add to the strengths and resources that starve the problem; they may choose to keep it at home or in the therapist's office; they may act out hostility toward the problem (stomping or squashing it); they may choose to embrace the problem or explore their relationship with it in greater detail; they may remark upon their changing relationship with it and use visual means to express change (putting it in a box or a cage, closer or further away; removing its "fangs"); or they may symbolize the emergence of a new story not dominated by the problem through ritual (burying or burning the problem, tearing it up, throwing it away, writing a farewell letter, leaving it forever at the therapist's office).

From a narrative perspective, clients may be invited to move away from the focus on the problem to focus on the emergence and thickening of the new, preferred story. They may also wish to perform the new story in various ways, such as archiving or inviting others to witness their new story (White & Epston, 1990).

Contraindications

As mentioned in the instructions, it is important to join with clients and attend to their pain before starting this intervention. For some clients, the use of art-based interventions and imagination may seem childish, and the initial playfulness of this approach may make some clients feel that the therapist is not taking them seriously. Respect and sensitivity can improve the chances for success. In addition, this intervention is not appropriate for clients who are in crisis or unstable due to psychotic episodes or delusions.

References

Bermudez, J. M., & Bermudez, S. (2002). Altar-making with Latino families: A narrative therapy perspective. *Journal of Family Psychotherapy, 13*(3-4), 329-347.

Carlson, T. D. (1997). Using art in narrative therapy: Enhancing therapeutic possibilities. *American Journal of Family Therapy, 25,* 271-283.

Freedman, J., & Combs, G. (1996). *Narrative therapy: The social construction of preferred realities.* New York: Norton.

Keeling, M. L., & Bermudez, J. M. (2006). Externalizing problems through art and writing: Experience of process and helpfulness. *Journal of Marital and Family Therapy, 32*(4), 405-419.

Keeling, M. L., & Nielson, R. (2005). Indian women's experience of a narrative therapy intervention using art and writing. *Contemporary Family Therapy, 27,* 435-452.

St. James O'Connor, T., Meakes, E., Pickering, M. R., & Schuman, M. (1997). On the right track: Client experience of narrative therapy. *Contemporary Family Therapy, 19,* 479-495.

White, M. (2000). *Reflections on narrative practice.* Adelaide, South Australia: Dulwich Center.

White, M., & Epston, D. (1990). *Narrative means to therapeutic ends.* New York: Norton.

Zimmerman, T., & Shepherd, S. (1993). Externalizing the problem of bulimia through conversation, drawing and letter writing in group therapy. *Journal of Systemic Therapies, 12*(1), 22-31.

Professional Readings and Resources

Bermudez, J. M., & Bermudez, S. (2002). Altar-making with Latino families: A narrative therapy perspective. *Journal of Family Psychotherapy, 13*(3-4), 329-347.

Buckman, R. (1997). Using art to externalize and tame tempers. In T. S. Nelson & T. S. Trepper (Eds.), *101 more interventions in family therapy* (pp. 437-439). New York: The Haworth Press.

Carlson, T. D. (1997). Using art in narrative therapy: Enhancing therapeutic possibilities. *American Journal of Family Therapy, 25,* 271-283.

Freedman, J., & Combs, G. (1996). *Narrative therapy: The social construction of preferred realities.* New York: Norton.

Keeling, M. L., & Bermudez, J. M. (2006). Externalizing problems through art and writing: Experience of process and helpfulness. *Journal of Marital and Family Therapy, 32*(4), 405-419.

Keeling, M. L., & Nielson, R. (2005). Indian women's experience of a narrative therapy intervention using art and writing. *Contemporary Family Therapy, 27,* 435-452.

Riley, S. (1997). Social constructionism: The narrative approach and clinical art therapy. *Art Therapy, 14,* 282-284.

Riley, S. (2003). Solution-focused and narrative approaches. In C. A. Malchiodi (Ed.), *Handbook of art therapy* (pp. 82–92). New York: Guilford.

Roth, S., & Epston, D. (1996). Consulting the problem about the problematic relationship: An exercise for experiencing a relationship with an externalized problem. In M. F. Hoyt (Ed.), *Constructive therapies* (Vol. 2, pp. 148-162). New York: Guilford.

St. James O'Connor, T., Meakes, E., Pickering, M. R., & Schuman, M. (1997). On the right track: Client experience of narrative therapy. *Contemporary Family Therapy, 19,* 479-495.

White, M. (2000). *Reflections on narrative practice.* Adelaide, South Australia: Dulwich Centre.

White, M., & Epston, D. (1990). *Narrative means to therapeutic ends.* New York: Norton.

Zimmerman, T., & Shepherd, S. (1993). Externalizing the problem of bulimia through conversation, drawing and letter writing in group therapy. *Journal of Systemic Therapies, 12*(1), 22-31.

Bibliotherapy Source for Clients

Huber, C., & Shiver, J. (1998). *How you do anything is how you do everything: A workbook.* Murphys, CA: Keep It Simple Books.

15

Putting Pressure on Procrastination

Howard G. Rosenthal

Type of Contribution: *Homework*

Objectives

Clients who put off tasks often feel unproductive and rarely reach their goals. Worse yet, they frequently use the fact that they procrastinate to further beat themselves, which in turn tends to lower their sense of self-esteem and self-worth. This scenario is so common that rational-emotive behavior therapy lists inaction and inertia as a major irrational idea that causes emotional discord, and Ellis (2004) points out that the easy way (i.e., putting things off) is truly the hard way over the course of time.

Rationale for Use

Many clients have tried to tackle their procrastination themselves with little result. When they engage therapists in their struggle to decrease procrastination, direct intervention with the problem often yields poor results. The therapist may become as frustrated as the client when direct intervention only yields "more of the same" responses from the client. Much to the therapist's chagrin, the client may even procrastinate or shirk homework assignments or interventions directly related to decreasing procrastination. It is at this point that the therapist may find paradoxical assignments beneficial.

The use of paradoxical assignments related to behavior and thinking is well documented in the literature (Haley, 1963), as is the use of shaping by successive approximations (Ferster and Skinner, 1957). This simple assignment makes use of both strategies, although historically they originate from two opposing camps of therapy (i.e., brief strategic therapy and Skinnerian behavior modification, respectively).

Instructions

First, the client is asked to describe the situation related to procrastination, such as cleaning the garage, riding an exercise bicycle twenty minutes a day, or perhaps finishing a term paper. After the client is allowed to talk about the situation and, ideally, explore feelings and the rationale for the behavior (or more likely the lack of it), a homework assignment is prescribed.

The homework assignment always consists of prescribing a small chunk of behavior (or successive approximation) in the direction of the ultimate goal. Nevertheless, the assignment always paradoxically prescribes a behavior that is so small, minute, paltry, infinitesimal, and minuscule that it is seemingly ridiculous.

The Therapist's Notebook, Volume 2
doi:10.1300/5550_15

For example, the client who is putting off cleaning his garage is asked to throw away one box, and only one box, between now and next week's session. The woman who is suffering from a "mañana complex" and has not set foot on her exercise bike is asked to ride the bike for just twenty seconds per day. More is forbidden. The individual who is paralyzed by a massive fifteen-page term paper is instructed to write the title or perhaps the first paragraph.

Brief Vignette

A therapist was able to utilize this strategy when confronted with a somewhat unusual case a few years ago. The client, who was very bright and successful, and lived in an affluent neighborhood, had a lawn that was several feet high. The subdivision association had strict rules for homeowners and maintaining a well-kept lawn was one of them. They had fined the client for his lack of lawn maintenance on numerous occasions and they were now suggesting that he needed to move.

He absolutely dreaded the act of cutting the lawn. However, when the therapist suggested he hire a lawn service, he stated that the idea of paying to get the job done was even more distasteful, since he owned an array of expensive lawn equipment.

The therapist asked him if on those rare occasions when he actually cut the lawn, he performed the work on a section-by-section basis. The therapist was especially interested in whether the lawn sported a tiny postage-stamp-sized section that might be easy to cut. Indeed, the lawn did have a small section near the driveway that took less than three minutes to cut. However, the client routinely tackled a large hilly section first, with the thought that he had to finish the entire job. The task would become overwhelming and, on most occasions, he would quit.

The clinician wrote a contract stating that the client was to cut the tiny section near the driveway prior to the next meeting. He was given a copy of the contract and informed that the therapist was keeping a copy in his file. A behavioral contract is not mandatory when using this strategy, but it can help. The therapist further suggested that if he finished the bonsai-sized portion of his lawn, he should reward (i.e., reinforce) himself. His choice of a positive reinforcement was renting a DVD to watch. Here again, like the written contract, positive reinforcement is not mandatory, but in very difficult cases like this it can be helpful.

During the next session, the client revealed that he felt a tad foolish quitting after he cut the small section near his driveway. He had timed the procedure and it took only a hair over two minutes. Instead of stopping, he completed the entire front lawn and rented a DVD from a video store.

The next day, as he put it, "I played the same mind game with myself and decided I was just going to cut a ten-by-ten-foot strip near the patio. I did it and quit. I then said to myself that as long as I had the lawnmower fired up I could do another small portion of my property. Before long, my entire backyard was finished."

The therapist then discussed other areas of the client's life where procrastination was causing him problems (it turned out there were quite a few of them) and outlined specific ways he could implement this technique in each of the particular situations.

One major plus is that this homework assignment paradigm almost guarantees success and the feelings that go with it. For example, a client who comes to the session and says, "I only wrote one paragraph this week," is reminded that he did more than was asked of him since the assignment merely consisted of constructing a title.

Just as an aside, this is an excellent self-assignment for therapists who, despite their vast theoretical knowledge and introspection, are still personally held captive by procrastination.

Suggestions for Follow-Up

In many—if not most—cases the therapist will be pleasantly surprised by the client's progress. Assuming the client did follow the assignment to the letter and performed only what was prescribed, another ever so slightly more difficult assignment is given. Hence, the client who writes a paragraph on his term paper is assigned to write another paragraph or two at the most.

Whenever possible, future assignments should progress as slowly as possible. For example, a client who rides her exercise bike for twenty seconds is asked to increase the amount to one minute during the next week and maybe a minute and a half for the week after that. A client who smokes a pack a day (twenty cigarettes) is asked to lower the number to nineteen during the next week, and then eighteen for the week after that.

Contraindications

If a client responds to direct interventions (see examples under Bibliotherapy Sources for Clients), paradoxical intervention may not be needed or called for. In addition, it goes without saying that a rapidly approaching deadline may negate the possibility of using this intervention.

References

Ellis, A. (2004). *Rational emotive behavior therapy: It works for me—It can work for you.* New York: Prometheus Books.

Ferster, C. B., & Skinner, B. F. (1957). *Schedules of reinforcement.* New York: Appleton-Century-Crofts.

Haley, J. (1963). *Strategies of psychotherapy.* New York: Grune and Stratton,

Professional Readings and Resources

Haley, J. (1991). *The art of strategic therapy.* New York: Brunner-Routledge.

Haley, J. (1991). *Problem solving therapy.* New York: Jossey Bass.

Wolpe, J. (1990). *The practice of behavior therapy* (4th ed.). New York: Pergamon Press.

Bibliotherapy Sources for Clients

Burka, J. B., & Yuen, L. M. (2004). *Procrastination: Why you do it, what to do about it.* Cambridge, MA: De Capo Press.

Emotional wellness matters. (n.d.). Retrieved March 25, 2006, from http://www.emotional wellness.com/procrastination.htm

Knaus, W. J. (2002). *The procrastination workbook: Your personalized program for breaking free from patterns that hold you back.* Oakland, CA: New Harbinger Publications.

Procrastination. (n.d.). Retrieved March 25, 2006, from http://mentalhelp.net/psyhelp/chap4/chap4r.htm

Rosenthal, H., & Hollis, J. (1993). *Help yourself to positive mental health.* Muncie, IN: Accelerated Development.

Tullier, M. (2000). *The complete idiot's guide to overcoming procrastination.* New York: Alpha Books.

16

The Situation Trigger Worksheet

Kolleen L. Simons

Type of Contribution: *Homework, Handouts*

The Situation Trigger Worksheet can be used as a homework assignment or as a guide for the therapist in session. This worksheet is based on cognitive-behavioral theory (Sundel & Sundel, 2005). It can be used with teenagers or adults and is best used with clients who value the role of insight in therapy. It is necessary that clients be aware of their behaviors and be willing to recognize the impact of their negative behaviors on their current situation.

Objectives

According to Sundel and Sundel (2005), the application of behavioral interventions allows new target behaviors to be developed, increased or strengthened, and maintained. Likewise, the focus of behavioral interventions is to identify, decrease, weaken, and ultimately extinguish any negative behaviors that interfere with the new target behavior. This is accomplished by initially identifying the trigger event for the negative behavior and then exploring positive alternative thoughts and behaviors. Trigger events are accompanied by thoughts, feelings, and actions that lead to consequences that hold the negative behavior in place. This worksheet can help the client identify trigger events and explore positive alternatives to increase the new target behavior.

Rationale for Use

This homework assignment (see Handout 16.1) is designed to aid clients in recognizing triggers and the impact of automatic thoughts on behaviors. According to Greenberger & Padesky (1995), automatic thoughts are "words and images that pop into our head throughout the day as we are doing things" (p. 49). This is a helpful point to identify when working with clients who feel they cannot control their behavior and want help in breaking that cycle. It is the awareness of the automatic thoughts that is the first step toward change and better problem solving (Greenberger & Padesky, 1995). Because the therapist will be confronting the consequences of the client's behavior, this tool is best used once rapport and trust have been established.

Instructions

Step 1: It is best to start by asking the client to identify behaviors that have had a negative impact on his or her life. For example, a good place to start is to reflect back on an incident where the client admits poor choices were made. For example, with a client who has a history of anger problems, it is helpful to ask him about what happened the last time that he lost his temper. For

doi:10.1300/5550_16

example, a fight with a loved one or altercation at work may have occurred. An event or situation described would be a trigger for the client and listed in the first column of the worksheet.

Step 2: After the trigger is identified, ask the client to reflect on the automatic thought that occurred at the time of the incident. The thought occurs within seconds and often clients feel that they are not aware that it is happening (Greenberger & Padesky, 1995). The client may respond with, "I don't know; I just did it." The therapist can ask the client to describe the trigger in more detail. Then the therapist can find out the type of thought that occurred to accompany the trigger. These self-statements are very automatic for the client; they are the internal dialogues that accompany the thoughts, feelings, and actions of the client. The therapist should write down the exact statement (or statements) made by the client, because this can be helpful at the conclusion of the worksheet. For example, the client might say, "She shouldn't have talked to me like that!" or "I should be treated better than that!"

Step 3: Ask the client to identify the underlying feeling that occurred with the thought and trigger. Be sure to ask the client to be specific and not to use the same emotion for each situation. It is easy to say, "I was just mad." It is more helpful to explore other emotions such as fear, shame, sadness, being overwhelmed, or jealousy. Ask the client to be specific about the event and subsequent feeling. For example, a common feeling for an individual with depression is hopelessness, and the client might feel convinced that the problems will go on forever and that things will never improve (Burns, 1999).

Step 4: Identifying the action or behavior that occurred following the trigger identified in Step 1, for example, drinking, using drugs, having unprotected sex, self-mutilation, or any other unhealthy behavior.

Step 5: Identify the consequences of the negative behavior. A consequence is defined as a stimulus that follows a behavior and can influence the future likelihood of the behavior (Sundel & Sundel, 2005). Consequences can be positive, negative, or neutral. There are two columns for consequences in the Situation Trigger Worksheet: positive and negative. Positive consequences can be gathered from the previous discussion about the behavior. For example, an individual who is engaging in self-mutilation may state that while cutting, her anger is gone. An alcoholic might state that a positive outcome of drinking is that it helps to reduce anxiety. Negative consequences can include relational problems, physical ailments, emotional difficulties, financial, and legal troubles.

Step 6: The therapist helps clients create alternative thoughts and behaviors to create their new target behavior. The alternatives that are created or explored should be written down (see Handout 16.2) on the worksheet, since the client can use these to reflect back on after the session. If used as a homework assignment, the client is instructed to complete the columns on the situation/trigger, thought, and behavior. The therapist should provide the client with instructions on completing the worksheet.

The therapist should pay special attention to the thought column. It is likely that a pattern will be revealed. For example, many thoughts include assumptions about what others think. It is not uncommon for this column to reflect low self-esteem that has yet to be expressed in therapy.

It is important that clients generate the list of alternatives to promote a sense of ownership and responsibility for their own recovery. The client should create a list of alternatives, rather than the therapist. The client must feel a sense of ownership; if not, the alternatives are less likely to be utilized.

The consequences and alternatives are to be discussed with the therapist at the follow-up appointment. Many times a discussion of the negative consequences of change can be fruitful. This means helping clients explore any negative consequences that might occur in giving up a harmful behavior. Although change has many positive benefits, there are hidden costs that must be discussed, lest they sabotage progress.

Brief Vignette

Sally has a history of bipolar disorder, alcohol dependence, and methamphetamine dependence. She came to therapy with approximately one year of sobriety. She reported that she did not understand why she kept making the same mistakes over and over again.

Step 1: The therapist provided Sally with a copy of the Situation Trigger Worksheet (see Handout 16.1) and she was asked to think about the behaviors that she felt that she repeated, and that she would like to change. According to Sally, they were obvious to her. They included drinking, using drugs, and inappropriate sexual relationships. It was easy for Sally to identify the trigger and to blame someone else for her drinking. For example, Sally would get angry with her mother and then would get drunk. She wrote this down in the first column of the worksheet.

Step 2: Sally was asked about what her thoughts were when she was angry with her mother. Her thought was, "Mom is always mad and I do not do anything right, so I should just do what she thinks I will do." There was no thought of the ramifications of this behavior or how this was a relapse of previous behavior. Sally denied that her thoughts and feelings caused her to drink. She felt that it was her mother that caused her to drink.

Step 3: When the therapist inquired how she felt, Sally replied that she felt hopeless when she drank and that things would never improve for her. This was written down in the Feeling column (see example in Handout 16.2).

Step 4: The action for Sally was consuming alcohol. She went on later to describe other unhealthy behaviors such as using drugs or having unprotected sexual intercourse. This was written in the Action column.

Step 5: The therapist and Sally discussed the purpose or role of alcohol in her life. The statements were listed in the Positive Consequence column of the worksheet. Sally stated that alcohol helped her to escape and forget, and believed nothing else did that for her. The therapist and Sally examined the reasons that she felt that she needed to escape from the moment. When asked about contacting a sponsor or going to an Alcoholics Anonymous meeting, Sally had several excuses about why she could not do that at that time. It is important that Sally felt that she could trust the therapist because she was being confronted about her behavior. The therapist pointed out that in a previous session she talked about entering her sponsor's phone number into her phone address book. Sally was able to list several negative consequences of her behavior. For example, Sally got arrested for driving while intoxicated.

Step 6: Once the handout was completed, Sally's feelings and thoughts were discussed in more detail. The therapist explored how Sally coped with her feelings and acted upon them without often thinking about the consequences. She was able to list several alternatives that she felt that she could do. For example, she listed that she could attend an AA meeting. Sally began to recognize that it was not her mother's fault that she drank and that she needed to take responsibility for her actions.

The therapist and Sally then explored additional triggers and situations, which were also listed on the handout. The therapist was also able to use the worksheet as a tool for future discussions when Sally would express that she had no choice but to drink or take drugs. Sally was provided a copy of the handout to keep with her and reflect on if she began to experience a similar trigger.

Suggestions for Follow-Up

Once this activity is completed, it should be reviewed in subsequent sessions and can be reflected upon when a client engages in negative behavior. Additional items can always be added. As stated previously, negative consequences of change can also be discussed. The ultimate goal is that the client will begin to implement the alternatives to replace the prior negative or unhealthy behaviors.

Contraindications

Clients with limited abilities for insight likely will not benefit from this activity.

References

Burns, D. (1999). *The feeling good handbook* (rev. ed.). New York: Penguin.
Greenberger, D., & Padesky, C. (1995). *Mind over mood: A cognitive therapy treatment manual for clients.* New York: Guilford.
Sundel, M., & Sundel, S. (2005). *Behavior change in the human services: Behavioral and cognitive principles and applications.* Thousand Oaks, CA: Sage.

Professional Readings and Resources

Greenberger, D., & Padesky, C. (1995). *Clinicians guide to mind over mood.* New York: Guilford.
Hepworth, D., Rooney, R., & Larsen, J. (2002). *Direct social work practice: Theory and skills.* Belmont, CA: Wadsworth.
Sundel, M., & Sundel, S. (2005). *Behavior change in the human services: Behavioral and cognitive principles and applications.* Thousand Oaks, CA: Sage

Bibliotherapy Sources for Clients

Burns, D. (1999). *The feeling good handbook* (rev. ed). New York: Penguin.
Greenberger, D., & Padesky, C. (1995). *Mind over mood: A cognitive therapy treatment manual for clients.* New York: Guilford.

HANDOUT 16.1

SITUATION TRIGGER WORKSHEET

Situation/Trigger	Thought	Feeling	Action	Positive Consequence	Negative Consequence

Alternatives:

Simons, K. L. (2007). The situation trigger worksheet. In L. L. Hecker, C. F. Sori, & Associates, *The therapist's notebook, volume 2: More homework, handouts, and activities for use in psychotherapy* (pp. 119-124). Binghamton, NY: The Haworth Press.

HANDOUT 16.2

EXAMPLE: SITUATION TRIGGER WORKSHEET

Situation/Trigger	Thought	Feeling	Action	Positive Consequence	Negative Consequence
I got angry at my mom	She is always mad at me. I do not do anything right.	Hopeless	Drank alcohol	Helped me to forget and escape from life	Cost money; I relapsed, got arrested, late to work, hangover
Getting paid, extra money	I could use this money to get high.	Scared	Used drugs	Helped me to escape and reduced anxiety	Disappointed in myself, worried about work finding out, disappointing my daughter
First date with new guy	He will only like me if I have sex with him.	Fear of rejection	Sexual intercourse	Enjoyed experience and felt that he liked me	STD, possibly pregnant, he did not call

Alternatives:

1. Communicate with my mother about my feelings
2. Develop anger management skills
3. Go to AA meeting
4. Call sponsor or friend
5. Reach out to a co-worker
6. Make first date a group date to help reduce possibility of having sex on first date

Simons, K. L. (2007). The situation trigger worksheet. In L. L. Hecker, C. F. Sori, & Associates, *The therapist's notebook, volume 2: More homework, handouts, and activities for use in psychotherapy* (pp. 119-124). Binghamton, NY: The Haworth Press.

17

Active Imagination

Marita Delaney

Type of Contribution: *Activity, Handouts*

Objectives

The purpose of this activity is to expand self-awareness and open up communication between the conscious and unconscious mind. Clients may benefit from increased self-awareness if they hold limiting beliefs or perceptions about themselves and others. The development of a broadened outlook leads to greater self-acceptance and self-understanding, as well as more generosity and tolerance toward others.

Rationale for Use

Psychological life expresses itself through images, and the spontaneous images that arise from dreams reflect the autonomous nature of psychic life. When individuals behave in a way that is contrary to conscious values and intentions, it is often because they are unaware of an aspect of their individuality. By engaging the conscious mind in a dialogue with these aspects of themselves, clients develop an enriched sense of self-awareness and a deeper integration of the personality.

In psychotherapy with a Jungian or depth psychological orientation, clients learn that their conscious ideas about themselves, their viewpoint of the world, their attitude, and their self-awareness only represent a portion of their Self. (Carl Jung referred to the Self as the totality of the individual, including the conscious and unconscious mind.) One of the mechanisms for becoming conscious of other parts of oneself is through the process of active imagination, a technique originally developed by Carl Jung (1968). Active imagination, as Jung initially conceptualized it, is when an individual develops a relationship with a part of the psyche that seems strange or unfamiliar, such as a threatening dream figure or an animal that appears in a dream (Jung, 1970). A client can also do active imagination with a living person who represents characteristics with which he or she is uncomfortable or unfamiliar, such as an overbearing boss or a rambunctious child. The activity can also be done with an object, such as an unridden bicycle, or a box of doughnuts purchased but uneaten. These people or objects can represent aspects of the self. By entering into a conversation with an alien part of the self, a person, or an object, a relationship develops with the previously unfamiliar figure or object. The client's self-awareness grows in tandem with the developing relationship with a formerly unknown part of the psyche. The result is a broadened perspective on life, including deepened self-acceptance and tolerance toward others.

The Therapist's Notebook, Volume 2
doi:10.1300/5550_17

Instructions

The therapist should explain to the clients that they are going to be presented with an exercise that may help them get better acquainted with other parts or aspects of themselves. It should be explained to the client that they need at least twenty minutes when they will not be interrupted to do this exercise. The only implements needed are a pencil or pen and a journal, or a computer. The therapist should instruct the client to relax, take some deep breaths, and allow the mind to drift in reverie.

Ask the client to imagine a person about whom the client dreamed, a person in the outer world, or an object that elicits ambivalent thoughts or feelings. Encourage the client to enter conversation with the chosen figure. Use Handout 17.1 to guide the client in asking questions, including these:

- Who are you?
- Why are you so important to me?
- Why do you keep showing up in my dreams?
- What do you want from me?
- Where do you come from?
- Is there anything you need?
- Have I been neglecting you?
- How can we get along better?

Have the client keep a record of the conversation on the handout and journal about it at a later time, or discuss it in therapy.

If the active imagination was done with a dream figure, ask your client to give a name to the dream figure. If your client names the dream figure Albert, refer to Albert in future sessions. For example, if your client was struggling with concern about a work situation, the therapist might ask, "What would Albert think of this situation?" or "What would Albert do?" Use Handout 17.2 (Active Imagination Exercise) to help the client better integrate the experience of the conversation.

Brief Vignette

The client was a twenty-eight-year-old woman who was struggling with writing her doctoral dissertation. She had a dream in which a man kept stealing her purse and taking her checkbook. This dream recurred until she sat down and did the active imagination activity with the man in the dream.

In her active imagination exercise, the man in the dream said that he had in fact been neglected and that he was angry about it. He had much to offer that would enrich her life, but she had not taken advantage of his gifts. He insisted that she hand over her checkbook to him so that he could purchase what he needed, which was a new computer. (In fact, she had an ancient computer that caused her endless difficulty and time spent fixing glitches.) She realized that she did need a new computer, and investing in it would be an act of affirming the value of her work, as well as solve a time- and energy-draining problem. She realized that she had in fact devalued her work by not investing in a suitable tool with which to compose her dissertation.

After doing the active imagination activity, she purchased a new computer. She immediately sat down to do the work and was successful in completing her dissertation within the next six months.

Listening to the dream figure allowed her to free the creative energy encapsulated in the figure of the man in the dream. She developed the awareness that the man in the dream was in fact a neglected part of herself. As she began to relate to this disavowed part of herself, she reclaimed creative energy and power. By taking the concrete step of purchasing a new computer, she freed the psychic energy within herself and directed it to meet her goals.

In another instance, a sixty-year-old woman had a recurring dream about a snake. The snake had a sword in its mouth, and every direction it turned, it cut something. She sat quietly and envisioned the snake in her mind. Holding a journal, she prepared herself to write down her conversation with the snake. When she asked him what he wanted from her, he exclaimed, "I'm hungry!" Later, when she shared this comment with her therapist, the therapist responded that if the snake was hungry, he ought to be fed. Her therapist suggested that she would become better acquainted with the snake's intent if she listened to the snake's words. With the encouragement of her therapist, she constructed a small snake out of clay and placed it at a dollhouse table and chair set. She set the table and put a pink bow around its neck. She symbolically fed the snake. In talking about it with her family, she said, "I wonder if he symbolizes something about my speech, like I have a cutting tongue." Her family members burst into laughter, since they had been aware for many years of this individual's tendency toward sharp words. She was able to accept the observation and realized that this snake figure was helping her come to greater self-awareness. This snake held both inner wisdom and insight that led her to greater self-knowledge and appreciation of the impact of her sharp words on others.

Suggestions for Follow-Up

The conversation that began in the active imagination exercise may continue in future therapy sessions. If the exercise was fruitful, it is likely that the client will bring up the exercise spontaneously and discuss what information was learned from the conversation.

If the therapist is responsive to the insights shared by clients, it will help clients become more comfortable with the aspect of themselves about which they have just learned. The therapist may discuss how this figure is now a more conscious part of the individual. The therapist can continue to cultivate clients' awareness of this aspect of themselves by discussing the qualities held by this figure.

Often the figure represents a positive growing edge of the person, and it is helpful to the therapeutic process to continue talking about the figure in therapy. In the course of the conversation with the therapist, the client comes to internalize and relate to a newly conscious aspect of his or her individuality. Eventually, the client asks these questions of himself or herself, without the prompting of a therapist. "What would Albert say about this bounced check? How would he handle it?"

If the figure is negative or destructive and may harbor malevolent intent, the therapist should work with the client to help contain the energy by continuing to talk about this figure. It is likely that in an active imagination exercise, the figure will explain its behavior, such as, "I act this way because I am so angry at being ignored." By continuing to discuss the dream figure and its comments, the therapist helps the client to recognize the energy contained in this figure and continue to relate to it. The more clients can discuss an aspect of themselves without judgment or self-criticism, the more they will become at ease with themselves.

Contraindications

This exercise should be avoided when clients have a tendency toward dissociation or psychosis. Such individuals need to develop ego strength and a strong reality orientation so that they may better cope with everyday life. The therapist should have a clear sense of whether there is a tendency toward dissociation before proceeding with this exercise.

References

Jung, C. G. (1968). *Analytical psychology: Its theory and practice. The Tavistock lectures.* New York: Random House.

Jung, C. G. (1970). Mysterium coniunctionis (2nd ed.). In H. Read (Ed.), *The collected works of C. G. Jung* (R. F. C. Hull, Trans.; Vol. 14, pp. 495-496, 528-530). Princeton, NJ: Princeton University Press.

Professional Readings and Resources

Jung, C. G. (1965). *Memories, dreams, reflections.* New York: Random House.

Jung, C. G., & Chodorow, N. (Ed.). (1997). *Jung on active imagination.* Princeton, NJ: Princeton University Press.

Stein, M. (Ed.) (1984). *Jungian analysis.* Boulder, CO: Shambhala.

Bibliotherapy Sources for Clients

Hannah, B. (2001). *Encounters with the soul: Active imagination as developed by C. G. Jung.* New York: Chiron.

Johnson, R. (1986). *Inner work: Using dreams and active imagination for personal growth.* San Francisco: Harper.

HANDOUT 17.1

ACTIVE IMAGINATION EXERCISE

Having decided what figure you wish to talk to, pose the following questions. Try not to edit, rationalize, or make the answer more socially acceptable. Write down or type what comes to mind immediately.

Who are you?

Why are you so important to me?

Why do you keep showing up in my dreams?

What do you want from me?

Where do you come from?

Is there anything you need?

Have I been neglecting you?

How can we get along better?

Delaney, M. (2007). Active imagination. In L. L. Hecker, C. F. Sori, & Associates, *The therapist's notebook, volume 2: More homework, handouts, and activities for use in psychotherapy* (pp. 125-130). Binghamton, NY: The Haworth Press.

HANDOUT 17.2

ACTIVE IMAGINATION EXERCISE

In this exercise, record both the questions you want to ask and the responses that you hear. Take some time for reflection on what you have experienced.

What questions do I want to ask?
What did she/he/it say to me in response to my questions?
My reflections on this conversation:

Take some crayons or markers, and on the reverse side of this page, draw a picture of whom or what you spoke to.

Delaney, M. (2007). Active imagination. In L. L. Hecker, C. F. Sori, & Associates, *The therapist's notebook, volume 2: More homework, handouts, and activities for use in psychotherapy* (pp. 125-130). Binghamton, NY: The Haworth Press.

18

Discovering Hidden Immigrants

Elise Cole

Type of Contribution: *Activity, Handout*

Objectives

As the world becomes more global, an increasing number of children are growing up outside of their home countries. This results in an increasing population of hidden immigrants, which includes but is not limited to missionaries, military families, political ambassadors, and families working for U.S. companies abroad.

Hidden immigrants are persons who appear physically the same as people in their home country (this is most often the parents' country of origin), yet they are immigrants because they have lived in another culture the majority of their life. These persons are hidden by the color of their skin. They look the same as others in their home country, and therefore the social expectation is that they are in fact the same. Hidden immigrants are often in the process of learning the culture of their home country for the first time as teenagers or adults. The objective of this activity is to provide therapists with tools to better understand the context of the hidden immigrant. When therapists have a better understanding of clients' contexts, they are able to help them more effectively and in a culturally appropriate manner.*

Rationale for Use

Hidden immigrants face a number of struggles. People often overlook their unique experiences and do not understand their sense of feeling different because they look so much like those in the dominant culture around them. However, many hidden immigrants feel that they never fully comprehend or adapt to their new culture; they continue to remain on the outside.

Some of the common characteristics that shape the hidden immigrant experience include being raised in a cross-cultural world, being highly mobile, experiencing distinct differences in the cultures they bridge, expecting repatriation but identifying with the culture in which they grew up, and representing something greater than themselves in their communities (Pollock & Van Reken, 2001).

Hidden immigrants are raised in host cultures that are often very different from their parents' home country. As children they learn to assimilate this host culture and make it their own. Much of their energy is spent on learning cultural rules and surviving. Hidden immigrant children often grow up feeling that they belong to the host culture, yet society makes it clear to them that because they appear physically different from others in this host culture, they are not of that cul-

---

*I am quite aware of the experience of being a hidden immigrant. I am a white American who grew up in Kenya. I am presently a hidden immigrant living in America.

ture. Their family tells them that their culture is someplace else, and they will return to this home country permanently someday. However, while hidden immigrant children may believe they are familiar with their home culture because they have heard stories of their home country and visited it occasionally, often they do not truly know the culture of their home country. Often shortly after these children and young adults arrive in their parents' home country to live they are shocked with the realization that they do not fit in there either. Their home country does not feel like home, and they begin to struggle with the question of where home is. Many hidden immigrants have a difficult time settling down; they keep searching for a place that feels like home.

The jobs that take families away from their home countries are highly mobile jobs; therefore the children in these families often end up living in several different places. This means that they themselves, as well as the people in their lives, keep coming and going. Hidden immigrant children often become marginal; either they do not get involved in relationships or they try to form deep relationships with others too quickly. Often they have not been anywhere long enough for a relationship to deepen.

After living in various countries, hidden immigrants develop an expanded worldview, but this can leave them confused about their identity, values, politics, and patriotism. They often develop so many personas that they may not know who they really are (Pollock & Van Reken, 2001).

Hidden immigrants often grow up conscious of representing something greater than themselves in their communities. Their families represent their home culture to the host culture. Likewise, children of these families represent their parents' work or reasons for being there. This can be a heavy burden for children, to represent an entire country or culture they do not know, or the work their parents do. This is usually a role they hadn't expected and are ill equipped to carry out.

Instructions

Clinicians may wish to use the discussion questions in the handout to help hidden immigrants explore their experiences and challenges. These questions are door openers and not the entirety of therapy. They should help clinicians identify issues that they can explore together with the client.

This activity is designed to be an in-session task, which begins with the clinician introducing the activity as an opportunity for the client to learn more about himself or herself. Clinicians will ask the client a series of questions regarding the experience as a hidden immigrant. Before asking questions, the clinician should give the handout to the client and ask that questions be rank ordered according to the level of importance to the client's experience as a hidden immigrant.

Next, the clinician asks the client the questions on the handout. Clinicians may wish to spend more time on questions that the client appears to struggle with and on questions that the client has ranked as an important part of their hidden immigrant experience. With the permission of the client, the clinician may wish to make notes on the handout regarding the client's responses.

After reviewing the handout questions, the clinician processes the activity with the client. The clinician and the client can decide together which issues to explore in future sessions.

Brief Vignette

Sue, whose parents were American missionaries, had lived in several African countries most of her life. At the age of eighteen, her family bought her a plane ticket to go to the United States to begin college. Sue had been to the United States before with her family on short trips to visit family and friends, but Malawi was where she considered home to be. Sue had lived in the United States for a year and a half when she began therapy. She felt confused and down and was unsure why, because she finally felt that she fit into the American culture, and she enjoyed school.

After a period of joining with Sue, her therapist, Jana, thought they might gain more insight on Sue's struggles by going over the handout with questions for hidden immigrants at the end of this chapter. Jana explained the handout activity to Sue, and Sue agreed to participate. Sue ranked Questions 1, 4, and 18 as the highest in importance:

1. What was your family's pattern of moving?
4. What have been some of the benefits of growing up outside your home country? What have been some of the challenges of growing up outside your home country?
18. Do you continue to have ties with old friends or persons from your host country? Tell me about them.

Jana asked Sue the questions while she listened and took brief notes on the handout. Sue explained that she ranked Question 1 the highest because her family moved so much when she was growing up and it had been strange, almost a struggle, for her to stay in one location (her college) for the past year. Sue ranked Question 4 high also because she believed she was exposed to some wonderful privileges overseas, as well as some unique challenges. Sue ranked Question 18 high because she felt she was beginning to lose contact with some of her friends overseas, and she was sad about this.

Jana and Sue spent time processing the questions. Sue realized that she was experiencing some unresolved grief (Question 12) in relation to her home country as well as her family and friends overseas. Sue knew that she was not able to deal with stress (Question 13) in America the same way that she had overseas, but through this activity she realized that she had not yet built up a support system as helpful as the one she had previously to help her cope with stress. In addition, she used to run along the beach when she was stressed, but since coming to America Sue had not found any physical exercise to replace this activity. Last, Sue found that she had great difficulty answering Question 7, "How do you currently view your identity?" This surprised Sue; she had grown up feeling very confident in herself, but she realized that her identity was beginning to confuse her. She had adapted more to American culture in order to fit in, but Sue wondered if this was making her less African. Jointly, Sue and Jana picked out the questions and topics they would explore further in future sessions.

In short, the questions stimulated reflection and conversation that Sue needed. The therapist, through these questions, opened the door for Sue to begin considering her roots, cultures, and assumptions, and to explore what aspects of her previous life she wanted to change or keep the same. This helped her gain a sense of direction for her future.

Suggestions for Follow-Up

The clinician should check in with the client regularly. The client may exhibit nonverbal behaviors that are unlike the nonverbal behaviors with which the clinician may be familiar. It is best that clinicians not assume that they are reading the client correctly. Also, the clinician should recognize the impact of the surrounding systems on the client, and the fact that the surrounding culture may not be altogether familiar to the client.

After the client has shared his or her story, the clinician should focus on the narrative's ability to integrate disparate aspects of the client's life into a unified whole, and help the client identify areas of the narrative that may need to be adapted in this new phase of life.

As areas of strength and perseverance are identified for clients, clinicians can begin to discuss with clients how these strengths might be employed as clients integrate their experiences and learn to cope with their new culture and home.

Reference

Pollock, D., & Van Reken, R. (2001). *Third culture kids: The experience of growing up among worlds.* Boston, MA: Nicholas Brealey.

Professional Readings and Resources

Ancis, J. (2004). *Culturally responsive interventions.* New York: Brunner-Routledge.
Freedman, J., & Combs, G. (1996). *Narrative therapy: The social construction of preferred realities.* New York: Norton.
Harper, F., & McFadden, J. (2003). *Culture and counseling: New approaches.* Boston, MA: Pearson Education.

Bibliotherapy Sources for Clients

Bell, L. (1997). *Hidden immigrants: Legacies of growing up abroad.* Notre Dame, IN: Cross Cultural Publications.
Pollock, D., & Van Reken, R. (2001). *Third culture kids: The experience of growing up among worlds.* Boston, MA: Nicholas Brealey.

HANDOUT 18.1

HIDDEN IMMIGRANT HANDOUT

1. What was your family's pattern of moving?

2. How did you deal with transitions? (Has there been closure for each transition?)

3. What educational settings did you grow up in, and how often did you see your parents? (In some countries it is common for children to attend boarding schools.)

4. What have been some of the benefits of growing up outside your home country? What have been some of the challenges of growing up outside your home country?

5. What are your current relationships to people in the host countries where you lived, as well as to those in your home country?

6. What continues to be difficult for you now about living in your home country?

7. How do you currently view your identity?

8. Did your family receive any reentry services when they came back to their home country?

9. What are your typical routines?

10. What are your fears or losses?

11. What strengths do you have because of growing up in a different culture? How are you able to use these strengths today?

Cole, E. (2007). Discovering hidden immigrants. In L. L. Hecker, C. F. Sori, & Associates, *The therapist's notebook, volume 2: More homework, handouts, and activities for use in psychotherapy* (pp. 131-136). Binghamton, NY: The Haworth Press.

12. Is there unresolved grief (related to lost relationships, lost homes)?

13. How have you learned to deal with stress?

14. What have been the characteristics of relationships in your life? Do you see themes? Are there any you would like to change? Do you see any relationship between these themes and growing up in other countries?

15. What do your relationships with your family members look like now?

16. What is your involvement with relatives and your community? (Explore if the person is maintaining a marginal stance.)

17. Did you grow up with family traditions? What were they? Are they still carried out?

18. Do you continue to have ties with old friends or persons from your host country? Tell me about them.

19. What aspects of the foreign culture in which you lived did your family adopt? Which are still utilized in your family today (e.g., rituals, customs, celebrations, beliefs, etc.)?

20. How did this experience in a foreign culture enrich your individual/family life?

Cole, E. (2007). Discovering hidden immigrants. In L. L. Hecker, C. F. Sori, & Associates, *The therapist's notebook, volume 2: More homework, handouts, and activities for use in psychotherapy* (pp. 131-136). Binghamton, NY: The Haworth Press.

SECTION IV:
GROUPS

19

Creating a Special Place

Lorna L. Hecker
Catherine Ford Sori

Type of Contribution: *Activity, Handout*

Objectives

The purpose of this activity is to provide clients with a relaxation exercise followed by a guided imagery activity that allows clients to create a mental oasis from stress. The exercise can be done in groups, families, or with individuals.

Rationale for Use

Relaxation and guided imagery exercises have found widespread use in the field of psychotherapy in a group format (e.g., Sori & Biank, 2003) or for both adult and child clients in individual or couple sessions (e.g., Piercy & Tubbs, 1996; Sori, Piercy, & Tubbs, 1998). Since anxious children often have anxious parents, relaxation and visualization exercises can be taught to children and adult clients in family sessions as well, and then continued in the home (Sori & Biank, 2003).

Relaxation and visualization exercises have been used to treat a variety of presenting problems, including anxiety disorders (e.g., Campbell, 2001), post-traumatic stress disorder (e.g., Bevin, 1991), childhood depression or fear (Deutschle, Tosi, & Wise, 1987; Kendall, 1993), trauma or abuse (e.g., Maher, 2006), sleep problems (e.g., McManamy & Katz, 1989), and physical illnesses (e.g., Naparstek, 1994), and to promote spiritual growth and healing (e.g., Maher, 2006; Tuskenis & Sori, 2006). Some have trained parents to use imagery and relaxation with their children prior to surgery or hospitalization (Peterson & Shigetomi, 1981). It is important to note that studies have found guided imagery to be associated with increased health, reduced stress, better coping ability, response to treatment, and even longevity in some cancer patients (Fawzy, Fawzy, Hyun, & Elashoff, 1993; Naparstek, 1994; Shrock, Palmer, & Taylor, 1999; Spiegel, Bloom, Kraemer, & Gottheil, 1989).

Helping clients to relax by focusing on alternately tensing and then releasing various muscle groups is important to reduce physical stress and is an essential prelude for clients to enter a state of relaxation or altered consciousness, where they then can "flow" through a guided imagery activity (see Naparstek, 1994). The deep breathing that is incorporated in this activity increases the flow of oxygen to the bloodstream, promoting a sense of relaxation and well-being. Naparstek points out that when a sensory image of an original event (such as a positive memory) is evoked, "the mood, emotions, physiological state, and blood chemistry associated with the original event reverberate in the body" (p. 18).

The Therapist's Notebook, Volume 2
doi:10.1300/5550_19

Guided imagery exercises help clients tap their inner resources, promote self-discovery, and often allow new and unique perspectives to emerge (Sori et al., 1998). According to Naparstek (1994), when clients reach the powerful altered state of consciousness that often occurs, they "are capable of more rapid and intense healing, growth, learning, and change" (pp. 22-23).

When doing an imagery exercise, it is important not to focus just on the visual image but to help clients elicit perceptions from all the senses (Naparstek, 1994; Sori & Biank, 2003; Tuskenis & Sori, 2006). Tuskenis and Sori point out that imagery is enhanced when many of the clients' senses are used, as it enhances the experience and makes it feel more real. This is also important because people often have a primary preferred sensory modality from which they experience the world. Some may relate better to visual images, others to auditory images, while others may best relate through tactile or kinesthetic experiences.

This activity may be used with a variety of clients who present with numerous complaints. It can be used at the beginning of a session to help relax and ground clients. Conversely, we have found it to be especially helpful to clients at the end of a session to help center them.

Instructions

The therapist may read the handout to a group or individual client. It is best to set the mood by lowering the lighting and having comfortable seating, or allowing clients to recline in comfort. Sometimes soft background music is helpful to induce relaxation.

Clinicians should try to use a soft, evocative, lower-pitched voice, and to speak slowly, allowing for the pauses that are indicated in the handout. It is often helpful to practice and then record one's own voice, and then to try out the exercise oneself using the recording, before utilizing this activity with clients.

Suggestions for Follow-Up

Many clients like to practice relaxation and visualization at home, and it can be a key component in treating anxiety and sleep disorders. One way to facilitate this is for clinicians to record themselves reading this activity. In this way, the therapist's voice goes with the client in the manner of a transitional object, which can help to promote change between sessions.

Some clients may benefit from doing a sand tray following this activity, in which they build their special place in the sand. Sand is a sensory modality, and this can deepen the discussion of what the special place was like, who or what objects were there, and what feelings (e.g., of safety, peace, or joy) were evoked. Therapists can then take a picture of the special place to give to the client.

Other clients, especially children or adolescents, may enjoy drawing their special place, or doing a free drawing just using colors to express the feelings evoked. These art products may deepen the experience, and they may be useful to induce a relaxed state for clients who practice this activity at home.

Contraindications

Clients who dissociate may not be good candidates for this activity, depending upon their ability to tolerate focusing on their body in the present moment.

References

Bevin, T. (1991). Multiple traumas of refugees—Near drowning and witnessing of maternal rape. In N. B. Webb (Ed.), *Play therapy with children in crisis* (pp. 92-110). New York: Guilford.

Campbell, G. (2001). The anxious client reconsidered. *Psychotherapy Networker, 25*(3), 40-45.

Deutschle, J. Jr., Tosi, D., & Wise, P. (1987). *The use of hypnosis and metaphor within a cognitive experiential framework: Theory, research, and case applications with impulse control disorders.* Paper presented at a meeting of the American Society for Clinical Hypnosis, Las Vegas, NV.

Fawzy, F. I., Fawzy, N. W., Hyun, C. S., & Elashoff, R. (1993). Effects of an early structured psychiatric intervention, coping, and affective state on recurrence and survival 6 years later. *Archives of General Psychiatry, 50,* 681-689.

Kendall, P. (1993). Cognitive-behavior therapies with youth: Guiding theory, current status, and emerging developments. *Journal of Consulting and Clinical Psychology, 61,* 235-247.

Maher, A. B. (2006). Impact of abuse on internalized God-images: Spiritual assessment and treatment using guided imagery. In K. B. Helmeke & C. F. Sori (Eds.), *The therapist's notebook for integrating spirituality in counseling I: Homework, handouts, and activities for use in psychotherapy* (pp. 87-112). Binghamton, NY: The Haworth Press.

McManamy, C., & Katz, R. C. (1989). Brief parent-assisted treatment for children's nighttime fears. *Journal of Development and Behavior Pediatrics, 10,* 145-148.

Naparstek, B. (1994). *Staying well with guided imagery.* New York: Warner Books.

Peterson, L., & Shigetomi, C. (1981). The use of coping techniques in minimizing anxiety in hospitalized children. *Behavior Therapy, 12,* 1-14.

Piercy, F., & Tubbs, C. (1996). Tapping internal resources: Guided imagery in couple therapy. *Journal of Systemic Therapies, 15,* 53-64.

Shrock, D., Palmer, R. F., & Taylor, B. (1999). Effects of a psychosocial intervention on survival among patients with stage I breast and prostate cancer: A matched case-control study. *Alternative Therapies, 5*(3), 49-55.

Sori, C. F., & Biank, N. (2003). Soaring above stress: Using relaxation and visualization with anxious children. In C. F. Sori, L. L. Hecker, & Associates, *The therapist's notebook for children and adolescents: Homework, handouts, and activities for use in psychotherapy* (pp. 25-359). Binghamton, NY: The Haworth Press.

Sori, C. F., Piercy, F. P., & Tubbs, C. (1998). A picture of health: Using guided imagery to facilitate differentiation. In T. S. Nelson & T. S. Trepper (Eds.), *101 more interventions in family therapy* (pp. 360-367). Binghamton, NY: The Haworth Press.

Spiegel, D., Bloom, J., Kraemer, H. C., & Gottheil, E. (1989). Effect of psychosocial treatment on survival of patients with metastatic breast cancer. *Lancet, 2,* 888-891.

Tuskenis, A., & Sori, C. F. (2006). Enhancing reliance on God as a supportive attachment figure. In K. B. Helmeke & C. F. Sori (Eds.), *The therapist's notebook for integrating spirituality in counseling II: Homework, handouts, and activities for use in psychotherapy* (pp. 47-61). Binghamton, NY: The Haworth Press.

Professional Readings and Resources

Naparstek, B. (1994). *Staying well with guided imagery.* New York: Warner Books.

Piercy, F., & Tubbs, C. (1996). Tapping internal resources: Guided imagery in couple therapy. *Journal of Systemic Therapies, 15,* 53-64.

Sori, C. F., Piercy, F. P., & Tubbs, C. (1998). A picture of health: Using guided imagery to facilitate differentiation. In T. S. Nelson & T. S. Trepper (Eds.), *101 more interventions in family therapy* (pp. 360-367). Binghamton, NY: The Haworth Press.

Sori, C. F., & Biank, N. (2003). Soaring above stress: Using relaxation and visualization with anxious children. In C. F. Sori, L. L. Hecker, & Associates, *The therapist's notebook for children and adolescents: Homework, handouts, and activities for use in psychotherapy* (pp. 25-359). Binghamton, NY: The Haworth Press.

Bibliotherapy Source for Clients

Naparstek, B. (1994). *Staying well with guided imagery.* New York: Warner Books.

HANDOUT 19.1

GUIDED IMAGERY

Instructions: Read the following to client in a very slow-paced, soothing voice. Pause for several seconds whenever "..." appears in the script, and for longer periods between paragraphs.

Today you are going to go to a special place. . . . It is a place that you will be able to go to anytime you desire. . . . You can take a break anytime you want from stresses or strains in your life. . . . You will create the place, and it will always be your special place to go.

Settle into comfort. Relax all your muscles. Get comfortable where you are.

Now, you're going to tighten all the muscles in your face. Scrunch your face, and really scrunch!

And relax.

Tighten the muscles in your mouth and neck. Tighten, tighten!

And relax.

Now make tight fists with your hands. Tighten, tighten!

And relax.

Now pull your arms into your body, and tighten your arms and torso. Pull all the muscles in so your shoulders push against your torso and neck. Tighten, tighten!

Hecker, L. L., & Sori, C. F. (2007). Creating a special place. In L. L. Hecker, C. F. Sori, & Associates, *The therapist's notebook, volume 2: More homework, handouts, and activities for use in psychotherapy* (pp. 139-145). Binghamton, NY: The Haworth Press.

And relax.

Next pull your thighs in together so you can feel your hips tighten, and you feel your buttocks tighten as well. Tighten, tighten!

And relax.

Next tighten your lower legs and push your ankles and feet together. Tighten, tighten!

And relax.

Next flex your feet into an L shape with your toes pointing toward the sky. . . . Push your feet into the ground. Push, push, push!

And relax.

Fully relax your body.

Now we are going to go on a journey in your imagination. I want you to imagine your favorite place in the world. It can be an imaginary place, or a real place that you find wonderful. . . . Relax into the image. . . . Look around your image, and take in the sights. . . . Look all around and see the special beauty in the place you have chosen. . . . What do you see?. . . Notice all the colors you see . . . and the textures. . . . Just take time to take it all in . . .

Next become aware of the smells in your special place. . . . Take in a deep breath, and slowly notice what scents you detect. . . . Take time to notice all the smells in this, your special place. . . . Breathe deeply and relax into your special place.

Hecker, L. L., & Sori, C. F. (2007). Creating a special place. In L. L. Hecker, C. F. Sori, & Associates, *The therapist's notebook, volume 2: More homework, handouts, and activities for use in psychotherapy* (pp. 139-145). Binghamton, NY: The Haworth Press.

Next, listen to the sounds of your special place. Are there birds chirping? Is there any music? Do you hear surf? Do you hear any animals making sounds? Listen closely. What do you hear? Take time to notice the sounds. . . . Enjoy the sounds here, and . . . relax.

Now as you settle into the beauty of your special place, look around again. Touch something in your special place that gives you a lovely feeling. Touch it with your hands, and notice how it feels to you. . . . Is it cool or warm? . . . Does it feel as you expected it would? Is it soft, . . . hard, . . . textured, . . . or smooth? Does it have a scent? Take some time to enjoy the feeling of what you touched.

Now settle into your special place and enjoy the sights, the smell, and the sounds of your special place. . . . Relax deeply as you sense everything in your special place. . . .

Allow yourself to sink into your special place and just enjoy the sights, the smells, the sounds, and the sensations. . . . Breathe.

You have created a very special place. This place is yours, and yours alone. No one can come into the special place, unless you invite them. . . . You can go to your special place any time you want to. . . . You just close your eyes and imagine it. . . . It is relaxing and beautiful here. It is yours. . . . You can allow your body just to be here, with no worries, . . . no stresses, . . . just the pleasant feelings that come to you from this place you have created. It is a lovely place. It is a pure place; it is your special heaven on earth. . . . You enjoy this place so much. You feel at peace here. You feel joy in being in this place.

Again, allow yourself to relax in your special place and take in everything about it.

Now it is time to leave your special place, to leave it and come back to the present moment. . . . Knowing you can always come back here, you can leave your special place in peace.

When you are ready, you may open your eyes.

Hecker, L. L., & Sori, C. F. (2007). Creating a special place. In L. L. Hecker, C. F. Sori, & Associates, *The therapist's notebook, volume 2: More homework, handouts, and activities for use in psychotherapy* (pp. 139-145). Binghamton, NY: The Haworth Press.

20

Say It with Flowers: An Innovative Group Therapy Activity for Adults and Children

Jolene Oppawsky

Type of Contribution: *Activity*

Objectives

The objectives of this activity are to aid in the expression of feelings within a group, create a positive atmosphere for therapeutic exploration, and increase group solidarity and interaction. In addition, this activity will foster personal and spiritual introspection by having the clients identify with the characteristics of flowers.

Rationale for Use

Flowers are vehicles to express feelings, both positive and negative, due to the universality of their characteristics and the acceptance of their beauty and scent characteristics by most people, regardless of social or cultural differences. Flowers are universally accepted as something known, nice, and pleasurable, which evokes a sense of safety in a group. These feelings of familiarity, pleasure, and safety promote a safe group environment for therapeutic work.

According to Relf (2001), "as a result of repeated successes of practitioners, horticulture is being widely accepted as an effective therapeutic tool" (p. 1). Most counseling, homeopathic, and occupational therapies use flower essences and plants as therapeutic tools. For example, at a nursing home, Pratt (2002) used cut flowers, having patients "touching, arranging, and playing with sizes and colors of the beautiful blossoms" (p. 1). Yet fresh flowers are underused in psychotherapy, despite their appropriateness for use in group therapies with children and adults with an array of psychological problems. They have universal characteristics and the ability to evoke olfactory and visual memories.

Flowers are nonthreatening and nondiscriminatory tools; therefore, they make excellent mediums to promote personal and spiritual introspection in clients by helping them discover positive and negative characteristics in themselves as they identify with the characteristics of particular flowers, such as deep roots, delicate petals, or rough or thorny stems. This uncovering and exploring of self helps clients recognize their inner beauty and specific positive traits, as well as their negative characteristics. Furthermore, the descriptions of flowers and the identification with a flower's characteristics can help clients reveal threats or unconscious material that are causing them distress.

Fresh flowers stimulate olfactory and visual memory. Olfactory memory is a strong source of memory and is underutilized in psychological counseling and psychotherapy. The limbic system, particularly the hypothalamus, plays a role in emotional conditions such as stress and de-

doi:10.1300/5550_20

pression. This means that flower odors trigger limbic responses, which can affect clients' physical, mental, and emotional well-being (Pines, 1997). Smith (2004) stated, "Recognition of the odor occurs in the limbic system when the signal is interpreted through a comparison to past experiences with the odor and relation of the smell to the emitting substance" (para. 4).

This recognition can be used in group counseling to evoke life events and life reviews. In life reviews, clients look back over their lives, visualize ups and downs, and recognize successes as well as failures. A life events approach focuses on how a life incident influences a person's life. How the client adapts to a life event is important. One client might react with stress or depression while another sees a life event as a new challenge or a chance for growth.

Stimulating the olfactory senses by using flowers in a group activity can open not only positive themes that promote psychological growth, but difficult and stressful themes as well, such as death and dying. Olfactory memory has a universality about it that can enhance group work. For example, the scents of flowers evoke universal memories of gardens, homes, churches, or funeral parlors, among others. Commonalities of memories can enhance group cohesiveness.

Flowers, as therapeutic tools, with their visual characteristics and practicality, can promote verbal talk and group interaction. Clients are discouraged from hiding, masking, or numbing their feelings. Moreover, they help clients overcome a fear of expressing their feelings because they are talking through the metaphor of a flower.

Flowers are more suitable to group work than for individual therapy because flowers are colorful, aromatic, and beautiful, and these characteristics often enhance clients' receptiveness to responses from other people. Therefore, using flowers in a group promotes an atmosphere where group participants can relate to one another easily. This positive atmosphere stimulates clients to exhibit empathy toward group peers and helps clients share feelings. Flowers cross social and cultural lines, which diminish age, sex, racial, and minority group barriers or tensions within the group and lead to positive interactions among group members.

This activity can be adapted for use in many ways. Some significant horticulture studies, while not using fresh flowers, have already been done on gerontology clients (Beckwith & Gilster, 1996), clients with drug and alcohol problems (Benson, 1996), children and adolescents (Bunn, 1986; Doutt, Airhart, & Willis, 1989), and service providers suffering from burnout (Smith, 1986). Flowers promote social behaviors, making them appropriate for educational groups such as groups working on developing social skills.

Instructions

A variety of real, colorful flowers of different sizes is needed. The amount needed depends on the group size. Donations from private gardens, nurseries, and flower shops reduce costs.

The group opens by having the clients select their flowers. Then the clients take turns discussing why they chose a particular flower and how their flower represents them or their personality. Identification with the flowers' characteristics helps clients share personal information and helps them to discover or elaborate on their positive and negative characteristics. For example, "The rose is yellow and mellow, as I am most of the time; however, the thorns can prick and draw blood."

It is important to expose the feelings that might be elicited by the presence of the flowers. For example, flowers may help stimulate a positive atmosphere in which clients can reveal threatening subjects or unconscious material.

The clients are then encouraged to let their flowers stimulate olfactory and visual memories, which have a universality about them, such as the smells and look associated with Grandma's garden, weddings, home, or funerals. These often vivid olfactory and visual memories are then used as life reviews or event reviews.

An important and innovative group task is to ask the clients to identify times when they felt similar to and different from the other flowers in the room (V. Hansen, personal communication, March 16, 2003). These tasks help the clients differentiate their personality characteristics and help them discover just how multifaceted they are, as well as helping them better identify their feelings. By identifying how they feel alike, these vehicles help clients exhibit empathy toward their group peers by feeling connected to them. Asking clients how they see themselves differently promotes differentiation of self, helps clients identify boundaries, and helps them understand and accept differences.

The group closes with each client giving an affirmation connected to the flower they chose, ending the group on a positive note.

After-session homework is important to extend the positive results of group work. The clients are asked to take their flower home and journal on any changes they observe in the flower, such as the bloom getting bigger, wilting, fading, or dying, or a small bud opening (V. Hansen, personal communication, March 16, 2003). Clients are also asked to document how these changes reflect any changes in their lives. In the following session, these elements are shared and discussed in group. These elements are especially poignant and helpful when dealing with life span development issues, grief, grief work, death, and dying.

This group activity can be used for different populations in much the same format or by adapting the activity to fit any special needs of a new population. It has a wide multiplication factor for expanded use in other helping fields such as hospital or medical groups on wellness, gerontology programs, school programs on self-esteem, educational groups, focus groups or special topic groups, crisis intervention groups, cultural diversity groups, groups for the developmentally disabled, church groups on self-enhancement and spiritual development, and partnership seminars.

Suggestions for Follow-Up

In the subsequent group session, each member is given an opportunity to express how the flower activity affected them. The members should be encouraged to tell the group how they plan to incorporate the personal and spiritual introspection won in the flower activity into their daily life.

Contraindications

Clients should be screened to rule out allergies to flowers. In addition, some clients may not like flowers or may have strong negative memories associated with flowers that might preclude them from benefiting from this activity. Fresh flowers can be costly at certain times of the year; therefore, donations may need to be solicited. At other times of the year, wildflowers may be used.

References

Beckwith, M. E., & Gilster, S. D. (1996). The paradise garden: A model for designing for those with dementia and Alzheimer's disease. *Journal of Therapeutic Horticulture, 8,* 45-52.

Benson, R. (1996). What's a nice guy like me doing in a place like this? A landscape architect and recovering alcoholic's thoughts on designing therapeutic landscapes. *Journal of Therapeutic Horticulture, 8,* 88-91.

Bunn, D. E. (1986). Group cohesiveness is enhanced as children engage in plant stimulated discovery activities. *Journal of Therapeutic Horticulture, 1,* 37-43.

Doutt, K. M., Airhart, D. I., & Willis T. W. (1989). Horticulture therapy activities for exceptional children. *Journal of Therapeutic Horticulture, 4*(1), 10-14.

Pines, M. (1997). *Seeing, hearing and smelling the world—New findings help scientists make sense of our senses.* Retrieved February 6, 2004, from http://www.hhmi.org/senses

Pratt, W. (2002, July 8). Flowers as therapy at GCNH. *LeRoy Penny Saver and News.* Retrieved January 31, 2004, from www.lerogny.com/news/2002/0708/front_page/008.html.

Relf, D. (2001). *Dynamics of horticulture therapy.* Retrieved October 12, 2003, from http://www.hortvt.edu/ht5a.html.

Smith, A. (2004). *The olfactory process and its effect on human behavior.* Retrieved February 8, 2004, from http:/serendip.brynmawr.edu/bb/neuro/neuro99/web2/Smith.html.

Smith, R. (1986). Understanding and overcoming burnout. *Journal of Therapeutic Horticulture, 1,* 15-24.

Professional Readings and Resources

Simson, S. P., & Straus, M. C. (1998). *Horticulture as therapy: Principles and practice.* Binghamton, NY: The Haworth Press.

Wells, S. E. (1997). *Horticultural therapy and the older adult population.* Binghamton, NY: The Haworth Press.

Bibliotherapy Source for Clients

Richey, R. (2002). *Take time to smell the roses book of poetry.* Bloomington, IN: Authorhouse.

21

Taking Out the Trash

René A. Jones

Type of Contribution: *Activity*

This is an activity for group therapy for adolescents or adults to improve body image and self-esteem.

Objectives

To assist clients in ridding themselves of negative and destructive self-thoughts and to empower clients to control the negative thoughts that they have about themselves.

Rationale for Use

Most people can easily list negative aspects of themselves but have difficulty stating the positive. This is due in part to negative messages from the media, family, and friends, and social expectations. Another component is that acknowledging our strengths may be considered bragging, a social faux pas. It has become fashionable to point out the flaws and spend time, energy, and money to correct them. The attempts to achieve unrealistic body images affect self-esteem, sexual functioning, and general happiness.

White middle-class American women are most likely to try to achieve the "perfect body" (Kelly, 1996) and there are very few positive messages for women related to the body and even fewer related to other aspects of the person, like careers. Therefore, many believe that they are not okay the way they are (Kelly, 1996). These negative self-images for women trickle down to girls as well, who are dieting at younger ages.

Though there is a sizable gap between the percentage of women and men who diet, 80 percent and 25 percent respectively, the number is increasing for men (Kelly, 1996). Men receive the message that they need to be muscular to find a partner and be happy. In addition, males and females promote this image to each other. This creates unrealistic expectations and places a person's value at the physical level.

Negative body image and low self-esteem can impact a relationship, especially in the sexual arena. Many believe that in order to enjoy sex they need to be beautiful and thin, and so they may deny themselves the pleasures of love and intimacy (Hutchinson, 1985). It is nearly impossible to surrender to sexual abandon while worrying if one's stomach is protruding.

This activity is designed to assist people in feeling better about themselves. It promotes the positive aspects of individuals while aiding in ridding them of the negative. This activity provides a venue for the participants to normalize feeling good about themselves and to process negative feelings.

doi:10.1300/5550_21

Instructions

The following materials will be needed for this activity:

- Index cards in bright colors (one for each person, but not everyone has to have the same color)
- Bright colored paper (all the same color and one for each person)
- Pens of the same color (one for each person)
- Clean garbage can or bag

Prior to doing this activity there should be a sense of trust and community within the group. The participants should sit in a circle so they can see one another in order to promote discussion and a sense of unity (Hedgepeth & Helmich, 1996). The circle also increases discussions and use of the group as a legitimate source of ideas and information (Hedgepeth & Helmich, 1996).

The entire activity has three parts: Positive Thoughts, Taking Out the Garbage, and Taking Control.

Positive Thoughts

The first part acknowledges the positive points of each person. The facilitator should pass out the index cards and tell the group that they should take their favorite color. Then hand out the pens. When each person has both handouts, the therapist should explain that they are to write on the cards at least three things about themselves that they are proud of (proud cards). What they write needs to be about themselves, not about their kids, husband, wife, or dog. What about themselves are they proud of?

When everyone is done writing, each one around the circle should read what is on the card. When everyone is done, the group should applaud themselves. This is a possible scenario:

THERAPIST: How do you feel after doing this?

GROUP: Good. Proud. I didn't realize I had this much to be proud of. I felt uncomfortable talking about what I do well.

T: Why do you think it may be difficult or uncomfortable to talk about what we do well?

G: Because people might think we are bragging. Because it is something that we do not normally do. Usually we talk about what is wrong with us: "I am too fat. I don't like my teeth."

T: What is the difference between bragging and acknowledging what you do well?

G: Bragging is talking about oneself without listening to other people. "It is all about me." Acknowledging is recognizing what one has accomplished. It does not have to be told to other people and when it is told the intent is to share the success, not steal the spotlight.

T: Very good. However, the two have gotten very confused and so we often do not acknowledge our good points and instead focus on the parts of ourselves that we do not like, such as "I am too fat, or I wish I didn't laugh so loud." I call these thoughts garbage thoughts. What is garbage?

G: Waste, material that we no longer need.

T: What do you do with garbage that you have at home?

G: Throw it out.

T: What would happen if you did not throw it out?

G: It would build up, make it difficult to move around the house. It would smell.

T: Just as there is physical garbage, there is also mental garbage. These are messages or thoughts that are of no use and that are negative. Can someone give me an example of some mental garbage?

G: You need to be a size five to be happy. Blondes have more fun. You have to look good to have someone love you.

T: Where do you get these messages?

G: TV, magazines, friends, family.

T: How much mental garbage do you accumulate in a day?

G: A lot!

T: How much acknowledgment do you gather in a day?

G: Very little.

T: So if you have all this garbage building up and taking up all the space, what happens to the acknowledgments?

G: They get buried in the garbage.

T: So you are getting all this mental garbage and it is starting to build up and starting to smell. What would it be like to live inside your mind?

G: Unpleasant and uncomfortable.

T: So what do we need to do with the mental garbage?

G: Take it out.

T: Exactly, and that is what we are going to do now.

This leads into the next segment.

Taking Out the Garbage

This is an anonymous activity. Therefore it is important that everyone have the same color paper. The therapist hands out a piece of paper to each participant and checks that everyone still has the same pen handed out earlier.

T: I would like you to put away your cards. We will use them later, but keep your pens out. I want you to think of all the self "garbage" you store in your head and then I want you to write it down on the paper. Some of you may not have any garbage and if that is true then you should write "the garbage was taken out."

While the participants are writing the therapist should get the garbage can. Once everyone has stopped writing, the therapist says with conviction,

T: Now I want you to take that garbage and crumple it up and throw it into the garbage can.

If a participant throws it lightly into the can, give it back and have the participant throw it out emphatically. This is somewhat of a symbolic activity. Members are ridding themselves of their garbage and negativity and the items that are preventing them from accepting their bodies and selves. It should feel good to crumple up the negativity and throw it away.

Once all the papers are in the can, the therapist passes out the papers randomly to the participants. Remind the participants that if they receive their own paper that they should not say anything. The participants uncrumple the papers and read them. After they are done, here are some process questions:

T: Any comments about this activity?

G: I couldn't believe how much garbage I had. It was sad to hear that other people think that way about themselves because I don't see anyone that way. It was good to hear I was not alone. It felt good to crumple it up.

T: What did it feel like writing down all that garbage?

G: Sad. It felt good to get it out.

T: What was it like hearing all that garbage?

G: Like I said, it was sad to hear that other people think that way about themselves because I don't see anyone that way. It was good to hear I was not alone in my feelings.

T: Where do these thoughts come from?

G: Other people like family, friends, boyfriends or girlfriends, media.

T: Are they all true?

G: No, but when it is told over and over it becomes easy to believe.

T: So what does this tell you about the power of words?

G: They are very powerful.

T: So if others' words were such a powerful influence on you, what kind of power do your words have over others?

G: A lot.

T: You have the ability to empower or disempower others with your words. In the same way, you have the ability to empower or disempower yourself by deciding whether or not to believe what others are saying. By deciding whether or not to keep the garbage or throw it out. So if you have the power not to keep the garbage, why do you still keep it?

G: I don't even realize that I am keeping it. All my friends complain about themselves so it feels normal.

T: You're right. We are taught that we (especially women) should be talking about what we need to improve upon rather than what we already have right. What do we do when someone gives a compliment?

G: Usually we don't accept it.

T: Right. So instead of keeping all this garbage, what would you like to keep instead?

G: Acknowledgments, positive thoughts, empowering thoughts.

T: What would you like to do with all that garbage?

G: Throw it out!

T: All right! I want you to crumple the papers back up and throw them out like you mean it.

The therapist goes around the circle with the garbage can and the participants throw the paper in again. This exercise normalizes that almost everyone carries negative thoughts about themselves and this unifies the group and creates a bond between them. This activity provides the opportunity to let the participants know that they have control over whether or not they accept these messages and carry them around. It provides another alternative way to think about themselves and about the power that they give to the messages that surround them.

Taking Control

In this section, the therapist empowers the clients so they realize the control they have regarding their own self-image and body image.

T: If these messages are so detrimental to each of us, why are the magazines still out there?

G: The answer is that we buy them.

T: So what are we telling the industry when we buy these magazines?

G: That we believe these messages.

T: Who decides whether or not you believe and accept these messages?

G: I do.

T: Who decides how much garbage you keep in your head?

G: I do.

T: That's right. You decide what you believe about yourself. Now that you have thrown out your garbage, you need to fill that space with some acknowledgments, positive thoughts, and so on.

Suggestions for Follow-Up

This activity examines the negativity that each person carries inside. This activity provides a venue to discuss the negativity and deconstruct it so that it no longer has as much power or control over people. Since they just eliminated the negative, empty space now needs to be filled with something positive or mental treasures. The group should write these mental treasures on the other side of the proud card.

Everyone can write down something they are going to do for themselves before the next meeting and read this to the group. This reinforces the positive and commits the participants to own what is positive about them.

Each person can write a want ad about himself or herself. For example: a smart young woman who loves to laugh and play sports. The purpose of the ad is not to seek someone else but to highlight and enforce the qualities that the person currently possesses. If the client is unable to do it, then the members of the group are each to write a want ad for that person. After each person writes the ad, he or she gives it to the client who was unable to write an ad.

Contraindications

This activity would not be productive for a group that lacks trust. It should not be used early in a group's formation.

References

Hedgepeth, E., & Helmich, J. (1996). *Teaching about sexuality and HIV.* New York: New York University Press.

Hutchinson, M. G. (1985). *Transforming body image.* Freedom, CA: The Crossing Press.

Kelly, M. (1996). *My body my rules: The body esteem, sexual esteem connection.* Ithaca, NY: Planned Parenthood.

Professional Readings and Resources

Hutchinson, M. G. (1985). *Transforming body image.* Freedom, CA: The Crossing Press.

Kelly, M. (1996). *My body my rules: The body esteem, sexual esteem connection.* Ithaca, NY: Planned Parenthood.

Northrup, C. (1991). *Women's bodies, women's wisdom.* New York: Bantam Books.

Pipher, M. (1995). *Reviving Ophelia: Saving the selves of adolescent girls.* New York: Ballantine Books.

Bibliotherapy Sources for Clients

Covey, S. (1990). *The 7 habits of highly effective people.* New York: Fireside.
Northrup, C. (1991). *Women's bodies, women's wisdom.* New York: Bantam Books.
Pipher, M. (1995). *Reviving Ophelia: Saving the selves of adolescent girls.* New York: Ballantine Books.

SECTION V:
TRAUMA AND ABUSE RECOVERY

22

Exploring Relationships: An Eco-Map Activity for Adult Survivors of Incest

Abigail T. Christiansen
Andrea K. Wittenborn
Günnur Karakurt
Syidah Abdullah
Chunhong Zhang

Type of Contribution: *Activity, Handouts*

Objectives

The objective of this activity is to help adult incest survivors explore their current relationship network. Within this network, participants identify which relationships are supportive and provide comfort during difficult times. They also identify the relationships in their network that are not supportive. Participants work to identify their own needs in each relationship and enhance their awareness of their own relationship skills. This activity can be used in either individual therapy sessions or group therapy format.

Rationale for Use

When incest occurs there is a betrayal of trust by the perpetrator, who is often someone the survivor relied on for the satisfaction of basic needs (e.g., a parent or primary caregiver; Kirschner, Kirschner, & Rappaport, 1993). It often causes problematic attachment relationships when children need to depend on someone for survival who is also the cause of pain and hurt (Loewenstein, 2004). To resolve this discrepancy, children may need to hold onto the belief that their parents are good and it is they themselves who are bad (Loewenstein, 2004). This can have a profound and lasting impact on one's self-image.

As adults, women who have survived childhood sexual abuse are often more introverted and less open to new experiences (Talbot, Duberstein, King, Cox, & Giles, 2000). Alexander (1993) found that survivors lacked secure attachment styles as adults. When someone has a secure attachment style, they are comfortable trusting and interacting with others. Clearly, incest affects a survivor's capacity to trust and to comfortably interact with others. Cole and Putnam (1992) found that incest had negative effects on social functioning and in particular on one's sense of security and trust in relationships.

For many, the experience of childhood sexual abuse qualifies as trauma (Courtois, 2000). Trauma survivors are most likely to experience distress in their closest relationships (Johnson, 2002). Childhood abuse contaminates relationships with "the terror of past trauma" (Johnson,

doi:10.1300/5550_22

2002, p. 14). However, it is those who are able to turn to others for support that deal well with their past trauma (Johnson, 2002).

By identifying supportive relationships, survivors may feel greater connection to significant others, foster a sense of trust, improve their self-concepts, and have an increased acknowledgement of their own needs. Survivors can use this information to further develop their support network and strengthen relationships. Conversely, identifying tenuous and stressful relationships provides information that one can use to protect oneself from potentially harmful interactions and make decisions about continuing or improving these difficult relationships. It is also helpful to determine which relationships are most supportive during specific life experiences (e.g., happy times, sad times, distressing times, etc.). For example, discussing the stress and joys of raising children with other parents can normalize one's own experiences and be a positive source of social support.

This activity helps incest survivors explore their current relationships in two ways. First, an eco-map is used to visually display relationship networks (Hartman, 1978). Using an eco-map helps participants to get a clear understanding of the structure and extent of their relationship network. The eco-map (Hartman, 1978) in this activity has been adapted for use from that used in the Kinship Care Practice Project (n.d.) for use with incest survivors. It is limited to the survivor's personal relationships and does not include the larger social systems such as church, work, health care, or government agencies that are often included in eco-maps (Hartman, 1978; Kinship Care Practice Project, n.d.). However, this eco-map could easily be adapted to include these larger systems if the therapist so desires.

The second way that survivors explore relationships in this activity is by answering questions about their relationship network. Survivors are asked about whom they can turn to and whom they avoid when experiencing certain emotions. They are also asked to specifically identify ways others can support them when they are experiencing these emotions.

Instructions

Individual clients or group members can be approached with the following introduction:

> The relationships we have in life can be safe havens when things go awry. However, our relationships can also feel unsupportive or stressful at times. It is helpful to assess your relationships and determine who is most helpful during specific experiences in our lives. Realistically assessing your relationships with others can help you during both negative and positive encounters in life. For example, it might be helpful to know whom you can count on for support if you were to lose a job or if someone close to you passed away. It also might be important to know who will support you during positive life events, such as getting a promotion.
>
> Using Handout 22.1, place yourself in the circle labeled You. Then draw a circle for each person you come in contact with on a fairly regular basis within the larger circle labeled Your World, and put that person's name in the circle. Once you are done, indicate the nature of the relationship between you and each person by using the following lines: ——— ——————— for a close relationship, ------- for a tenuous relationship, -/-/-/-/-/-/-/-/- for a stressful relationship, or you can make up different types of lines to better describe your relationships. Once you've completed the diagram, take a minute to think about your different relationships with the following list of questions in mind (see Handout 22.2 for the list of questions).

Individuals should complete this activity on their own. This can be done at the beginning of the meeting or completed outside of the meeting time. Then the activity can be discussed in session. If this activity is used in the context of a support group, it should be made clear that if clients feel uncomfortable they are not obligated to self-disclose. The questions in Handout 22.2 can be used to facilitate discussion. Additional questions that could be used to facilitate a discussion:

- How did it feel to complete this activity?
- Were you surprised by any of the relationships you listed?
- Are there more or fewer relationships listed than you expected? Why do you think that is?
- Which relationships feel supportive? Why?
- Which relationships feel unsupportive? Why?
- What ways do you support the people in your diagram?
- Is there anything you would like to change about this diagram? If so, what?
- If there is something that you want to change about your diagram, what is one step you could take to work toward that change?

Brief Vignette

This activity was used with a support group for adult female survivors of childhood incest. At the time of the activity, the support group had eight members, each of whom had participated in the group for at least six years and had worked on recovery for much longer. The length of group membership was partly due to the fact that this was a community support group, not a therapy group in the strict sense. All group members were living functional lives. Group members mainly used this group for community, support, and continued growth. Each group member was either engaged in individual psychotherapy or had completed individual psychotherapy at the time of the activity. Given the length of time the group members had worked together, they were very familiar with one another. There was a strong sense of support and safety both during and outside group sessions. The group meetings were held twice per month in a semistructured format that alternated between sharing sessions and activity sessions.

Group members had mixed reactions when the activity was introduced. Some group members showed enthusiasm and interest while others were concerned about their ability to do the activity since they were unmarried or did not perceive themselves as having significant relationships. Group members then took the activity home and worked on it individually over a period of weeks. During the next activity session, group members had positive responses to the activity. They reported that the eco-map helped them think about all of the different relationships they had, not just with significant others. Handout 22.2 helped group members identify whom they could share feelings with, and whom they avoided at times. The women reported feeling both encouraged by the supportive relationships they did have and saddened by their unsupportive relationships.

During the activity session, the group members took turns sharing their experiences with the activity. Some group members discussed individual questions, but most described the insights they had after reviewing their responses to sets of questions or the eco-map as a whole. The eco-maps of some group members were full of people and different types of lines, while those of others only had a few people. Some group members had extensive answers written out for Handout 22.2, while others left some questions blank because they did not feel like they had anyone with whom they could share certain feelings. One group member did not complete the activity because she did not feel like she had any relationships in her life. She did not even include the other group members whom she had known for years. The rest of the group protested that they cared about her. This led to a discussion of how scary relationships have been for her.

Of the women who felt generally supported, one woman, Sarah, reported feeling happy to know that she had a few important people in her life to turn to during emotionally intense situations. Similarly, Helen reported that she was impressed with her support network and had not realized that she had so many people around her who cared about her, who supported her, and with whom she could share her feelings. Lisa appreciated that she had the members of the group to rely on in times of need.

Conversely, others felt somewhat discouraged when examining their social support networks. Sally stated that the questions about whom she avoids gave her perspective into how she shuts others out during important times in her life. By looking at her responses on Handout 22.2, Tracy realized how disconnected she was from her husband. By looking at her eco-map, she realized how small her support network had become. Rebecca shared that this activity gave her a chance to process her grief over the recent move of her best friend.

Overall, group members felt the activity was helpful. Those who were proud of their support system processed their paths of recovery and saw the payoff from the challenging work they had completed to get to that point in their lives. Moreover, the women who didn't seem to have strong support networks were able to determine which relationships needed nurturance, and they began exploring ways to strengthen these important relationships. Likewise, they began indicating which relationships were hindering their growth.

Suggestions for Follow-Up

This activity was followed by another activity focusing on relationships. Group members were asked to focus on one relationship. It could be any type of relationship (e.g., friend, partner, parent-child, or co-worker). It could be a relationship they felt was particularly strong or weak. Group members were then asked to think about the questions below with regard to the target relationship. Their thoughts and reactions were discussed at a subsequent group meeting.

1. How long have you had this relationship?
2. How did this relationship start?
3. What are some of the struggles you have faced together?
4. What are some of the good times you have shared together?
5. What do you value about this relationship?
6. What do you dislike, or would want to change, about this relationship?
7. In an ideal world, what would you want this relationship to look like? (What types of things would you be able to talk about? What would you do together? How would you resolve this conflict?)
8. What changes would you need to make so this relationship could be more like your ideal relationship? What is the first step you would be willing to take?
9. What changes would the other person need to make for this relationship to be more like your ideal relationship?
10. How could you talk to this person about improving your relationship?

Contraindications

If this activity is to be used successfully with a group, the group needs to be perceived as a safe place. If intragroup conflict exists, it is important to resolve it as much as possible. We have found that reducing intragroup conflict and increasing safety leads to more participation and self-disclosure by group members. Second, group facilitators need to set the tone for valuing sharing and diversified experience. Although the likelihood of this activity turning into a competition is low (e.g., who has the most friends), it is still best for group facilitators to take precautions. If a sense of competitiveness arises, facilitators could reemphasize that number of friends does not equal quality, and that each person's situation is unique.

Depending on the nature and intensity of the trauma, the activity may not work well with individuals who are just embarking on their healing and are still overwhelmed with intense emotions, flashbacks, or crises, as often is the case with incest survivors during the awareness stage (Bass & Davis, 1990). This activity takes a considerable amount of energy and may not be appropriate for beginners on the healing journey who have more urgent things to deal with.

References

Alexander, P. C. (1993). The differential effects of abuse characteristics and attachment in the prediction of long-term effects of sexual abuse. *Journal of Interpersonal Violence, 8,* 346-362.

Bass, E., & Davis, L. (1990). *The courage to heal: A guide for women survivors of sexual abuse.* New York: Perennial Library, Harper & Row.

Cole, P. M., & Putnam, F. W. (1992). Effect of incest on self and social functioning: A developmental psychopathology perspective. *Journal of Consulting and Clinical Psychology, 60,* 174-184.

Courtois, C. (2000, October/November). The sexual after-effects of incest/child sexual abuse. *SIECUS Report, 29,* 11-16.

Hartman, A. (1978). Diagrammatic assessment of family relationships. *Social Casework, 59,* 465-576.

Johnson, S. (2002). *Emotionally focused couple therapy with trauma survivors: Strengthening attachment bonds.* New York: Guilford.

Kinship Care Practice Project. (n.d.). *Genograms and eco-maps: Tools for developing a broad view of family.* Retrieved March 28, 2005, from http://www.vitaedesigns.com/kinship/unit1/unit1_discussion8.html

Kirschner, S., Kirschner, D. A., & Rappaport, R. L. (1993). *Working with adult incest survivors: The healing journey.* New York: Brunner/Mazel.

Loewenstein, R. J. (2004). Dissociation of the "bad" parent, preservation of the "good" parent. *Psychiatry, 67,* 256-260.

Talbot, N. L., Duberstein, P. R., King, D. A., Cox, C., & Giles, D. E. (2000). Personality traits of women with a history of childhood sexual abuse. *Comprehensive Psychiatry, 41,* 130-136.

Professional Readings and Resources

Cameron, C. (2000). *Resolving childhood trauma: A long-term study of abuse survivors.* Thousand Oaks, CA: Sage.

Chew, J. (1998). *Women survivors of childhood sexual abuse: Healing through group work.* Binghamton, NY: The Haworth Press.

Courtois, C. A. (1996). *Healing the incest wound: Adult survivors in therapy.* New York: Norton.

Kriedler, M., & Fluharty, L. (1996). The "New Family" model: The evolution of group treatment for adult survivors of childhood sexual abuse. *Journal for Specialists in Group Work, 19,* 175-181.

Marotta, S. A., & Asner, K. K. (1999). Group psychotherapy for women with a history of incest: The research base. *Journal of Counseling and Development, 77,* 315-323.

Meekums, B. (2000). *Creative group therapy for women survivors of child sexual abuse: Speaking the unspeakable.* London: Jessica Kingsley.

Roth, S., & Batson, R. (1997). *Naming the shadows: A new approach to individual and group psychotherapy for adult survivors of childhood incest.* New York: Free Press.

Silverman, S. W. (1999). *Because I remember terror, Father, I remember you.* Athens, GA: University of Georgia Press.

Bibliotherapy Sources for Clients

Bass, E., & Davis, L. (1990). *The courage to heal: A guide for women survivors of sexual abuse.* New York: Perennial Library, Harper & Row.

Chew, J. (1998). *Women survivors of childhood sexual abuse: Healing through group work.* Binghamton, NY: The Haworth Press.

Davis, L. (1991). *Allies in healing: When the person you love was sexually abused as a child.* New York: HarperCollins.

Rich, P. (1999). *The healing journey through grief: Your journal for reflection and recovery.* New York: John Wiley & Sons.

Silverman, S. W. (1999). *Because I remember terror, Father, I remember you.* Athens, GA: University of Georgia Press.

Taylor, C. L. (1991). *The inner child workbook: What to do with your past when it just won't go away.* New York: Jeremy Tarcher.

HANDOUT 22.1

AN ECO-MAP FOR EXPLORING RELATIONSHIPS

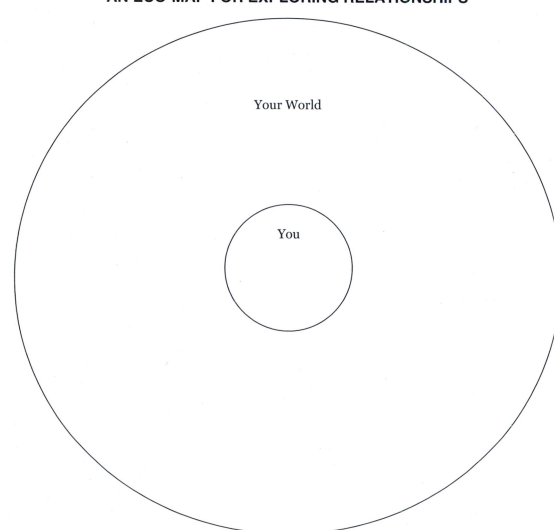

Your World

You

Instructions

To complete this eco-map, write your name in the middle of the circle labeled You. Then draw a circle for each person you come in contact with on a fairly regular basis within the larger circle labeled Your World and write that person's name in the circle. Once you are done, connect your circle to the circles you added with lines to indicate the type of relationship you have with each person: ——— for a close, strong relationship, - - - for a tenuous or distant relationship, and -/-/-/-/- for a stressful relationship. You also have the option of making up your own types of lines to better describe the nature of each relationship.

Christiansen, A. T., Wittenborn, A. K., Karakurt, G., Abdullah, S., & Zhang, C. (2007). Exploring relationships: An eco-map activity for adult survivors of incest. In L. L. Hecker, C. F. Sori, & Associates, *The therapist's notebook, volume 2: More homework, handouts, and activities for use in psychotherapy* (pp. 159-168). Binghamton, NY: The Haworth Press.

HANDOUT 22.2

QUESTIONS FOR EXPLORING RELATIONSHIPS

The relationships we have in life can be safe havens when things go awry. However, our relationships can also feel unsupportive or stressful at times. It is helpful to assess your relationships and determine who is most helpful during specific experiences in life. Realistically assessing your relationships with others can help you during both negative and positive encounters in life.

Questions

1. Whom do you go to for help? _____

   How can they help you? _____

   _____

   _____

   Whom do you avoid when you need help? _____

   Why? _____

   _____

   _____

2. Whom do you go to when you're sad? _____

   How can they comfort you? _____

   _____

   _____

   Whom do you avoid when you're sad? _____

   Why? _____

   _____

   _____

3. Whom do you go to when you're angry? _____

   How can they be there for you? _____

   _____

   _____

   Whom do you avoid when you're angry? _____

   Why? _____

   _____

   _____

Christiansen, A. T., Wittenborn, A. K., Karakurt, G., Abdullah, S., & Zhang, C. (2007). Exploring relationships: An eco-map activity for adult survivors of incest. In L. L. Hecker, C. F. Sori, & Associates, *The therapist's notebook, volume 2: More homework, handouts, and activities for use in psychotherapy* (pp. 159-168). Binghamton, NY: The Haworth Press.

4. Whom do you go to when you feel hopeless? _____

   How can they share this with you? _____

   _____

   _____

   Whom do you avoid when you feel hopeless? _____

   Why? _____

   _____

   _____

5. Whom do you go to when you're excited? _____

   How can they share this with you? _____

   _____

   _____

   Whom do you avoid when you're excited? _____

   Why?_____

   _____

   _____

6. Whom do you go to when you're nervous or anxious? _____

   How can they be there for you? _____

   _____

   _____

   Whom do you avoid when you're nervous or anxious? _____

   Why? _____

   _____

   _____

7. Whom do you go to when you're worried? _____

   How can they be there for you? _____

   _____

   _____

   Whom do you avoid when you're worried? _____

   Why? _____

   _____

   _____

Christiansen, A. T., Wittenborn, A. K., Karakurt, G., Abdullah, S., & Zhang, C. (2007). Exploring relationships: An eco-map activity for adult survivors of incest. In L. L. Hecker, C. F. Sori, & Associates, *The therapist's notebook, volume 2: More homework, handouts, and activities for use in psychotherapy* (pp. 159-168). Binghamton, NY: The Haworth Press.

8. Whom do you go to when you're feeling peaceful or calm? _____

   How can they be there for you? _____

   _____

   _____

   Whom do you avoid when you're feeling peaceful or calm? _____

   Why? _____

   _____

   _____

9. Whom do you go to when you're scared? _____

   How can they be there for you? _____

   _____

   _____

   Whom do you avoid when you're scared? _____

   _____

   _____

10. Whom do you go to when you're happy? _____

    How can they be there for you? _____

    _____

    _____

    Whom do you avoid when you're happy? _____

    _____

    _____

Christiansen, A. T., Wittenborn, A. K., Karakurt, G., Abdullah, S., & Zhang, C. (2007). Exploring relationships: An eco-map activity for adult survivors of incest. In L. L. Hecker, C. F. Sori, & Associates, *The therapist's notebook, volume 2: More homework, handouts, and activities for use in psychotherapy* (pp. 159-168). Binghamton, NY: The Haworth Press.

23

Using Art and Metaphor in Spiritual Restoration After Trauma

Lisa A. Hollingsworth
Mary J. Didelot
Caryn Levington

Type of Contribution: *Activity, Handout*

Objectives

This activity can be used with clients who need a foundation for healing from trauma in their lives. When psychotherapists hear clients express experiences of trauma, clients often describe feeling shattered or not whole. The proposed intervention helps clients describe which parts of their lives have been affected by a traumatic event (e.g., relationships, self-esteem, safety, a sense of connection and trust in the world) and understand how different parts of the Self were changed and challenged by the trauma. By creating a plaque representing the trauma, recovery, and a new sense of Self, this activity produces a tangible metaphor that clients may keep and re-fer to when other challenging or traumatic events in their lives cause them to question whether or not they can recover. For clients who have experienced trauma, yet do not perceive their lives as being shattered, this intervention may also work to encourage them to explore the effects of the trauma upon the Self.

Rationale for Use

After the experience of trauma, it is common to hear a client say, "My life is in pieces," "I feel like I have to put the pieces of my life back together again," or "I am shattered." Addressing the experience of trauma by integrating the spiritual metaphor of the broken vessels from the Kabbalah (a book of Jewish mysticism), current principles of psychotherapy after trauma, and theories from art therapy generates an experiential and metaphorical approach to healing. Cur-rent literature promotes the psychotherapist's need for creativity in adapting to the individual needs of clients but rarely makes use of the client's creative potential in healing (Blatner, 2003). According to Gerity (1999), art therapy works particularly well with clients who have experi-enced traumas and anxieties, and with clients diagnosed with dissociative and post-traumatic stress disorders.

Creativity, in essence, is a reflection of the spiritual Self. Therefore, in relationships between psychotherapists and clients, clients cannot be understood as human, spiritual beings unless therapists are sufficiently aware of a client's basic answers to the meaning and purpose of life, which compose the human condition. This is of particular significance for psychotherapists who work with clients who have experienced trauma. These answers might involve responses to the questions: Who am I to myself? Who am I to others? Who am I in the world? Who or what am I after death? Few experiences shatter these core answers more completely than do experiences of trauma, beckoning the Self to experience new states of disintegration, change, reintegration, and potential transformation.

To these ends, the Kabbalah, a philosophical and psychological vision of Jewish mysticism, may lend perspective to psychotherapy. Although borrowed from the Kabbalah, this conceptual framework is effective for both those of the Jewish faith and those of different spiritual or religious backgrounds. It also can bring healing to atheists because the exploration is based on the higher Self, and not religion or dogma. Of all the Kabbalistic scholars, Isaac Luria developed original theosophical systems that give insights into both God and the nature of humanity (Drob, 2000).

One of Luria's most notable metaphors contributed to the Kabbalah is the *Shevirat ha-Kelim* or the Breaking of the Vessels (Drob, 2000). Luria held that world was created through a negative act that involved the shattering of vessels. This act involved an attempt by darkness to destroy the beauty of humanity. These vessels are called Crown, Will, Wisdom, Understanding, Loving-kindness, Strength, Judgment, Beauty, Compassion, Glory, Splendor, Foundation, and Kingship. These were Luria's thirteen archetypal elements, the elements of holiness. The restoration of these shattered vessels was charged to humankind. Redemption of the world is dependent upon the restoration of these symbolic vessels.

Using Luria's Kabbalistic shattered vessel metaphor (Drob, 2000), valuable insights into the process of healing after trauma can take place. Taking this metaphor into the realm of psychotherapy, every individual becomes a spiritual vessel (Self) full of sparks of holiness. Each vessel becomes a boundary of the spiritual Self. If this spiritual vessel is shattered by trauma or anxiety, the sparks of holiness are hidden within the shards of the vessel, which are chaotically scattered and seemingly irretrievable. Some clients may even perceive these shards as lost forever. There exists an emptiness of the spiritual Self, which can lead to a sense of hopelessness (Drob, 2000).

However, it is this state of emptiness, according to Luria (cited in Drob, 2000), that provides a strong potential for restoration of the spiritual Self. If applied to psychotherapy, the client now has, because the emptiness allows for new beginnings, a powerful opportunity to re-create (restore) the Self, one shard at a time. Each shard symbolizes a dimension of the Self that carries with it a spiritual meaning. By restoring each shard with great care, one at a time, and using Loving-kindness as the cement of insight and wisdom, the shard can generate a vessel (spiritual Self) that is more beautiful and far stronger than the original vessel (Self). The vessel, through this restorative process, is recreated. The spiritual Self is helped to heal. Traumatized clients, though they feel broken or shattered, may use this metaphoric activity to rebuild their sense of Self.

Instructions

Combining the metaphor of the vessel and art therapy generates an innovative and effective strategy to restore the spiritual Self. It should be noted that this new intervention is incompatible with the pathological forces that allow the suffering to continue: fear, psychic pain, shame, and sadness. The following are general step-by-step directions for psychotherapists using this original strategy. Psychotherapists must use their own experiences and knowledge concerning particular clients throughout this process. Before the session, however, the psychotherapist needs to procure the following materials, which can be found at most building supply stores:

- A hammer or rubber mallet
- A piece of light beige or white tile, at least 8" × 8" dimension
- A set of permanent color markers
- A piece of plywood or stiff cardboard, at least the dimension of the tile

- A clean piece of cloth, minimally larger than the tile dimension
- A container of glue for porous material, such as Elmer's or any epoxy

In the session before the actual activity, the psychotherapist should fully explain the teachings and the metaphors of the Kabbalah's Breaking of the Vessels. The following is a sample dialogue:

> With your permission, I would like to use with you a very effective strategy that involves the Kabbalistic shattered vessel metaphor. Before you give your consent, allow me to tell you a bit more about this. I personally find this to be a very powerful and healing strategy after trauma. Many clients, like you, come in to speak with me after a traumatic event. Many have told me, like you, that they feel their lives have been shattered or they feel as if their lives are in pieces. After a trauma, many of my clients have told me that they also began questioning themselves and their lives: Who am I to myself? Who am I to others? Do I have any meaning in my life? All of these questions and their answers are really important in healing. Sometimes individuals who have experienced trauma also feel terribly alone and start to mistrust everyone, including themselves and their own judgment. Do you feel this way too? You may even have asked yourself some of these same questions. This project will help you to understand yourself, to heal, and to become connected or reconnected to yourself, others, and the world. Would you like to continue?
>
> Have you heard of the Kabbalah? It is a book of philosophical and psychological vision that has been around since medieval times. It is filled with ancient traditions, secrets, teachings, and transformations. Most important, it is filled with ways to know yourself as a spiritual being and how you fit into the nature of humanity. It is a book that helps us find beauty in life.
>
> One of the most important metaphors in this book is the Breaking of the Vessels. It is believed that all good was contained in thirteen vessels: Crown, Will, Wisdom, Understanding, Loving-kindness, Strength, Judgment, Beauty, Compassion, Glory, Splendor, Foundation, and Kingship. These were elements of holiness. When the world was created through a negative act, all the vessels were shattered. The restoration of these shattered vessels and their content was a charge to all of us humans.
>
> You've stated in the past that you see yourself as broken or shattered. [Use the client's own language here.] This is part of the symbolism we will explore together during our next few sessions as we do this project. We are going to restore, or heal, your vessel shattered by the negative, traumatic event that happened to you, and fill it with the elements of holiness to empower you to be your self again, whole and strong. The most wonderful part of this metaphor is that even though the vessel was shattered, it is believed that any vessel put back together, piece by piece, with care, gentleness, and loving-kindness becomes even more beautiful and far stronger than it was originally.
>
> Do you have any questions? Is there any part of this I can further explain to you? Remember, I will be with you and walk with you through every step of this process. Although it may be painful at times, it will be a very healing experience for you. We will take this at your pace.

At the next session, have all the materials available. Explain to the client that the tile itself is symbolic of the vessel of his or her life. Review with the client the relationship between the metaphor in the Kabbalah and the client's shattering of the vessel, or the tile. Also tell the client that he or she is going to symbolically shatter the tile with the hammer or the mallet, just as the traumatic event shattered his or her life. To do this in a safe manner, place the tile itself on the wood or cardboard. Then cover the tile with a cloth. This will not only prevent shattered pieces from scattering but will dull the sound of the tile breaking. Remind the client how this shattering symbolizes the traumatic event that shattered his or her Self. Also, warn the client that some shards may be sharp, so they must be handled with care. If there are concerns about the client using a hammer or handling the shards, the psychotherapist may break the tile for the client.

Once the tile is shattered, have the client carefully take a shard and, using markers, color each shard with a symbol, picture, words, or a combination of significant symbols relating to the traumatic event. The psychotherapist may wish to offer the client some paper towels, a clean cloth, or a lapboard not only to balance the shards but to keep from marking on his or her clothing should the markers slip off the edge of the tile. Allow the client the freedom to think freely and draw freely in this process. If there are not enough shards, make more. If there are too many, use the extras as mosaic of single colors to complete the project.

When the client is finished with the drawing, or as the client is drawing, have him or her discuss with you the relevance and meaning of the shard symbolism in his or her life. Ask the client to discuss (a) the symbol, word, or parts of the drawing, (b) the choice of colors used, and (c) the learning about the spiritual Self and other things that can be gleaned from each shard representation. As the discussion continues, remind the client:

> Remember, everything in the Kabbalah is a metaphor, just as in your drawings. With this first drawing on the shard, let me help you to draw the relationship between your trauma experience and the vessels. Allow me to go over these with you. I have written these vessels down on this sheet of paper that you can use as a guide, but let me go over them with you verbally, so if you have any questions, I can answer them immediately (see Handout 23.1). It's important that as you create the shards, we explore the meaning in the symbolism you are using. By exploring these representations, we will both come to an understanding concerning the traumatic event, the ramifications of the event for you, and a healing through spiritual growth.

The psychotherapist and the client will repeat the process for each shard. Through each session, the psychotherapist should be encouraging reflection on each shard, the symbolism, and the spiritual meaning for the client.

When all the shards are completed, the client should glue them onto the plywood or cardboard while again discussing how each reflects the client's life, what he or she has experienced, and how those experiences and this experience of the vessels have facilitated spiritual growth. The client may then take the newly created mosaic, or vessel, home as a symbol to serve as a continual reminder of healing, strength, beauty, and spiritual growth.

This is a new practice that can easily be used by any psychotherapist without any further training. As a caveat, however, the psychotherapist should know that this process requires the following:

- All the artwork must be done in session; this should not be perceived as a homework project, as processing this in session is imperative.
- Reflection and process are completed by the counselor immediately after each session. Since a portion of the progress a client makes will be seen on a preverbal level, it is particularly important that the psychotherapist gives attention to and reflects upon the client's nonverbal messages.
- The psychotherapist keeps questioning to a minimum while the client is formulating the symbol to be drawn onto each piece, as questioning at this point will interrupt the process and may be perceived as intrusive by the client.

Using the metaphor of the broken vessels from the Kabbalah can be an effective new practice in helping clients heal after trauma or rebuild an identity. This practice from ancient tradition has not lost its modern relevance. It can give definition, understanding, and tangible results to ease the suffering resulting from the events. This strategy can bring many beneficial insights concerning the trauma and the Self to both therapists and clients. The simplicity of this very successful strategy lends itself to a myriad of therapeutic settings and requires no further training.

Brief Vignette

Using this strategy within a clinical practice can be illustrated by the case of Darlene (a pseudonym), a forty-seven-year-old single professional woman who was experiencing psychic suffering due to the death of her mother. Darlene's mother was not only the maternal nurturing figure in her life; her only relationship maintained in the last twenty years was with her mother. The very long, painful death of her mother shattered Darlene's Self. Darlene, like many clients who experience this level of suffering, could not find the words to describe her feelings. Therefore, after the strategy was explained and the tile shattered, Darlene was given the worksheet and asked which vessel she would like to use to begin her healing process.

Darlene had a very evident need in the area of Loving-kindness, so this is where the therapeutic process was initiated. She drew an empty heart. This act of drawing, the concreteness of the thought, elicited a strong emotional response. The question was then posed, "What do you need to do for yourself to support yourself emotionally?" Her response was, "I desperately need to connect with people." From there, Darlene and the therapist discussed possible intersections for connection and allowed for her willingness to be involved in a local philanthropic organization of other professional women with similar interests who supported women with breast cancer. From these experiences within the organization, Darlene came to the realization that she was far more than her physical self, and that the connections she made with other women were on a deep, spiritual plane that she could feel emotionally. Darlene still missed her mother terribly, but was able to connect through others to her higher Self. This connection gave her spiritual comfort.

Next, Darlene discussed the vessel of Beauty and drew a picture of a flower on the next shard. She discussed feeling off-balance since her mother died, and anxious. Her work environment was stress producing and life had been extremely busy. When asked what strategies she could use to calm herself, she began to discuss her yoga class and how she had strayed from her daily meditation practice. As she continued to draw the flower on her shard, she resolved to return to her meditation and yoga practice as a way to calm herself and return to her vessel of Beauty.

The therapist and Darlene continued to discuss her loss and the relevance and meaning of the shard symbolism in her life. When all the shards were completed and glued into mosaic form, Darlene decided to take her completed mosaic home to put in her garden as a tribute to the many strengths her mother had given her.

Contraindications

Whenever a psychotherapist works with clients, attention must be given to harm awareness and harm reduction (Geppert, 2003). Using sound clinical judgment to ensure the appropriateness of this strategy with each individual client, several ideas that relate to harm awareness and reduction are crucial when using this approach. From this perspective, all clients have strengths. Clients will, in most cases, act on those strengths if supported and affirmed. The client is the expert on his or her experience and resolution. For some psychotherapists, this requires a significant change in perspective: from fixer to collaborator (Bell, 2003). It is the client who defines mental health and what actions he or she needs to take to become healthy (Bartoli, 2003).

Risks that may be germane to this strategy may include a vivid reexperiencing of an event and perhaps intense emotions. If this does occur in the middle of the therapeutic process, the psychotherapist must help the client put all materials down and ground in the here and now. If the psychotherapist has any concerns regarding the client hurting himself or herself with the recommended materials, several other materials may be substituted for the tile (e.g., paper, cardboard, or cloth). These substitute materials would not necessitate the use of a hammer. The strategy, however, would still be effective.

Last, some clients from other faiths may be reluctant to take part in this activity. The objection to the use of the Kabbalah may be countered with the idea that this book may be looked to as a self-help book that contains wisdom for daily living, or the metaphor itself can be used as a part of Hebrew culture and wisdom alone without mention of the Kabbalah itself or religion.

References

Bartoli, E. (2003). Psychoanalytic practice and the religious patient: A current perspective. *Bulletin of the Menninger Clinic, 67*(4), 347-366.

Bell, H. (2003). Strengths and secondary trauma in family violence work. *Social Work, 48*(4), 513-522.

Blatner, A. (2003). Using creativity to explore in psychotherapy. Special report: Creativity and psychiatry. *Psychiatric Times, 20*(6), 35-36.

Drob, S. L. (2000). *Kabbalistic metaphors: Jewish mystical themes in ancient and modern thought.* New York: Jason Aronson.

Geppert, C. M. A. (2003). Do no harm. *Psychiatric Times, 20*(7), 91-92.

Gerity, L. A. (1999). *Creativity and the dissociative patient.* Philadelphia: Jessica Kingsley.

Professional Readings and Resources

Blatner, A. (2003). Using creativity to explore in psychotherapy. Special report: Creativity and psychiatry. *Psychiatric Times, 20*(6), 35-36.

Drob, S. L. (2000). *Kabbalistic metaphors: Jewish mystical themes in ancient and modern thought.* New York: Jason Aronson.

Frankl, V. (1963). *Man's search for meaning: An introduction to logotherapy.* New York: Washington Square Press.

Gil, E. (1988). *Treatment of adult survivors of childhood abuse.* Rockville, MD: Launch Press.

Herman, J. (1997). *Trauma and recovery.* New York: Basic Books.

Levine, S. K., & Levine, E. G. (1998). *Foundations of expressive arts therapy: Theoretical and clinical perspectives.* London: Jessica Kingsley.

Moon, B. (1994). *Introduction to art therapy: Faith in the product.* Springfield, IL: Charles C Thomas.

Rogers, N. (1993). *The creative connection: Expressive arts as healing.* Palo Alto, CA: Science & Behavior Books.

Bibliotherapy Sources for Clients

Berg, M. (2002). *The way: Using the wisdom of Kabbalah for spiritual transformation and fulfillment.* New York: Kabbalah Centre.

Gil, E. (1988). *Outgrowing the pain: A book for and about adults abused as children.* New York: Dell.

Laitman, R. M. (2003). *Kabbalah for beginners.* Ontario, Canada: Laitman Kabbalah Publishers.

Whitfield, C. L. (1990). *A gift to myself.* Deerfield Beach, FL: Health Communications.

THE VESSELS

This is a list of all the vessels, their representative meaning in your life, and some questions for you and your therapist to address. For example, if you have drawn an empty heart to represent your need for connectedness in a relationship, you and your therapist would be exploring the shard of Loving-kindness.

- **The Crown:** your soul
  How do you see your soul within yourself?
  What does the soul mean to you?
  What symbol might you use for your soul?

- **The Will:** your intentions
  What intentions are you focusing upon right now?
  What symbol might you use for your intentions?

- **Wisdom:** your inspirations
  How do your inspirations come to you?
  What would motivate you to actually act upon your inspirations?
  What symbol might you use for your inspirations?

- **Understanding:** nourishment/nurturance
  What actions do you need to take in your life to nurture yourself?
  Who do you look to for nurturance?
  Who do you feel responsible to nurture?
  What symbol might you use for your nourishment/nurturance?

- **Loving-kindness:** your emotional, physical, and spiritual support and/or supporters
  What do you need to do for yourself to support yourself emotionally?
  What do you need to do for yourself to support yourself physically?
  What do you need to do for yourself to support yourself spiritually?
  Who might help support you in any of these areas?
  What symbol might you use for your emotional support? Physical support? Spiritual support?

- **Strength:** your self-discipline and ability to stay focused on the person you wish to be
  Who do you wish to be?
  What steps are you taking to become the person you wish to be?
  What strategies are you using to stay true to the person you wish to be?
  Where does your strength of character come from?
  What symbol might you use for the person you wish to be?

- **Judgment:** your decision-making skills; your ability to use factual information wisely in the decision-making process
  How do you distinguish fact from opinion?
  How do you recognize the truth?

Hollingsworth, L. A., Didelot, M. J., & Levington, C. (2007). Using art and metaphor in spiritual restoration after trauma. In L. L. Hecker, C. F. Sori, & Associates, *The therapist's notebook, volume 2: More homework, handouts, and activities for use in psychotherapy* (pp. 169-176). Binghamton, NY: The Haworth Press.

How can you use facts in your decision-making process?
Are there any strategies that you can think of to weigh facts?
What symbol might you use for factual decision making?

- **Beauty:** your sense of peace and calm
  What strategies can you use to calm yourself when you feel anxieties arising or you
    are in anxiety-producing situations?
  Where (physical location) are you most at peace?
  What are some calming activities you can involve yourself in?
  Who are you connected (any and all interpersonal relationships) to in your life?
  How can you nurture those connections?
  How do those connections nurture you?
  What symbol might you use for peace and calm?

- **Compassion:** your acceptance of yourself and others
  Do you accept yourself?
  Who accepts you?
  Who do you accept?
  What qualities do you possess that help you establish relationships?
  What qualities do you look to in others before you establish a relationship with them?
  What symbol might you use for acceptance?

- **Glory:** your emotional reactions to situations
  How would you describe your emotional self?
  Would there be any changes you would like to make to your emotional reactions to
    negative and positive situations/experiences?
  What symbol might you use for your emotional reactions?

- **Splendor:** your meaning and purpose in life
  What brings you meaning in your life?
  What do you feel is the purpose of your life?
  What symbol might you use for your meaning in life? Purpose?

- **Foundation:** your social desires and sexual desires
  What do you desire socially for yourself in the future?
  Are your current social desires being met?
  Are you sexually satisfied?
  What symbol might you use for all your desires?

- **Kingship:** your spirituality
  What are your spiritual beliefs?
  What role do spiritual beliefs play in your life?
  Are you comforted by your spiritual beliefs? Why? Why not?
  What symbol might you use for your spirituality?

Hollingsworth, L. A., Didelot, M. J., & Levington, C. (2007). Using art and metaphor in spiritual restoration after trauma. In L. L. Hecker, C. F. Sori, & Associates, *The therapist's notebook, volume 2: More homework, handouts, and activities for use in psychotherapy* (pp. 169-176). Binghamton, NY: The Haworth Press.

24

Writing the Script for Survivor Therapy

Mary Bratton

To survive the unsurvivable, to continue to live in a family where they are being physically, emotionally, or sexually assaulted, victims of childhood abuse have to fragment their experiences, their feelings, and, ultimately, themselves. The duality of a parent who is both caring and threatening, the contrast between the public "looking good" family and the private hell, and the conflict between love and hate or love and fear all require the child to ignore huge chunks of reality and to suppress both awareness and emotion. This gives rise to a sense of distance from life and a loss of wholeness and identity. It is also the taproot of a more significant separation from self.

For most survivors of childhood abuse, splitting the self has nothing to do with split personality or dissociative identity disorder. Splitting the self comes out of the struggle to endure ongoing deprivation or attack. To cope with the fragmentation all around them, survivors have to fragment themselves, too. They have to censor and compartmentalize their behaviors, feelings, perceptions, and beliefs (Herman, 1992; Shengold, 1989). The shards of self that result are reflections of the events that formed them. They are normal and understandable defensive states, or personas, that can be shrugged on and off to suit the circumstances.

If the survivor had to be a parent to parents or to siblings in childhood, there might be an efficient, controlling persona who can take charge and run the world, or, on the other hand, an undependable, indecisive persona who runs from responsibility. If the survivor was sexualized as a child, there might be a seductive persona who attracts and discards lovers like a candle lures moths to its lethal flame or an isolated, lonely persona terrified of intimacy. If the survivor had to disappear as a child, there might be a timid, apologetic persona who withdraws, turtlelike, at the slightest sign of conflict or danger. Or there could be an exuberant, impatient, immature persona who emerges, ever so briefly, to dance in the sunlight. All of these are understandable responses to what was demanded in childhood.

Underneath the masks shown to the outside world lies a trio of personas that more truly mirrors the disconnection from self dictated by trauma. Three broad themes run consistently through survivors' descriptions of themselves—part empty and mechanical, part impulsive and even fun loving, part dark and menacing shadow that overhangs life and threatens existence. The first is the Adult; the second is the Child; the third represents the hurtful legacy of family dysfunction and abuse, the Destroyer (Bratton, 1999). Naming and personifying the triumvirate of defensive states makes them less vague and intimidating and more approachable and workable.

When a child is being abused and no one is taking responsibility or protecting that child, the entire abusive drama is absorbed by the child. The child internalizes the triangle of players—the victim, the abuser, and the nonprotective bystander (Miller, 1981, 1994). The victim becomes the persona of the Child, the abuser and the abuser's distorted reality become the Destroyer, and the bystander who should have protected but didn't becomes part of the Adult.

The Therapist's Notebook, Volume 2
doi:10.1300/5550_24

Splitting the self is necessary for survival in the crucible of abuse. The survivor manages to mold three levels of self, three distinct and coherent internal pieces, to deal with the chaos outside.

The first part, the Adult, grew from the limited part of self that the survivor was allowed to expose. It reflects the false front the family showed to the world and the family's inability to value or protect their child. The second part, the Child, the vulnerable, real self, was forced into hiding by the third part, the Destroyer. The Destroyer is the sum total of family dysfunction—the disapproval, condemnation, altered reality, rejection, and violence, which were internalized as rules for the game of life. The survivor intuitively and sensibly presented to the world only what the family decided was acceptable—the Adult. The survivor intuitively and cleverly hid a part of self—the Child—to keep feelings, creativity, and spontaneity intact. The survivor intuitively and wisely played by the family rules and believed the distortion and denial—the Destroyer.

Survivors need to understand that the three-part defense, Adult, Child, and Destroyer, is not a sickness or craziness. Rather, it bears testimony to the strength and brilliance of the children they were. It explains their ongoing ability to hold opposing beliefs and engage in incongruent behaviors. It is the triumph of their will to survive.

Healing launched from the viewpoint of the incomplete Adult, which is only a portion of the total being, will also be incomplete and doomed to failure. It is the Child who heard and felt the abuse; it is the Child who believes the excuses and rationalizations, the ridicule and condemnation. The Adult may intellectually deny shame and guilt about the abuse, but until the Child is convinced, recovery will be superficial and short-lived. Healing modes that fail to include the hidden Child or take into account the unstated family manual for living that is the Destroyer will produce piecemeal recovery at best.

This chapter focuses on the roles of the Adult and Child personas in the healing process. Integrating these two parts, augmenting the power of the Adult to protect and honor the Child and increasing the Child's worthiness to be honored and protected, is a pivotal task in healing. The progressive dialogue between these two personas becomes the script for every ensuing stage of therapy.

The Adult is often experienced as an empty shell, devoid of many feelings, deprived of many responses, and drained of energy and life force, moving through the world like a robot, just an observer. The survivor's first response to accessing this part of self to initiate healing is often negative, because the Adult, the only self the survivor knows, is a shadow with no substance or worth. Writing and drawing exercises are helpful for the therapist to learn the survivor's entry-level view of the Adult.

Jessica described herself as "dead":

> I've always known I was different. I know now it's because I died a long time ago. When you're dead inside you're not like other people. You laugh when you're supposed to and smile when you're supposed to, and on rare days you even cry when you're supposed to. But you're never really there. There's no energy inside, no life energy.

Chris presented a blank page as a picture of herself. Sadie drew a tiny stick figure with no mouth and no eyes, surrounded by a "forest of fear."

But the Adult is not a void. The Adult is window to the Child and the self-destructive family mythology. More important, the Adult is the bearer of the self-parenting skills that will be used to reconnect with the Child, as well as to protect the Child from the threats and rules the family used to smother that Child. Although the Adult internalized the family's failure to protect and value the Child from the nonprotective bystander in the abusive drama, in reality, survivors were forced to parent themselves long before they were ready to do so. Recovery is not about learning all new self-parenting skills; it is about beginning to deliberately use the incredible skills already in place.

Kevin recognized those skills in his first tentative letter to the Child:

Dear Child,

    I am learning that I have always been your loving parent. Even when we were little and felt so isolated and invisible, I hoped that somewhere there would be a better and safer place and knew that it was worth it to hang on. The nights I spent alone in my room listening to the radio, I was really taking care of you, although I didn't know it then. And yesterday, when I stood up for myself and wouldn't take the blame for someone else's mistake, I hope you heard that I will never let you or me be blamed unjustly again. I am teaching people how to treat us. No one can make me a doormat unless I lie down.

Love,
Kevin

Once the survivor can identify and own self-parenting skills, reconnection to the Child can begin. There may be several different pieces of the inner Child that dwell in this segment of self. The Child was formed in moments of trauma, when the survivor had to freeze and go numb and then "forget" the feelings. The Child may have had to freeze and fragment repeatedly. If trauma occurred over and over again, feelings had to be repeatedly cut off from ongoing reality. If there was no chance for rescue or debriefing, emotions had to be continually shut down and encapsulated. There may be a series of wounded Children, each holding feelings for separate episodes of trauma. The survivor may need to work with an angry seven-year-old who was physically assaulted and a frightened nine-year-old who was emotionally abandoned. Survivors need to be reminded that this fragmentation is not craziness; it represents a brilliant survival defense.

Survivors may find that even thinking about the discarded Child is frightening. The Child was frozen and laid to rest a long time ago and doesn't want to be resurrected. When Troy first tried to find the Child, he could only visualize a tiny child being flattened under a sheet of ice, cold and lifeless. Missy's Child was stiff and resistant and didn't want to be held or hugged.

Survivors may also have a sense that the Child is unlovable. They were taught to hate and reject themselves as children. If the eyes in which they saw themselves mirrored only distortion, then their self-view became distorted, too. If the people around them treated them in ways that suggested disgust and loathing, then they learned self-disgust and self-loathing, too.

The most important word in that last sentence is *learned*. Survivors need to understand that what they learned is not who they really are. Just because they were rejected does not make them rejectable. That was learned, and it can be unlearned. The Adult must teach the Child the truth about self and the world.

Greta had considered herself stupid for laughing at her parents' threats to abandon her at an orphanage, because her parents beat her for her laughter. When she recognized her laughter was a clever and lifesaving defense, she shared her discovery with the Child:

Dear Little Greta,

    Laughing at the threat of being sent to the orphanage kept you from being abandoned physically. Even though you got beaten and abandoned emotionally, you did not get abandoned physically. Not being abandoned physically was an instinct of survival. You knew you had to have people to keep you alive. You couldn't do it yourself. If you stop and think about it, you weren't dumb. If you think of the human needs, survival has to come first. If you don't survive, none of your other needs can be met.

Love,
Greta

Considering the Child as separate from self eases reconnection. The Child has been lost inside for so long that unless the Child is held at arm's length and looked at in the light, it will be too easy for the Child to remain just a figment of the imagination. Techniques that emphasize this separateness actually speed reunification.

Art can facilitate reconnection with the Child. Most adults are predominantly verbal, and many of the blocks against talking, feeling, and trusting are stored in the verbal cognitive system. A switch to another modality, such as art, bypasses the verbal censors. Drawing tends to evoke spontaneous expression of feelings beyond the constraints of words and meanings. For survivors who need their work to be "perfect," an assignment to draw the Child as a child might draw may relax the inhibitions.

Diane drew a smiling, neatly dressed facade holding schoolbooks labeled "sad" and "lonely" to illustrate the childhood hero role that held the seeds of her perfectionist Adult persona. Lana's cage, labeled "lonely" and holding a little girl behind bars, showed how trapped she felt when she was little.

Perceptions of the self at varying ages in childhood should also be explored. In the labyrinth of an abusive family, children may have been accepted until some critical developmental stage was reached and rejection suddenly occurred. Often the onset of sexual maturity evokes disgust and humiliation. Some survivors may find it fairly easy to welcome themselves as very young children but may disown their teenage selves. Young children can hide in defenses of imagination and fantasy; they can fragment reality in the privacy of their own minds and keep the family secret by playing alone. But school-age children have to interact with the world and still keep the secret. They may use more aggressive and less attractive defenses to keep people at bay, lest the secret slip out inadvertently. Defenses such as rebellion or sexual flamboyance, which bring the attention so desperately craved but no closeness or intimacy, are less likable but no less brilliant. After much struggle, Laura finally realized the teenage "siren" she hated was really the source of her strength and courage.

A dialogue initiated between Adult and Child provides both foundation and direction for healing. A technique that can help is alternate-hand journaling (Kritsberg, 1985; Bradshaw, 1990). If survivors are right-handed, they will write to the Child with their right hand, but they will let the Child respond with their left hand. They may produce awkward printing or an almost unreadable scrawl. Neatness is not the point of this exercise. It is a tool to connect with the Child. Since each hemisphere of the brain controls the opposite side of the body, using the left hand to write for the Child allows survivors to access the right hemisphere of the brain, the side that is the seat of creativity and imagination, the natural dwelling place of the Child. If survivors are left-handed, they will still benefit from trying this alternate-hand method to journal with the Child. The switch to the nondominant hand focuses concentration on coordination rather than content and releases unexpected discoveries. If alternate-hand journaling does not seem to work, survivors can be encouraged to use different colored markers or pens for each persona.

Jessica's first alternate-hand dialogue introduced a little person who used childlike language and incomplete sentences, in contrast to Jessica's articulate adult style. It also indicates the first contact with the Child may not be the joyful reunion hoped for. It is unrealistic to expect instant trust and affection from a part of the self that has been ignored or hurt. Even if the worst the Adult provided for the Child was benign neglect, that Child was taught to disappear. The Child learned not to talk because no one was really safe or caring. Speaking up and believing someone will listen after so many years of silence may not come easily or quickly for the Child.

Little Girl,

Hi. I decided I needed to talk to you. Maybe because I think you know some things I need to know. I think you've been separate from me for a long time, and I want to get to know you. You look real sad. What was happening to you? Why are you crying?

Jessica,

Why are you writing now? You never cared about me before. You treat me bad. You don't like me. You say I'm gross and disgusting. Why should I tell you anything?

Little Girl,

How can I protect you if I don't know you? I do like you. It's me I don't like. It's me that's gross and disgusting, not you. You're only a baby.

Jessica,

I'm not a baby! I take care me [sic]. Daddy don't. Mommy don't. I do. If you don't like you, how can you like me? You're just like them—you just want to hurt me.

Over time, Jessica's alternate-hand journaling provided positive connection with the Child and direction for the recovery process. The Child confronted Jessica's eating disorder with power no therapist could muster:

Little Girl,

I do like you. I don't like what I've become. I don't like me. You're not me. I won't hurt you, I promise. I need to know what you know.

Jessica,

I am you. I'm you twenty years ago. You are hurting me. You shove food in my mouth and it hurts. Please stop it. How can I tell you anything if you shove things in my mouth?

Little Girl,

I don't want to hurt you. I try to stop—I try. I never thought that I was hurting you—only me. I don't care if I'm hurt. I don't care if I die. You need to live.

Jessica,

If you die, I die. If you hurt, I hurt. I don't think you try. You still have that medicine stuff [syrup of ipecac]. You're the one who needs to stop it. You make me hurt.

After years of fruitless therapeutic interventions, Jessica responded almost immediately to the Child's plea:

Dear Little Girl,

It's me again. I got rid of the syrup of Ipecac and I haven't binged or purged. It's weird—since I've talked to you I haven't really wanted to, and the few times I have, I've thought of you. I won't let them hurt you anymore.

Dear Jessica,

I know you haven't hurt yourself. I thought you would from what I told you. I feel safe.

Catherine summarized her newly forged partnership with the Child in a poem, "To Little Catherine":

> I need you as much as ever,
> I need you to see the light.
> I need you to know the answers,
> In the middle of the night.

I need you to do the seeing,
To hear and feel and love.
I need you to help discover,
A Higher Power above.

I need you to face discomfort,
When we go to school.
I need you to teach me how,
To disobey a rule.

The rules we always thought,
Were engraved in stone,
The ones that said to be afraid,
When we were alone.

You are the one I'll always need,
The one to teach me life.
For you're the one who knew just how,
To exist among the strife.

Now use your courage to grow beyond,
The pain and discontent.
Use your energy to live this life,
For it was heaven sent.

Don't be afraid we'll lose each other;
We were not attached through fear.
We lived their lie long enough,
And I love you, dear.

I care about just what you want,
Even though I cannot give,
Immediately you treasures,
I'll be here while you live.

I'll never leave you—no, not me;
I'll be right here for you.
And if you're napping, when you wake,
I'll be here—yes, it's true.

I love you every time you say,
I just can't make it one more day.
I love you even though you doubt,
And wonder what this life's about.

I love you when mistakes are made;
I'll always make time for you.
And I knew you could do anything,
When you learned to tie your shoe.

And when we die, nobody knows,
Where we will really be . . .
Though wherever we may travel,
It will still be YOU and ME.

This dialogue between Adult and Child must continue as healing progresses. It will serve as both the driving force for recovery and an ongoing measure of progress. It will become a tool to accomplish resolution of trauma and repair of developmental damage. The Adult will rescue the Child in fantasy from memories of abuse. The Adult will lead the Child through developmental stages that were absent or corrupted during childhood, replacing distrust with trust, worthlessness with purpose, inadequacy with self-sufficiency, and isolation with connection. Most important, it is the alliance between Adult and Child that will empower the survivor to challenge the cognitive distortions about self and world learned in the cauldron of abuse—the Destroyer. As those false beliefs are confronted and discarded, the survivor will build a solid and whole identity and become ready to claim a rightful place in the world.

References

Bradshaw, J. (1990). *Homecoming*. New York: Bantam Books.

Bratton, M. (1999). *From surviving to thriving: A therapist's guide to stage II recovery for survivors of childhood abuse*. Binghamton, NY: The Haworth Press.

Herman, J. (1992). *Trauma and recovery*. New York: Basic Books.

Kritsberg, W. (1985). *The ACoA syndrome*. Deerfield Beach, FL: Health Communications.

Miller, A. (1981). *The drama of the gifted child*. New York: Basic Books.

Miller, D. (1994). *Women who hurt themselves*. New York: Basic Books.

Shengold, L. (1989). *Soul murder: The effects of childhood abuse and deprivation*. New Haven, CT: Yale University Press.

SECTION VI:
DIVORCE AND STEPFAMILIES

25

Dos and Don'ts of Divorced Parents

Lorna L. Hecker
Catherine Ford Sori

Type of Contribution: *Handout*

Objectives

The objective of this handout is to decrease behaviors of divorced or divorcing parents that negatively affect their children. In addition, positive behaviors are outlined as suggestions for parents traversing the unfamiliar territory of postdivorce life with children.

Rationale for Use

How parents navigate the waters of divorce can strongly affect children's transition to the divorce, for better or worse, depending upon how the parents manage the transition. Ahrons (1999, p. 391) noted several major factors that have been identified which clearly contribute to the healthy adjustment of children. She notes that in order to transition well, children need:

- to have basic needs met, both economic and psychological,
- support for maintaining important familial relationships with immediate and extended family, and
- parents who have a cooperative relationship.

This handout was developed to help parents accomplish these goals in order to benefit their children, as well as themselves. It is targeted for families undergoing the transition of divorce, or for parents who continue to have problems navigating postdecree family life with regard to their children.

Instructions

This handout can be given in conjunction with therapy or used as a psychoeducational tool in numerous settings. Attorneys and judges also appreciate having a handout with guidelines that they can utilize with families who may be conflictual or doing things that harm the children. Court programs teaching parents about postdivorce life and the impact of parental conflict on children may also find this handout helpful.

When used in therapy with one or both parents, the therapist should be sure to go through the handout and discuss each item, noting which areas may be particularly difficult and should be addressed in future individual or conjoint sessions. Each partner should be given a copy of the handout for future reference.

The Therapist's Notebook, Volume 2
© 2007 by The Haworth Press, Inc. All rights reserved.
doi:10.1300/5550_25

Suggestions for Follow-Up

The therapist can check in with clients and make sure that they understand the points on the handout and can integrate the ideas into their lives. If only one parent is attending therapy, the therapist may also encourage the client to share the handout with his or her ex-spouse, but should realize that the client may need help in approaching the ex-spouse constructively in sharing the guidelines.

Contraindications

Some of the dos and don'ts in this handout do not apply if the parent was in an abusive relationship.

Reference

Ahrons, C. R. (1999). Divorce: An unscheduled family transition. In B. Carter & M. McGoldrick (Eds.), *The expanded family life cycle: Individual, family, and social perspectives* (3rd ed) (pp. 381-398). New York: Allyn & Bacon.

Professional Readings and Resources

Ahrons, C. (1998). *The good divorce*. New York: Harper Paperbacks.
Carter, B., & McGoldrick, M. (Eds.). (1999). *The expanded family life cycle: Individual, family and social perspectives* (3rd ed). New York: Allyn & Bacon.
Coates, C. A., Duval, B. B., Carla, B., Garrity, E. T., Johnson, E. R., Lacross, M. A., & Baris, M. A. (2001). *Working with high-conflict families of divorce: A guide for professionals*. Lanham, MD: Jason Aronson.
Hecker, L. L., & Sori, C. F. (2003). The parent's guide to good divorce behavior. In C. F. Sori, L. L. Hecker, & Associates, *The therapist's notebook for children and adolescents: Homework, handouts, and activities for use in psychotherapy* (pp. 323-329). Binghamton, NY: The Haworth Press.
Hecker, L. L., & Sori, C. F. (2006). Divorce and stepfamily issues. In C. Sori (Ed.), *Engaging children in family therapy: Creative approaches to integrating theory and research in clinical practice* (pp. 177-204). New York: Routledge.

Bibliotherapy Sources for Clients

Ahrons, C. (1998). *The good divorce*. New York: Harper Paperbacks.
Brown, M. T., & Brown, L. K. (1988). *Dinosaurs divorce: A guide for changing families*. Boston, MA: Little, Brown.
Emery, R. (2003). *The truth about children and divorce: Dealing with the emotions so you and your children can thrive*. New York: Viking Adult Press.
Krementz, J. (1988). *How it feels when parents divorce*. New York: Alfred A. Knopf.
Lansky, V. (1996). *Divorce book for parents: Helping your children cope with divorce and its aftermath*. Minnetonka, MN: Book Peddlers.
Long, N., & Forehand, R. (2002). *Making divorce easier for your child: 50 effective ways to help children adjust*. New York: McGraw Hill.
Stahl, P. M. (2000). *Parenting after divorce: A guide to resolving conflicts and meeting your children's need*. Adascadero, CA: Impact Publishers.
Tabor, E. (2001). *Helping children cope with divorce*. New York: Jossey Bass.

HANDOUT 25.1

THE DOS AND DON'TS OF DIVORCE

1. *Do* encourage your children to have contact with and to love the other parent.
2. *Do not* speak negatively about your ex-spouse to the children or within earshot of the children. Your children know that they are half you, and half your ex-spouse. Therefore, if you speak negatively about your ex, you are simultaneously hurting your children's self-esteem.
3. *Do* find developmentally appropriate ways to tell your child about the divorce, preferably with the other parent present. Avoid blaming your ex-spouse for the divorce. Remain calm when explaining the divorce to children, using simple language and a matter-of-fact tone of voice. For preschoolers you can use metaphors (e.g., their orange juice and milk mixed together would not taste good, and Mommy and Daddy just don't mix well together either).
4. *Do* explain to children how the divorce will affect them in the short term, for example, who they will live with, if they will remain in their home, or if they will have to change schools.
5. *Do* understand that divorce means children experience significant and multiple losses that they need to grieve. Work with your spouse to minimize the number and significance of the losses.
6. *Do* reassure children that they will always be loved and taken care of.
7. *Do* address children's egocentric thinking by reassuring them that they did not cause the divorce, and that there is nothing they can do to fix things. Children need repeated reassurance that they aren't being divorced.
8. *Do* encourage children to express their feelings both verbally and nonverbally in an atmosphere of acceptance. Children's books such as *Dinosaur's Divorce* are excellent tools to help children understand and express their emotions.
9. *Do* understand that some children regress during this time. For example, children may wet the bed or experience separation anxiety. Be calm and reassuring, and assure children that they will feel better soon and you will be a happy family again.
10. *Do* allow for transition time between houses. Don't assume if children act out when they return home that it is your ex's fault. Children need time to adjust. A transitional object they can take from home to home is a good idea (e.g., a favorite stuffed animal, a blanket, etc.).
11. *Do* put the needs of the children first when making arrangements for holidays and vacations. Be flexible and demonstrate your willingness to cooperate with your ex-spouse in front of the children.
12. *Do* set boundaries for your children and don't be afraid to discipline. Many single parents are afraid to discipline because they feel guilty for hurting their children by their decision to divorce. This does children no good. Especially with the transition of divorce, children need firm boundaries to help them feel secure. This means setting clear rules and consequences that are age appropriate, and also being clear with rewards for good behavior. Note: Discipline should never involve taking away daily quality time with a child.
13. *Do not* ask your children to carry messages or relay phone messages between you and your ex. You are the adult and need to do the negotiations for visitation times, school conferences, and so on. Your child should not have that responsibility. It puts your child in an adult position and is unhealthy for the family.
14. *Do* assume that you can have a healthy family after divorce. Most people mistakenly view divorce as giving one a broken home. There is transition, but not breakage. Children have a good chance to grow up to be healthy adults, especially if you work on their behalf to deal with the divorce and be a healthy adult yourself. Consider that your child now has a binuclear family—two homes with two loving adults.

Hecker, L. L., & Sori, C. F. (2007). Dos and don'ts of divorced parents. In L. L. Hecker, C. F. Sori, & Associates, *The therapist's notebook, volume 2: More homework, handouts, and activities for use in psychotherapy* (pp. 187-191). Binghamton, NY: The Haworth Press.

15. *Do* take care of yourself. If you are constantly tired, you are doing your children no favors. Try to take some time for yourself each day, even if it is just fifteen minutes. Follow up on health issues. This is even more important now that you are a single parent.

16. *Do not* stay in the legal system any longer than needed. The legal system is by nature adversarial; your postdivorce family needs to be cooperative. To continue with an adversarial stance can do long-term damage to your family. Give in on issues that are not that important in the larger scope of things. Do not give in on things that have lifelong ramifications that you will have a hard time living with.

17. *Do not* put your child in the parent's role. A parentified child is one who acts in the parent role. It is an unhealthy role for a child because it thwarts development as a child. Do not have your older child do too much parenting; the older children should not have to do any more parenting than absolutely necessary, and they need to know they are acting under your direction, not theirs. In addition, do not confide in your children as if they were your friends. Children may like the feeling of power being your confidant gives, but again, this truncates their growth and development and robs them of the chance to experience a childhood with a parent who establishes clear boundaries, rules, and consequences.

18. *Do* remember children have a social life too. Not every weekend should be totally family focused, as this would not be a normal family life. Children have social lives that need to be tended to, and adults need to allow them to have some independence. While the adult might not like that the child is occupied, or may wish to spend time with the child, the child's developmental needs trump the adult's wishes.

19. *Do* keep a calendar clearly marked with the parenting time arrangements so children will know when they will be with each parent.

20. *Do* give children plenty of advance notice when they will be leaving your home. You would not like to have to unexpectedly pack up what you are doing in the middle of something, nor will your children. This will decrease problems with the transition between homes as well.

21. *Do not* treat your child as a guest in your home. Do normal things, and have normal rituals and routines for the child. Carry on some family rituals and traditions, and involve children in making some new ones as you wish. Chores and rules need to be in place in both homes; the more similar the better, but consistency of rules is more important than similarity.

22. *Do not* ask your children about the activities of your ex-spouse. They will feel pressured by this and it puts them in a loyalty conflict to be loyal to you and tell you, thereby being disloyal to their other parent; or, if they keep information from you, they will fear being disloyal to you. It is a no-win situation for the child.

23. *Do not* let the children play you and your ex against each other. If children see a crack in a sidewalk, they will drive a bulldozer through it. Be sure you are coordinating parenting decisions as needed to keep this from occurring. Children may also bait you as they do in one-parent homes. They may say, "Well, Mom said it was okay," when indeed Mom did not say it was okay, and vice versa with Dad. If children begin acting out, it is even more important that you coordinate parenting with your ex. If your child is acting out, he or she needs you. You can't put your energy into fighting your ex without your own child suffering.

24. *Do not* expose your children to a new lover in your life, unless you are sure it is going to be a long-term relationship for you. If you allow this, your children will likely get attached to this new person, only to be left. They may reexperience being left in the same way their other parent left them. Do not have overnight visits with your boyfriend/girlfriend.

25. *Do not* expect your children to be as excited as you are about a new love in your life. Children may experience this as a threat to the time and attention they spend with you. Be sure to spend individual time with each child every week.

26. *Do* provide your child with ample love and individual attention during and after the transition of the divorce.

Hecker, L. L., & Sori, C. F. (2007). Dos and don'ts of divorced parents. In L. L. Hecker, C. F. Sori, & Associates, *The therapist's notebook, volume 2: More homework, handouts, and activities for use in psychotherapy* (pp. 187-191). Binghamton, NY: The Haworth Press.

27. *Do* work toward the goal of eventually letting go of any anger and blame you feel toward your ex-spouse, as this poisons you and will consequently affect your children. Express these feelings appropriately to caring adults, but do not allow your life to be organized around anger or revenge toward your ex-spouse. Instead, decide what should be central in your life and how you (not your ex) can be in charge of your emotions.

28. *Do* reframe your coparenting relationship as more of a business relationship. It may be advisable to arrange to pick up or drop off children in a neutral place, such as a fast-food restaurant. Be as pleasant and reassuring as possible during these exchanges.

29. *Do* assure your children that you will be enjoying yourself while they are visiting the other parent so they do not worry about you and can enjoy their time in the other home.

Hecker, L. L., & Sori, C. F. (2007). Dos and don'ts of divorced parents. In L. L. Hecker, C. F. Sori, & Associates, *The therapist's notebook, volume 2: More homework, handouts, and activities for use in psychotherapy* (pp. 187-191). Binghamton, NY: The Haworth Press.

26

Stepfamilies

Catherine Ford Sori
Lorna L. Hecker

Type of Contribution: *Handout*

Objectives

The purpose of this handout is to help adults and children adjust throughout the stages of stepfamily development. These guidelines provide a psychoeducational tool for therapists to use to help clients become aware of and avoid some of the common problems and pitfalls that plague many stepfamilies. Many adults enter into stepfamilies expecting children to share the same excitement about the new relationship that they do, while children may see the new marriage as a loss, not necessarily as a happy event. There is a minority for whom the transition to a stepfamily goes smoothly; this chapter is written for the majority of families who are faced with making a vast life transition with children who have burgeoning emotions.

Rationale for Use

Stepfamilies have many unrealistic expectations placed upon them by society and few resources from which to build a healthy family (see Hecker & Sori, 2006; Sori & Hecker, 2003; Visher & Visher, 1988). Often clinicians who treat stepfamilies make the mistake of trying to treat them like first-married families, ignoring many of the characteristics and problems that are unique to remarried families. This handout can be used as both a guide for clinicians to help identify some of the most critical and common pitfalls faced by stepfamilies, and also provides stepparents with practical advice and tips on how to form and maintain a healthy stepfamily.

Instructions

The handout can be used in couple or family sessions, or out of session as a psycheducational tool. It can also be used in a couples group therapy format.

Each adult should be given a copy of the handout, and clinicians should carefully go over each item, noting which areas may be particularly problematic for the family and should be addressed in follow-up sessions. Extra copies may be provided for ex-spouses who do not attend sessions and may be useful to motivate ex-spouses to attend a session if deemed helpful.

Suggestions for Follow-Up

After discussing the stepfamily handout with clients, clinicians should review how clients are following the guidelines throughout the course of therapy. It is important to note any hot issues

The Therapist's Notebook, Volume 2
doi:10.1300/5550_26

that arise or instances where couples have a difficult time implementing the suggestions. It is even more important to note times when families are able to follow the guidelines and to emphasize strengths and evidences of resiliency among children, adults, and the stepfamily as a whole. Often couples benefit from bibliotherapy, and *How to Win As a Stepfamily* by Emily and John Visher (1991) is especially recommended as an additional tool.

Contraindications

None noted. However, therapists should not allow parents to use the handout to blame or criticize ex-spouses for not following the guidelines in front of children.

References

Hecker, L. L., & Sori, C. F. (2006). Divorce and stepfamily issues. In C. F. Sori (Ed.), *Engaging children in family therapy: Creative approaches to integrating theory and research in clinical practice* (pp. 177-204). New York: Routledge.

Sori, C. F., & Hecker, L. L. (2003). Ten commandments for stepfamilies. In C. F. Sori, L. L. Hecker, & Associates, *The therapist's notebook for children and adolescents: Homework, handouts, and activities for use in psychotherapy* (pp. 330-335). Binghamton, NY: The Haworth Press.

Visher, E. B., & Visher, J. S. (1988). *Old loyalties, new ties: Therapeutic strategies with stepfamilies.* New York: Brunner/Mazel.

Visher, E. B., & Visher, J. S. (1991). *How to win as a stepfamily* (2nd ed.). New York: Brunner/Mazel.

Professional Readings and Resources

Bray, J. H. (1995). Children in stepfamilies: Assessment and treatment issues. In D. K. Huntley (Ed.), *Understanding stepfamilies: Implications for assessment and treatment* (pp. 59-72). Alexandria, VA: American Counseling Association.

Dunn, J. (2002). The adjustment of children in stepfamilies: Lessons from community studies. *Child and Adolescent Mental Health, 7*(4), 154-161.

Hecker, L. L., & Sori, C. F. (2006). Divorce and stepfamily issues. In C. F. Sori (Ed.), *Engaging children in family therapy: Creative approaches to integrating theory and research in clinical practice* (pp. 177-204). New York: Routledge.

Papernow, P. L. (1995). What's going on here? Separating (and weaving together) step and clinical issues in remarried families. In D. K. Huntley (Ed.), *Understanding stepfamilies: Implications for assessment and treatment* (pp. 3-24). Alexandria, VA: American Counseling Association.

Pasley, K., & Dollahite, D. C. (1995). The nine Rs of stepparenting adolescents: Research-based recommendations for clinicians. In D. K. Huntley (Ed.), *Understanding stepfamilies: Implications for assessment and treatment* (pp. 87-98). Alexandria, VA: American Counseling Association.

Pasley, K., Dollahite, D. C., & Ihinger-Tallman, M. (1993). Bridging the gap: Clinical applications of research findings on the spouse and stepparent roles in remarriage. *Family Relations, 42,* 315-322.

Pasley, K., & Ihinger-Tallman, M. (1992). Remarriage and stepparenting: What the literature has added to our understanding of this family form. *Family Science Review, 5*(3/4), 153-174.

Visher, J. (1994). Stepfamilies: A work in progress. *The American Journal of Family Therapy, 22*(4), 337-344.

Visher, E. B., & Visher, J. S. (1988). *Old loyalties, new ties: Therapeutic strategies with stepfamilies*. New York: Brunner/Mazel.

Visher, J. S., & Visher, E. B. (1989). Parenting coalitions after remarriage: Dynamic and therapeutic guidelines. *Family Relations, 38*, 65-70.

Visher, E. B., & Visher, J. S. (1990). Dynamics of successful stepfamilies. *Journal of Divorce and Remarriage, 14*(1), 3-11.

Visher, E. B., & Visher, J. S. (1995). Avoiding the mine fields of stepfamily therapy. In D. K. Huntley (Ed.), *Understanding stepfamilies: Implications for assessment and treatment* (pp. 25-34). Alexandria, VA: American Counseling Association.

Bibliotherapy Sources for Clients

Books for Children

Brown, L. K., & Brown, M. (1988). *Dinosaurs divorce: A guide for changing families*. Boston: Little, Brown.

Cain, B. S. (1990). *Double-dip feelings: Stories to help children understand emotions*. New York: Magination Press.

Evans, M. S. (1986). *This is me and my two families: An awareness scrapbook/journal for children living in stepfamilies*. New York: Magination Press.

Girard, L. W. (1987). *At Daddy's on Saturdays*. Morton Grove, IL: Albert Whitman.

Resources for Parents

Burns, C. (1986). *Stepmotherhood*. New York: Perennial Library.

Learning to Step Together. Palo Alto, CA: Stepfamily Association of America.

Mala, B. (1989). *Stepfamilies stepping ahead*. Lincoln, NE: Stepfamily Association of America.

Prilik, P. (1990). *Stepmothering—Another kind of love*. New York: Berkely.

Savage, K., & Adams, P. (1988). *The good stepmother*. New York: Crowne.

Stepfamily Association of America, Inc., 215 Centennial Mall South, Lincoln, NE 68505-1834.

Visher, E. B., & Visher, J. S. (1991). *How to win as a stepfamily*. New York: Brunner-Mazel.

HANDOUT 26.1

HEALTHY STEPFAMILY GUIDELINES

1. *Parents Should Be Partners First.* It is important to spend time together to strengthen your relationship as a couple. Spending time in activities you enjoyed together while dating and making efforts to keep the romance alive is the first crucial step in building a strong stepfamily. Time should be spent together weekly focusing on each other and *not* on problems or child-related issues. Spending positive time together is like putting money in the bank to be used when stressful issues arise (and they *will* arise!). Carve out time for yourselves; planning couple-only time is essential. Often babysitting can be exchanged with friends or families, and if money is tight, the date may be a quiet evening spent in front of the fire, holding hands and sharing dreams.

2. *Adjusting and Stabilizing.* One of the first tasks for new stepfamilies is for all family members to adjust to the many changes that occur when parents with children remarry. It is important for parents to establish the rules in a new household that includes children from previous relationships, with great sensitivity to how children often resent any new rules or ways of family life that are different from those to which they are accustomed. Each spouse brings at least two family histories (from their families of origin and from their first marriages) and unwritten rules and expectations as to how families should function, relate, and behave. Couples must recognize the loyalty each feels from their past and how they likely view their *own way* as the right way to be, before they can negotiate the rules and roles for their new stepfamily.

   New stepfamilies need time to adapt and create stabilization, and this is necessary before focusing on building relationships between stepparents and stepchildren. You may want to discuss and write down what each of your dreams is for your new family. In addition, you will want to discuss what rules are negotiable, nonnegotiable, or can be discarded. For example, a rule about clean rooms may be negotiable, but a rule about a teen staying out past a certain hour may not be negotiable. Some old rules from your previous family may simply no longer fit your new family and can be discarded.

3. *Give Relationships Time to Grow.* It is important to recognize that a spouse in a new stepfamily who has children from a previous relationship has a longer history of attachment, shared memories, and established roles and rituals than that of the newly wed couple. Children sometimes view the new stepparent as a threat to their close relationship with their parent—especially if they came from a single-parent household prior to the marriage. It takes time and care for attachment relationships to build—both between the couple, as well as between each stepparent and stepchild. Love between a stepparent and child is not spontaneous, so give it time to grow. Expecting instant love just because there is a marriage or stepfamily is unrealistic and creates unnecessary pressure and potential resentments.

4. *Avoid the "Don't Tell Me What to Do" Trap!* In new stepfamilies it is wise for the biological parent to do the majority of the parenting and disciplining for the first two years. This avoids another trap—where stepchildren often highly resent a stepparent who attempts to take over and tell them what to do. The stepparent's role during this time is twofold: (1) to support the parenting efforts of the biological parent, much like the cabinet supports and advises the president, or a babysitter who is temporarily in charge to follow the directives of the parents; (2) to begin to build one-on-one relationships with each stepchild by doing things together or spending time in pairs. These two steps are vital to lay the groundwork for successful co-parenting and harmonious stepfamily relationships.

5. *All for One, and One for All!* Children often complain to a biological parent about unfair treatment by a stepparent. Do not get pulled into an alliance with your child against your new spouse. Decide to support each other and act as a team, not taking sides with a child against a parent. Tell the child you support your spouse and will not listen to criticism, but will discuss

Sori, C. F., & Hecker, L. L. (2007). Stepfamilies. In L. L. Hecker, C. F. Sori, & Associates, *The therapist's notebook, volume 2: More homework, handouts, and activities for use in psychotherapy* (pp. 193-198). Binghamton, NY: The Haworth Press.

any complaints with your partner. Children feel secure when they see a good couple relationship that models a healthy boundary around the couple. Likewise, some stepparents can criticize a stepchild to their spouse. This is more likely to happen if the stepparent senses that their spouse's primary loyalty or affection lies with their child instead of them. Much of this can be avoided if spouses make a commitment to the primacy of their relationship—which hopefully will be strong long after the children leave home. Often it is better for a stepparent and stepchild to openly discuss their differences than to involve the biological parent in a triangle which forces him or her to choose sides.

6. *Kids' Transitions.* Be sensitive to how difficult it is for children to adapt to new family configurations—especially if they have gone through several transitions (for example, going from a first-married family to a single-parent family, moving, changing schools, and maybe even losing contact with a parent and extended family members). Expect that some children will regress by returning to behaviors from earlier stages of development that help them feel more secure. For example, some younger children may wet the bed or begin sucking their thumb again. Talking about these changes and encouraging children to share their reactions to these transitions and losses is vital in promoting children's healthy adjustment. Many children benefit from programs offered in schools; ask your child's school counselor or social worker if any programs are offered for children coping with loss or transitions.

7. *New Family Identity, Routines, and Rituals.* Once the stepfamily has some stability and has begun to foster ties among stepfamily members, you can focus on establishing your own unique identity. Children often have tremendous loyalties to their other parent and the routines and rituals of that household. Parents need to be sensitive and to incorporate routines and rituals from both former intact families as a way to help children identify with the new family. Learning what the daily routines for children were regarding bedtimes, tucking in, doing and checking homework, doing chores, and how free time was spent, and being cautious before changing these established routines can help children adjust to life in a new stepfamily. Openly discussing ethnic customs and how holidays and birthdays were celebrated in the past, and asking for input from children as to what they consider most important to incorporate in the new stepfamily can greatly increase a sense of belonging to the new family. For example, one new stepfamily where the children's mother had died was facing their first Thanksgiving together. Their mother had made a traditional ethnic bread, and that was what one preteen said she would miss the most. The family brainstormed and an aunt visited in order to teach the daughter how to make her mother's bread. The bread became a new ritual that bridged both families' traditions and helped identify how this new stepfamily celebrated Thanksgiving.

8. *Family Meetings.* It is wise to have regular family meetings that allow for input from everyone, including children who may only visit on weekends. Children may take turns chairing the meetings. Important topics include how space is configured and belongings are respected, rules, chores, and how to maximize resources for family enjoyment. For example, establishing a family night and allowing children to take turns choosing the family activity builds both respect and cohesion among family members. Children are often hypersensitive to the issue of fairness and should be allowed to give voice to any real or imagined injustices, and they are more likely to follow through on issues in which they have had input. Parents can function as benevolent dictators who listen and treat everyone with fairness, and who reserve the right to make final decisions based on the good of all.

9. *Easing Transitions.* Children who have shared custody or visitation are being asked to be exceptionally adaptive as they move in and out of homes that may have different and sometimes conflicting rules and expectations. Time should be taken to explain what is expected in each household and why, and parents should be sensitive to the difficulty some children experience in these ongoing transitions. Some children may act out before or after visiting a noncustodial parent, complain about that parent, or balk at coming back home. It is important to give the child the opportunity to express these feelings and any frustration at not having control over his or her own coming and going. If possible, parents can help by soothing their

Sori, C. F., & Hecker, L. L. (2007). Stepfamilies. In L. L. Hecker, C. F. Sori, & Associates, *The therapist's notebook, volume 2: More homework, handouts, and activities for use in psychotherapy* (pp. 193-198). Binghamton, NY: The Haworth Press.

children and by helping children learn how they can soothe themselves when upset or stressed. A transitional object, for example a teddy bear or favorite toy sent back and forth, may be helpful. Some children benefit from some alone time to decompress following a visit to the other parent's home. It is important to ask the child what would help in these transitions. Above all, avoid any open conflict with an ex-spouse whenever a child is being picked up or dropped off, as this intensifies split-loyalty conflicts that many children experience.

10. *"Surfing the Web" of New Steprelatives.* The web of relationships that often occurs in stepfamilies is difficult enough for adults to navigate, and can be much more confusing for children. Children may have new stepsiblings and stepparents at each parent's home. They may have several sets of new grandparents and extended family members, with whom they do not share a common history of shared memories or rituals. Some extended family members can be insensitive to stepchildren, especially during holiday or birthday celebrations. It is wise for stepparents to address this issue with their own families to help stepchildren begin to feel accepted in these extended stepfamily circles.

11. *"Good Fences Make Good Neighbors."* To paraphrase Robert Frost, fences make good boundaries that can improve relationships. This is especially true regarding relationships between divorced parents. Never criticize your ex-spouse in front of your children, and don't put your children in the position of sending messages back and forth over the fence. Talk directly to your ex-spouse regarding all matters involving your mutual children. Encourage your children to love their other biological parent. Sharing good memories about your former spouse and marriage, as well as what you loved about him or her, is a wonderful gift to give your children, and one that will help build their self-esteem and sense of trust.

12. *From Myth to Reality.* No family can live up to the unrealistic expectations of stepfamilies sometimes portrayed in the media, such as in TV's favorite stepfamily, the Brady Bunch. There are few real-life role models of healthy stepfamilies to follow, and too often couples mistakenly view stepfamilies and their complex relationships as the same as first-married families. Stepfamilies take time, commitment, and consistent hard work.

There are several books that can be helpful for adults as well as children, including the following.

Books for Children

Brown, L. K., & Brown, M. (1988). *Dinosaurs divorce: A guide for changing families.* Boston: Little, Brown.

Cain, B. S. (1990). *Double-dip feelings: Stories to help children understand emotions.* New York: Magination Press.

Evans, M. S. (1986). *This is me and my two families: An awareness scrapbook/journal for children living in stepfamilies.* New York: Magination Press.

Girard, L. W. (1987). *At Daddy's on Saturdays.* Morton Grove, IL: Albert Whitman.

Resources for Parents

Burns, C. (1986). *Stepmotherhood.* New York: Perennial Library.

Learning to Step Together. Palo Alto, CA: Stepfamily Association of America.

Mala, B. (1989). *Stepfamilies stepping ahead.* Lincoln, NE: Stepfamily Association of America.

Prilik, P. (1990). *Stepmothering—Another kind of love.* New York: Berkely.

Savage, K., & Adams, P. (1988). *The good stepmother.* New York: Crowne.

Stepfamily Association of America, Inc., 215 Centennial Mall South, Lincoln, NE 68505-1834.

Visher, E. B., & Visher, J. S. (1982). *How to win as a stepfamily.* New York: Brunner/Mazel.

Sori, C. F., & Hecker, L. L. (2007). Stepfamilies. In L. L. Hecker, C. F. Sori, & Associates, *The therapist's notebook, volume 2: More homework, handouts, and activities for use in psychotherapy* (pp. 193-198). Binghamton, NY: The Haworth Press.

27

Encouraging Children's Stories of Divorce

Nancee M. Biank

Catherine Ford Sori

Type of Contribution: *Handouts, Activity, Homework*

Objectives

These stories about children's experience of divorce can be used to stimulate children to express their feelings about events that are happening in their own family. As children draw pictures of and discuss their own experiences, the therapist can validate and normalize their feelings, and this information can be shared with parents. The stories themselves provide parents with several suggestions on how to help their children cope with the many difficulties that they are likely to encounter as they go through the divorce process. The completed pictures can be compiled into a story notebook that can be sent home each week for parents to use with their children between sessions. These stories can be used in family therapy, individual child sessions, or groups for children coping with divorce.

Rationale for Use

Divorce is a difficult experience for children as well as adults. Children often feel helpless simply because they have little input or control over all the decisions that must be made during a divorce. This feeling of helplessness can cause children to behave in ways in which they have never acted before. Some children become defiant, others lethargic and withdrawn, while still others strive for perfection.

During the stress of divorce, parents are by nature less available to their children. This can cause them to overlook children's needs at a crucial point in their development. Children can interpret this preoccupation as abandonment, and they may feel they have no one to turn to who can help them address their feelings and fears.

A combination of feeling helpless and abandoned is difficult to overcome. Children usually rationalize a solution by blaming themselves for their predicament. This provides them with a sense of control, and answers the question, "Why is this happening to me?"

Sometimes the above situation can resolve itself as parents get back on track and reestablish good parenting. Other times this situation lingers as the divorce process is prolonged for months or even years, and the fighting continues.

Two years of a parent's life that is preoccupied with a divorce can seem like a long time, but two years in the life of a six-year-old is one-third of their existence. This pressure and stress can have long-lasting effects on a child if not dealt with appropriately. Seeking the help of a skilled mental health professional can relieve some of the stress for children and help normalize their

The Therapist's Notebook, Volume 2
doi:10.1300/5550_27

feelings. It can also provide children with an opportunity to express their needs. Divorce means lifetime change for everyone, including the children.

The divorce stories that follow are basically designed to allow children to verbally and artistically express how they may be feeling regarding various aspects of their parents' divorce. The stories are designed to stimulate conversation between the child, therapist, and parents regarding the child's own unique experiences and emotions. They also guide children and parents to begin the healing process through both intimate communication and exploring coping skills.

This activity can be used in family therapy or children's groups. However, children often are initially reluctant to share their worries or feelings with parents, either because they don't want to cause a parent further pain or stress, or because they fear further emotional abandonment. Often it is useful to begin this activity in individual time with children in order to normalize and validate their feelings and to prepare them to share their stories with parents. Parents can also be educated about common reactions of children of divorce, and coached on how to support their child, address their concerns, and parent in a way that fosters emotional intelligence (see Gottman & DeClaire, 1996).

As therapists read the stories with children, they can encourage the children to share aspects of their own stories that may be similar to or different from what Jason or Allison experienced. They are encouraged to draw pictures to represent their own unique experiences and may add text to explain their drawings. Children's experiences and feelings can be validated, and they can be encouraged to share and discuss their stories with their parents.

Instructions

When children come into therapy, introduce the book to them and ask if they'd like to draw a picture about the pages you are reading. The pictures stimulate conversation, and the conversation is really what is important because it allows the therapist to discover what children are feeling about their own specific situation. Sections of the story are used over time, as it would be too overwhelming for a young child to draw all of the pictures in one setting. Children can make a notebook in which they add pages as they progress through therapy. In sessions with parents, children can be supported and encouraged to talk to their parent about their drawings.

Each story has a special emphasis. The Jason story (Handout 27.1) concentrates more on distress within the family and how a child can feel ignored or abandoned during this time. This story helps to alert parents to children's reactions to conflict and helps to refocus attention on children's needs during this difficult time. In the Jason story the child writes a letter to his parent at the end, and child clients are encouraged to do the same. This is another method to help the therapist understand what the child needs, and to examine the family dynamics through the eyes of the child. Children can read their letter to parents, and parents can write letters in response, which can be read and discussed in family sessions.

In the Allison story (Handout 27.2), families can be taught coping mechanisms that can help with issues regarding transitions in living arrangements. Coping mechanisms to help children through transitions are included in the stories, which, in effect, teach parents what the children need. The story can help therapists emphasize concrete things parents can do to help their children cope. For example, parents can help a child deal with loneliness by reading the child's favorite story into a tape recorder so the child can take it to the other parent's house and listen to it when the child is missing that parent. Together a parent and child can make a photograph book of the child's life that is continuous from birth to the present and includes transitions. The therapist can facilitate this by encouraging parents to bring pictures to a family session, where the photograph album can be constructed. The therapist can foster conversations that highlight the parents' ongoing love and delight in their child, that emphasize a promise of continued love and support, and that look to a future that holds bright promise of hope and happiness for the child.

This album provides the child with documentation of his or her life, whether the parents are together or not. Blank pages can be provided for children and parents to complete in the future.

Brief Vignette

Six-year-old Elnora was brought in for therapy by her mother, who was in the process of divorcing her husband. Elnora had been a vibrant, outgoing child until recent months. Following the separation, her father had lost his job and had moved in with a friend until he could find employment. Although he called her regularly and wanted her to visit, Elnora seemed uninterested in even talking to him on the phone. She had become increasingly withdrawn and reluctant to go to school, play outside, or be with friends. In sessions with her mother, Elnora was quiet and uncommunicative, and was unwilling to talk about events in her life.

Elnora agreed to meet with the therapist alone for part of a session, and the therapist asked if she would like to hear a story. The therapist began reading the story of Allison. After just a few pages, Elnora began to see things through the eyes of Allison. Suddenly she burst into conversation about her own story, because she identified with Allison. She took the book home with her and read it several times. The story validated Elnora's own feelings, and this empowered her to talk about her experience. Her feelings about herself changed.

The therapist met with each parent individually and educated them about children's common reactions to divorce, and what they might do to help their daughter (see "Parents' Guide to Good Divorce Behavior," Hecker & Sori, Chapter 25, this volume). In a family session, Elnora shared her own story and illustrations with her parents, so they could understand and talk with her directly about her feelings. In one session with just her father, Elnora brought in her favorite storybook, and the therapist recorded her father's voice reading the story, which Elnora played at home whenever she missed him. He soon found another job and was able to rent a small two-bedroom apartment. He allowed Elnora to help decorate her own room, and in a session with her mom, Elnora discussed which toys she wanted to leave at her new house with Dad. Her parents were able to support Elnora and address her worries and concerns. Gradually, Elnora began to enjoy school and friends once again, and looked forward to regular visits and calls from her father.

Suggestions for Follow-Up

This activity is used on an ongoing basis. Since feelings can change, it can also serve as a measuring stick to determine ongoing experiences of children going through a divorce experience. At termination, the booklet can be used to review a child and family's progress in therapy. Blank pages can be included for children and their parents to complete as new events unfold in the child's life.

Contraindications

There are no known contraindications for this activity. However, therapists should always be careful not to assume every child will feel like the children in the stories, since every child and every child's experience is unique. The stories should be used to invite children to share experiences that are similar as well as different, but never to suggest to children how they should be reacting to a divorce situation.

Professional Readings and Resources

Gottman, J. M., & DeClaire, J. (1996). *The heart of parenting.* New York: Simon & Schuster.

Wallerstein, J., Lewis, J. M., & Blakeslee, S. (2001). *The unexpected legacy of divorce: A 25 year landmark study.* New York: Hyperion.

Bibliotherapy Source for Adult Clients

Wallerstein, J., Lewis, J. M., & Blakeslee, S. (2001). *The unexpected legacy of divorce: A 25 year landmark study.* New York: Hyperion.

Bibliotherapy Sources for Children

Brown, L. K., & Brown, M. (1986). *Dinosaurs divorce: A guide for changing families.* Boston: Little, Brown.

Ives, S. B., Fassler, D., & Lash, M. (1994). *The divorce workbook: A guide for kids and families.* Burlington, VT: Waterfront.

CHILDREN OF DIVORCE—JASON AND HIS FAMILY

Once upon a time, there was a boy named Jason. He lived with his mother and father. He was very unhappy because his parents were always fighting.

Jason was also sad and confused. He thought that maybe if he was very helpful, his parents would stop fighting. He would set the table, clean his room, and try to be extra good. No matter how good he was, his parents kept fighting.

Biank, N. M., & Sori, C. F. (2007). Encouraging children's stories of divorce. In L. L. Hecker, C. F. Sori, & Associates, *The therapist's notebook, volume 2: More homework, handouts, and activities for use in psychotherapy* (pp. 199-222). Binghamton, NY: The Haworth Press.

Things got worse. Jason's parents tried to get along, but they just could not. Finally, they told Jason they had decided to get a divorce. Jason was not sure what a divorce was, but he knew it must be something pretty bad because his mom and dad told him that they would not be living together anymore.

Now Jason was very confused. He had so many questions.

Biank, N. M., & Sori, C. F. (2007). Encouraging children's stories of divorce. In L. L. Hecker, C. F. Sori, & Associates, *The therapist's notebook, volume 2: More homework, handouts, and activities for use in psychotherapy* (pp. 199-222). Binghamton, NY: The Haworth Press.

Jason hated everything about the divorce. He hated it so much that he started to act angry and do naughty things.

Even with the decision to divorce, Jason's parents continued to fight. Now they were fighting about money, the house, and even about Jason.

Biank, N. M., & Sori, C. F. (2007). Encouraging children's stories of divorce. In L. L. Hecker, C. F. Sori, & Associates, *The therapist's notebook, volume 2: More homework, handouts, and activities for use in psychotherapy* (pp. 199-222). Binghamton, NY: The Haworth Press.

Watching his parents act this way was upsetting to Jason. Not only was Jason confused, sad, and frightened, he was very angry. Sometimes he felt like crying and other times he felt like punching something.

However, most of the time he just wished that his parents would stop fighting and act nicer to each other.

Biank, N. M., & Sori, C. F. (2007). Encouraging children's stories of divorce. In L. L. Hecker, C. F. Sori, & Associates, *The therapist's notebook, volume 2: More homework, handouts, and activities for use in psychotherapy* (pp. 199-222). Binghamton, NY: The Haworth Press.

Jason's parents noticed that he was changing. He was no longer his helpful self. They became concerned. They decided to go visit Miss Anne, a counselor who helps children when their parents are divorcing.

Miss Anne met with Jason's parents and also with Jason. She talked and played games with Jason. Sometimes she even helped the parents stop fighting.

Biank, N. M., & Sori, C. F. (2007). Encouraging children's stories of divorce. In L. L. Hecker, C. F. Sori, & Associates, *The therapist's notebook, volume 2: More homework, handouts, and activities for use in psychotherapy* (pp. 199-222). Binghamton, NY: The Haworth Press.

Sometimes there was nothing that even Miss Anne could do. This helped Jason understand that the fighting was not his fault, because even another grown-up could not change the way his parents acted.

Jason began thinking. He understood that their fighting was not his fault, but he wanted his parents to know something about him.

Biank, N. M., & Sori, C. F. (2007). Encouraging children's stories of divorce. In L. L. Hecker, C. F. Sori, & Associates, *The therapist's notebook, volume 2: More homework, handouts, and activities for use in psychotherapy* (pp. 199-222). Binghamton, NY: The Haworth Press.

Jason talked with Miss Anne. They decided that she would help him write a letter to his mother and father.

Jason wrote:

Biank, N. M., & Sori, C. F. (2007). Encouraging children's stories of divorce. In L. L. Hecker, C. F. Sori, & Associates, *The therapist's notebook, volume 2: More homework, handouts, and activities for use in psychotherapy* (pp. 199-222). Binghamton, NY: The Haworth Press.

Jason felt better after he wrote his letter. He knew that his parents would not change, but now at least he was able to tell them what he needed. Being able to talk with Miss Anne and write about his feelings helped him learn more about the family.

Would you like to write or draw something about divorce?

Biank, N. M., & Sori, C. F. (2007). Encouraging children's stories of divorce. In L. L. Hecker, C. F. Sori, & Associates, *The therapist's notebook, volume 2: More homework, handouts, and activities for use in psychotherapy* (pp. 199-222). Binghamton, NY: The Haworth Press.

HANDOUT 27.2

ALLISON DISCOVERS WAYS TO FEEL BETTER

Once upon a time, there was a little girl named Allison. She was a very happy little girl. She loved her mother and father very much and they loved her. Allison spent much time with her parents.

Then one day things began to change. Mom and Dad did not talk to each other much. Sometimes Dad would come home very late. Sometimes Mom would talk on the telephone for hours. No one seemed to have much time for Allison anymore.

Biank, N. M. , & Sori, C. F. (2007). Encouraging children's stories of divorce. In L. L. Hecker, C. F. Sori, & Associates, *The therapist's notebook, volume 2: More homework, handouts, and activities for use in psychotherapy* (pp. 199-222). Binghamton, NY: The Haworth Press.

Allison did not know what was happening, but it did not feel right. Allison thought that maybe her parents did not like her anymore, or that she had done something very wrong to make them angry.

Soon, Mom and Dad took Allison for a walk. Allison thought that maybe her parents were going to be fun, just like before, but she was wrong.

Biank, N. M., & Sori, C. F. (2007). Encouraging children's stories of divorce. In L. L. Hecker, C. F. Sori, & Associates, *The therapist's notebook, volume 2: More homework, handouts, and activities for use in psychotherapy* (pp. 199-222). Binghamton, NY: The Haworth Press.

Mom and Dad told Allison that they had some sad news. Mom said, "Allison, Daddy and I love you very much, but we do not love each other anymore." Dad said, "Allison, we tried to love each other again, but it just did not work out. Mom and Dad are not going to live together anymore. We are getting a divorce."

Allison started to cry. She did not understand everything, but she knew that her family was changing. Dad told her that she would now have two houses, because he was going to move.

Biank, N. M., & Sori, C. F. (2007). Encouraging children's stories of divorce. In L. L. Hecker, C. F. Sori, & Associates, *The therapist's notebook, volume 2: More homework, handouts, and activities for use in psychotherapy* (pp. 199-222). Binghamton, NY: The Haworth Press.

Allison was confused. She did not want her Dad to leave. She thought, "Why is this happening to me? I am good! I love my mom and dad! Why can't they love each other? Why can't things stay the same?

Allison no longer felt happy. She was sad and angry and confused. She did not even want to play with her best friend.

Biank, N. M., & Sori, C. F. (2007). Encouraging children's stories of divorce. In L. L. Hecker, C. F. Sori, & Associates, *The therapist's notebook, volume 2: More homework, handouts, and activities for use in psychotherapy* (pp. 199-222). Binghamton, NY: The Haworth Press.

Soon, Dad moved to an apartment. Allison had a place to sleep there, but it was not like her own bedroom.

When she was with Dad, she missed Mom. When she was with Mom, she missed Dad. She was always missing somebody!

Biank, N. M., & Sori, C. F. (2007). Encouraging children's stories of divorce. In L. L. Hecker, C. F. Sori, & Associates, *The therapist's notebook, volume 2: More homework, handouts, and activities for use in psychotherapy* (pp. 199-222). Binghamton, NY: The Haworth Press.

Sometimes Dad would call and she would not talk with him because it made her sad to hear his voice.

At other times, she would call him and he would not be home. "This stinks!" she said. Allison was both sad and mad.

Biank, N. M., & Sori, C. F. (2007). Encouraging children's stories of divorce. In L. L. Hecker, C. F. Sori, & Associates, *The therapist's notebook, volume 2: More homework, handouts, and activities for use in psychotherapy* (pp. 199-222). Binghamton, NY: The Haworth Press.

One day, Allison began to cry. It felt like she could not stop. Mom tried to comfort her and tell her that it would be all right, just a little different. But Allison cried even more. She wanted her family back.

Allison's mother and father decided to talk with a counselor who specialized in helping families that are divorcing. Her name was Miss Judy. She met with Allison's parents and also with Allison.

Biank, N. M., & Sori, C. F. (2007). Encouraging children's stories of divorce. In L. L. Hecker, C. F. Sori, & Associates, *The therapist's notebook, volume 2: More homework, handouts, and activities for use in psychotherapy* (pp. 199-222). Binghamton, NY: The Haworth Press.

She played games and told stories to Allison that helped her understand that her mom and dad still loved her very much, but that sometimes grown-ups have problems that are not easy to solve.

Miss Judy helped Allison's mom and dad understand that Allison was a little girl who needed lots of love. She also said that Allison needed both a mom and dad for a very long time. Miss Judy then asked to meet with Allison and her mom and dad.

Biank, N. M., & Sori, C. F. (2007). Encouraging children's stories of divorce. In L. L. Hecker, C. F. Sori, & Associates, *The therapist's notebook, volume 2: More homework, handouts, and activities for use in psychotherapy* (pp. 199-222). Binghamton, NY: The Haworth Press.

The family came to talk with Miss Judy. She talked about divorcing families and love, and then said, "Let's do something to help Allison remember how much you, Mom and Dad, love her." Miss Judy asked, "How can we make Allison's new bedroom feel more like home?"

The family decided that Allison should bring some of her favorite toys over to Dad's house. She even decided to bring some of her clothes to hang in the closet. Now she really did have two houses.

Biank, N. M., & Sori, C. F. (2007). Encouraging children's stories of divorce. In L. L. Hecker, C. F. Sori, & Associates, *The therapist's notebook, volume 2: More homework, handouts, and activities for use in psychotherapy* (pp. 199-222). Binghamton, NY: The Haworth Press.

Miss Judy asked Mom and Dad to make a special picture album for Allison. This could be something that she could carry with her from house to house. She could also add new pictures any time that she wanted. The family made the album. Allison loved it. This helped Allison remember that her family had just changed. It did not disappear.

Allison was beginning to feel better. She did not cry as often. However, there was one more thing that she needed to talk with Miss Judy about. Allison sometimes missed her dad very much. She also wondered if Dad forgot about her when she was not with him. What could she do?

    Biank, N. M., & Sori, C. F. (2007). Encouraging children's stories of divorce. In L. L. Hecker, C. F. Sori, & Associates, *The therapist's notebook, volume 2: More homework, handouts, and activities for use in psychotherapy* (pp. 199-222). Binghamton, NY: The Haworth Press.

Miss Judy thought for a moment. Then she said, "Allison, the next time that you see Dad, bring your favorite books. You and Dad can tape record Dad reading your favorite story." Miss Judy then called Dad and told him about her suggestion. Dad thought that it was a great idea.

Allison came with her books and Dad had the tape recorder ready. They also made a tape of Allison singing songs, so that Dad could have it. Now Allison was pleased. She could listen to Dad anytime that she wanted. She also knew that Dad could listen to her. She no longer had to worry that he might forget her sweet voice.

Biank, N. M., & Sori, C. F. (2007). Encouraging children's stories of divorce. In L. L. Hecker, C. F. Sori, & Associates, *The therapist's notebook, volume 2: More homework, handouts, and activities for use in psychotherapy* (pp. 199-222). Binghamton, NY: The Haworth Press.

Allison is happier now. Things are not the same, but they have gotten better. Allison knows that she still has a family that cares very much and continues to love her. It has just changed.

Biank, N. M., & Sori, C. F. (2007). Encouraging children's stories of divorce. In L. L. Hecker, C. F. Sori, & Associates, *The therapist's notebook, volume 2: More homework, handouts, and activities for use in psychotherapy* (pp. 199-222). Binghamton, NY: The Haworth Press.

28

Using Movie Clips to Facilitate Discussion in the Postdivorce Family

Christie Eppler
Christopher Latty

Many important adaptive tasks face the postdivorce family (Kaslow & Schwartz, 1987; Peck & Manocherian, 1989; Schwartz & Kaslow, 1997; Wallerstein & Kelly, 1980). The modified family must establish new boundaries and build effective communication strategies to thrive after the divorce. Forming a new family structure is often a difficult task, and many postdivorce families seek family therapy following marriage dissolution.

In order to facilitate discussion in divorced families with school-aged children, the therapist may use typical family therapy strategies (e.g., joining, empathy, and circular questioning) to create dialogue about family functioning. However, many children are not responsive to directly talking about their thoughts and feelings. Displacing a child's situation onto a fictional character may ease the child into expressing his or her own story (Kalter, 1990). Additionally, bibliotherapy, or using literature as a therapeutic intervention, assists in displacement and teaches clients new information about their presenting problems, which encourages insight and understanding (Pardeck, 1990; Riordan & Wilson, 1989; Rubin, 1978). However, popular literature suggests that in today's fast-paced society, clients may not have the time to read and movies are a more efficient medium to present information (Hesley, 2000).

Objective

Showing movie segments in-session or assigning video viewing as homework accomplishes many therapeutic objectives. The video clips normalize clients' experiences by showing them that many of their problems are typical of postdivorce families. The video clips spark solutions by either suggesting appropriate behavior or creating an atmosphere where problems can be solved through dialogue. Additionally, the video clips may help clients see a problem that they were unable to face when looking directly at self and family.

Instructions for Using Video Clips in Therapy

When selecting the specific movie or video clip, it is important for the therapist to first determine the salient theme that the video will address (i.e., visitation logistics, emotions surrounding the divorce, sense of responsibility, etc.). Once the therapist has assessed the family's pattern of functioning, the therapist may intervene by showing a scene from a movie in session or by assigning family members to watch the film before the next session. Asking the family to view a movie between sessions may serve the dual purpose of creating a time when families share an activity while exposing them to information relevant for family development. In addition, fam-

The Therapist's Notebook, Volume 2

ily members who do not usually attend sessions could be included in the assignment. For example, a therapist may assign children to watch the video with the parent who does not attend conjoint sessions. After the clients watch the video or see the video clip, the therapist uses the next session or the remaining portion of the session, respectively, to debrief concepts germane to the postdivorce family's functioning (described below).

When choosing a movie or a segment, it is important to pick the right clip from the right movie. Cornett and Cornett (1980) suggest that the literature used in bibliotherapy should promote optimism, humor, abstract thinking, values clarification, empathy, and creative problem solving. These same principles apply when choosing video clips. Two movies that address divorce-related issues are *Stepmom* (Barnathan & Columbus, 1998) and *Mrs. Doubtfire* (Bradshaw & Columbus, 1993). These movies take both a serious and a lighthearted approach to divorce and postdivorce family adaptation.

A common situation with families who have experienced divorce is that one parent will talk negatively about the other in the presence of the children. Two critical scenes in *Mrs. Doubtfire* portray this interaction. Once scene takes place after the parents separate and the father is eating dinner with his children (twenty-seven minutes into the film). The father calls the mother a battle-ax and wishes that she would become ill. When the mother arrives at the father's apartment to pick the children up earlier than the agreed-upon time, the parents disagree about parenting styles and their conversation escalates into a fight that the children observe. In another scene with the same theme (forty-two minutes into the film), the mother tells the potential nanny (the father in disguise) that she wishes her ex-husband would get "a job and a decent apartment." The nanny politely admonishes the mother to step out of the room "before verbally bashing [the children's] father."

After showing either of these clips, the therapist could facilitate discussion related to what it is like for children to see parents fight or to hear negative thoughts about their other parent. Using displacement, the therapist could ask the clients what they thought the children in the film were feeling. The therapist could also direct a private conversation with the parents regarding establishing healthy boundaries by pointing out the inappropriateness of fighting when children are present, putting the other parent on the spot, not respecting the custody arrangement, not sabotaging the other's parenting efforts, and talking to each other about the children in a calm manner.

Another important issue for divorcing parents to address is that the separation is not the fault of the children. Parents need to reassure their kids that the children are not to blame. Both *Mrs. Doubtfire* and *Stepmom* address this issue. In *Mrs. Doubtfire* (twenty minutes into the film), as the father leaves home, the son says, "It is all my fault." The father replies, "You did nothing wrong." Similarly, a pivotal scene from *Stepmom* (seventeen minutes into the film) portrays a father discussing his divorce with his two children, highlighting that the children are not responsible for the divorce. As the father takes the children for a walk by a lake, he gently tells them that the divorce is not their responsibility, nor will he stop loving them although he no longer loves their mother in the way he used to.

After viewing one or both of these clips, the therapist and family may discuss the strengths of these scenes such as: (a) the father used child-friendly language to explain that the children are not responsible for the parents' breakup; (b) the parent answered the children's questions honestly and directly; (c) the dad explained to the children that he will always love them; (d) the father reassured the children that the divorce was not their fault and that they could not repair the marriage; and (e) the father began the discussion at an appropriate time. The clients could then brainstorm how they could apply these skills to their own situation. In addition, the therapist may reiterate to the parents that they need to give comforting messages to the children in order to relieve fears that the children may have cause the breakup and divorce.

Brief Vignette

George, thirty-eight, and his two sons, Milo, ten, and Reeves, eight, presented for family therapy four months after George and Mary, the children's mother, divorced. During the initial interview, George stated that he was worried about his sons as they were yelling at one another and were often sullen. George gave a detailed history of the family while the children remained silent in session. The therapist used humor, empathy, and positive regard to build rapport with the children, but they remained unresponsive.

During the second meeting, an individual session with George, the therapist learned that the father had a hard time communicating about emotions with his young sons. George stated that he and his sons never talked about their adapting family. When the therapist asked if George thought that his sons knew that they were not responsible for George and Mary's divorce, George stated that he had overheard his younger son say "This is all my fault" when the son was doing his homework. The client stated that he was unsure how to address this problem. First, the therapist normalized that children often feel responsible for their parents' breakup. The therapist educated George that children need to receive significant, comforting messages that contradict the belief that the children caused the divorce.

During the session, the therapist showed a brief scene from *Stepmom* where the father talks with his young children about the divorce. The therapist asked George what had gone well in the conversation. George stated that he liked how the dialogue occurred when the family was engaged in a relaxed activity. George also said he liked that the father directly communicated that the children were not responsible for the divorce. The therapist affirmed the client's interpretation of the scene and added that the film's father had used kid-friendly language and gave the children an opportunity to ask questions. The therapist and client then discussed how George would implement what he had learned into a conversation with his sons. George stated that he was still unsure exactly how to foster a conversation with Milo and Reeves. The therapist then talked with George about using books and videos to help the children talk about their thoughts and feelings. The therapist stated that often children talk about characters with more ease than they can talk about themselves. The therapist suggested that George and his children watch *Mrs. Doubtfire* before the next session.

During the following session, the therapist met with George, Milo, and Reeves. The therapist cued *Mrs. Doubtfire* to the scene where the son comments that the parents divorced because of his birthday party. The therapist asked Milo and Reeves what they thought was happening in the movie. Reeves stated, "The dad had to leave because the son was bad." The therapist reflected, "You think that the son may have caused the parents to split up." Milo interjected, "But the dad said that it wasn't his fault." The therapist directed the father to comment on the scene. George stated that it wasn't the son's fault. Then George stated that there was nothing Milo or Reeves did to make his divorce happen. Therapy continued for several weeks, addressing additional issues related to divorce and family adaptation. During subsequent sessions, the children, father, and therapist both directly and indirectly communicated about the emotions and the changes in the family structure.

Contraindications

There are some logistical concerns for showing a video clip. The therapy facility must be equipped with a TV and VCR or the family must have home access to the electronic equipment. In addition, the family must be open to seeing videos (e.g., some cultural values prohibit watching films).

References

Barnathan, M. (Producer), & Columbus, C. (Director). (1998). *Stepmom* [Video]. Available from Tristar.

Bradshaw, J. (Producer), & Columbus, C. (Director). (1993). *Mrs. Doubtfire* [Video]. Available from 20th Century Fox.

Cornett, C. E., & Cornett, C. F. (1980). *Bibliotherapy: The right book at the right time.* Bloomington, IN: Phi Delta Kappa Education Foundation.

Hesley, J. W. (2000). Reel therapy. *Psychology Today, 33*(1), 54-47.

Jalongo, M. R. (1983). Bibliotherapy: Literature to promote socioemotional growth. *Reading Teacher, 36,* 796-803.

Kalter, N. (1990). *Growing up with divorce.* New York: Ballantine Books.

Kaslow, F. W., & Schwartz, L. L. (1987). *The dynamics of divorce: A life cycle perspective.* New York: Brunner/Mazel.

Pardeck, J. T. (1990). Using bibliotherapy in clinical practice with children. *Psychological Reports, 67*(3), 1043.

Peck, J. S., & Manocherian, J. (1989). Divorce in the changing family life cycle. In B. Carter & M. McGoldrick (Eds.), *The changing family life cycle* (2nd ed., pp. 335-369). Boston: Allyn and Bacon.

Riordan, R. J., & Wilson, L. S. (1989). Bibliotherapy: Does it work? *Journal of Counseling and Development, 67*(9), p. 506.

Rubin, R. J. (1978). *Bibliotherapy sourcebook.* Phoenix, AZ: Oryx Press.

Schrank, F. A., & Engles, D. W. (1981). Bibliotherapy as a counseling adjunct: Research findings. *Personnel and Guidance Journal, 60,* 143-147.

Schwartz, L. L., & Kaslow, F. W. (1997). *Painful partings.* New York: John Wiley & Sons.

Tillman, C. E. (1984). Bibliotherapy for adolescents: An annotated research review. *Journal of Reading, 27,* 713-719.

Wallerstein, J. S., & Kelly, J. B. (1980). *Surviving the breakup: How children and parents cope with divorce.* New York: Basic Books.

Professional Readings and Resources

The resources for using films and videos in psychotherapy are not empirically tested. However, the practice is similar to bibliotherapy, or the clinical use of literature, which does have some efficacy data. Jalongo (1983), Pardeck (1990), Riordan and Wilson (1989), Rubin (1978), Schrank and Engles (1981), and Tillman (1984) detail the use of books in therapy. A variety of popular films may be used in place of books; however, empirical data are needed to test the outcomes of this intervention.

A good source to find movies relevant to the family's presenting problem is the Internet Movie Database (available online: http://www.imdb.com). By typing a keyword (i.e., divorce), the Web site gives a list of movies related to the theme. Also, the therapist may type in a specific movie and be given a list of similar films. It is important that the therapist watch the movie before showing it or assigning clients to watch the film.

The use of movies and video clips will not alleviate all symptoms in the postdivorce family. However, clients who participate in the intervention of interacting with films are afforded an opportunity to spark family discussion, normalize their situation, and see how others have solved similar problems. This, combined with talk therapy and additional interventions, may open the door to establishing healthy functioning for the adapting postdivorce family.

SECTION VII:
SPIRITUALITY

29

How to Defeat a Giant:
Using Spiritual Stories to Empower Children

Donald J. Olund

Type of Contribution: *Activity, Handouts*

Objectives

The purpose of this activity and intervention is to help children with Judeo-Christian beliefs use familiar spiritual stories as a narrative to overcome debilitating emotions and to promote positive behaviors. This is a postmodern approach combining spirituality and narrative theory to help kids create new constructs in dealing with personal problems. The activity can be used in family sessions or with children in individual counseling.

Rationale for Use

Children who are brought for therapy often carry negative perceptions about themselves. Inwardly they may wonder, "There must be something wrong with me. Otherwise, why would I be in counseling?" Consequently, children may believe others view them as having a problem or as being the cause of family problems. Furthermore, some parents may reinforce this belief in the manner in which they interact with their children. Here, parent-child interactions are primarily negative, drawing attention to the child's behavior. A complementary pattern may develop when parents' attempts to manage the children's behavior are matched by their children's resistance to parental control. Regrettably, parents and children often linger in problem-saturated stories that stigmatize children.

Developmentally, children are at risk of exhibiting low self-esteem and poor self-regulatory skills if they believe there is something wrong with them. This raises important considerations for therapists in determining a treatment approach. From a systems perspective, children are often the scapegoat or symptom bearer in disordered families (Minuchin, 1974). A child-focused approach may reinforce the family narrative; thus it is recommended that a family therapy treatment approach be utilized in addition to child treatment. A thorough assessment of the family is essential to formulate a proper diagnosis and treatment plan.

In the assessment phase of counseling, therapists hear the presenting problem, including contributing factors that maintain the problem. In addition, therapists look for clients' strength and resiliency. Among the various factors that contribute to family's strengths, spirituality has recently gained attention in the mental health field (Helmeke & Sori, 2006a,b; Miller, 2003). Research indicates clients with religious values and corresponding belief systems view them as a source of strength in addressing life issues (Tuskenis & Sori, 2006). Children are no exception.

The Therapist's Notebook, Volume 2

In many religious practices, children are taught beliefs at an early age through the reading of spiritual stories. For example, in Judaism, Tanakh or Written Torah faith-building stories of God's interaction with the people of Israel abound. Children raised in these spiritually based homes are often familiar with stories of Moses leading the Israelites across the Red Sea, David conquering the giant Goliath, Daniel in the lion's den, and Jonah and the whale. These stories help children see how impossible situations can be overcome with God's help.

Similarly, Christian themes can be found in both the Old and New Testaments. Stories of faith, courage, and overcoming obstacles are replete in the Gospels. Many of these stories can be used metaphorically with children to help them view problems differently. For example, children struggling with anxiety can learn how to apply their faith by observing how the apostle Peter's faith gave him the ability to walk on water while he kept his eyes on Jesus. When Peter took his eyes off Christ, focusing on the waves and the wind, he became afraid and began to sink. The wind and waves can be a way of externalizing fears and "keeping your eyes on Christ" a means of internalizing faith.

In addition to spirituality, narrative therapy helps children deconstruct negative self-attributions by approaching problems from a different direction. Through the use of externalization, therapists help children view the problem externally versus internally (Dermer, Olund, & Sori, 2006; Freedman, Epston, & Lobovits, 1997). Rather than having problems or being a problem, therapists encourage children to think in terms of struggling against a problem. Or as Nichols and Schwartz (2004, p. 333) aptly stated, "neither the patient nor the family is the problem: the problem is the problem!" Children with attention-deficit/hyperactivity disorder may be asked to talk about times when distraction tries to take hold of them. Proper use of externalization helps build self-esteem and self-confidence in children, while facilitating the development of effective coping skills. In family therapy, parents are encouraged to team up with children to discuss potential strategies to defeat the problem. Helping parents gain an externalized view of the problem depathologizes the child while increasing family cohesion (Dermer et al., 2006).

Another deconstructive approach in narrative therapy involves helping clients recall unique outcomes when they were able to triumph over a problem (Freedman & Combs, 1996). Children build self-confidence by paying attention to moments when they were not controlled by the problem. In therapy, children become authors of new narratives, composing scripts that portray them as conquerors. Through rehearsal of the new story, children develop adaptive behaviors that reinforce the narrative. Also, family members can serve as both an audience and supporting cast for the unfolding story.

Combining spirituality and narrative therapy in working with children to overcome problems is a collaborative process that requires matching a spiritual narrative with the problem. The best way to start is by asking children to talk about the spiritual stories they enjoy and what they like about them. Another method is to retell a familiar spiritual story that relates to the problem a child brings to counseling.

For example, most children from a Judeo-Christian background are familiar with the story of David and Goliath. A child with a problem with worry or fear can relate to the story of how the Israelite army was afraid to battle the giant Goliath. King Saul offered a handsome reward to any soldier who would go out and fight the giant. However, because all the soldiers were afraid, no one would answer the call. Along came David, a young shepherd boy who was bringing food supplies to his older brothers at the army camp, when suddenly he heard Goliath's challenge to meet him in battle.

David approached King Saul and offered to fight the giant, claiming that God would give him victory. His fear of the imposing giant was overshadowed by his faith in God's ability to help him win the battle. To convince the king, David described two unique outcomes in the past: God gave him courage to defend his sheep from an attacking lion and later, a ferocious bear. Reluctantly, King Saul agreed and offered David his own royal armor to wear in battle. However, David, feeling encumbered by the oversized armor, opted for his trusty slingshot and five carefully chosen smooth stones to face off against the giant. On the battlefield, determined David confronted the giant with a challenge: "Who are you to defy the armies of the living God?" As the story goes, David defeated the giant Goliath on his first sling.

Instructions

How to Defeat a Giant is a four-step activity therapists can use with children. (The activity sheet is located at the end of the chapter.) In the first step, children identify their giant by filling in the blank. For example, if their problem is worry, the deconstruction of worry can be rewritten as the Worry Giant that is trying to get in their way. In the second step, children place themselves in the narrative by choosing one of three characters in the narrative they want to emulate. The characters are Scared Soldier, Cowardly King Saul, and Determined David.

In the third step, children select five behaviors or traits they believe will help them defeat their giant. Here, therapists dialogue with children about times in the past when they felt powerful over the giant. Children uncover a narrative of behaviors formerly used to overcome their problem. In family therapy, parents and siblings are also encouraged to share evidence of unique outcomes they've witnessed. With the aid of therapists, children compose a new narrative by choosing five internal traits to defeat the external giant. These names are written on one of the five stones on the activity sheet. For example, a child who says that faith, courage, talking, action, and persistence help him defeat the Worry Giant can write these traits and behaviors on one of each of the five smooth stones.

An optional activity involves children selecting five large smooth stones and painting a name on each stone corresponding to one of the five traits. A linen pouch, ziplock bag, or pencil case can be used to store the stones. When the child begins to feel worry come near, the stones can serve as a mental reminder of what to think and how to act in the face of the Worry Giant.

In the fourth step, therapists and children collaborate on five action steps corresponding to the five stones to be used to overcome the giant. Children are encouraged to begin using these new behaviors. In succeeding sessions, these action steps can be used to measure their progress in defeating their giant.

Brief Vignette

Jon and Sheryl brought their only child, nine-year-old Jason, to counseling because they were concerned about a lack of social interaction with his peers. They stated that they first noticed the problem when Jason was two years old and placed in a day care center. They indicated that the problem continued when he transitioned into elementary school, as reported in succeeding years by his teachers. They stated that he demonstrated age-appropriate behavior when he interacted with adult family members. The couple also reported that they had had marriage problems since Jason was a toddler and had been separated for seven years.

In the first session with the family, Jason rarely made eye contact and gave short answers in a barely audible voice. When asked why he thought he was at counseling, he said his parents wanted him to come. Initial sessions involved building rapport with the family and gaining Jason's trust. The therapist utilized family play therapy to enter the family system, assess family structure and communication patterns, and to provoke interaction with Jason (see Dermer et al., 2006).

In succeeding weeks, Jason's interactions with the therapist showed minimal improvement. The therapist suggested to his parents an individual session with Jason. The goal was to get him to interact with the therapist without his parents being present. At the therapist's request, Jason brought a videotape of himself playing a game show host in a make-believe game of *Who Wants to Be a Millionaire?* with his family. This was the first observation of Jason interacting in what appeared to be an age-appropriate manner. On the tape he was vocal, humorous, and emotionally expressive. While viewing the tape, the therapist laughed numerous times, commented to Jason about his remarkable talent for playing a game show host, and asked open-ended questions to engage him in conversation. By the end of the session, Jason and the therapist were laughing and talking freely.

This interaction was a breakthrough in therapy, for the therapist was able to gain Jason's trust and it gave him a positive experience interacting with a person who was not in his family circle. Next, the therapist invited him to talk more openly about the problem he was having interacting with his peers. When asked to describe the problem, Jason called it shyness. Scaling questions were used to establish a baseline for his problem with shyness in various social situations: school, sports, neighborhood, and church (Selekman, 2000). Narrative therapy was used to find unique outcomes to his shyness problem. The remainder of the session was used to help Jason decide what he wanted to do about his problem and establish operational goals for overcoming shyness.

In the following weeks, Jason reported measured success in overcoming shyness. He reported incidents of initiating conversations, responding to kids who talked to him, and not lingering too long eating his lunch to avoid recess. Also, he stated that he liked going to church and was planning on being baptized. By exploring Jason's spirituality, the therapist discovered that he had recently begun attending church with his parents and enjoyed attending the children's services. He stated that he liked the Bible stories and believed in God.

Over the course of time, Jason appeared to be discouraged in his attempt to overcome shyness and expressed frustration over his lack of progress. The therapist could see he was getting down on himself and felt like he was failing. They talked about Bible characters who felt discouraged at times and put their hope in God to help them. The therapist talked about how David conquered the giant Goliath because he had faith that God would help him.

Using the activity sheet, the therapist guided Jason through the four-step process of defeating giants. In the first step, Jason was asked who Goliath might represent in his life. He answered, "He's the Shyness Giant." The therapist engaged Jason in a dialogue about how the Shyness Giant tried to keep him from having fun with his peers. This enabled Jason to form an externalized view of the problem.

In the second step, Jason was asked what character he wanted to emulate. He decided he was not going to be like the Scared Soldiers who ran from the giant, nor the Cowardly King who did not lead them in battle. Rather, he wanted to be like Determined David, able to overcome the giant with God's help.

In the third step, Jason was asked to think of five winning traits and behaviors (corresponding to David's five smooth stones) that might help him defeat the Shyness Giant. Jason talked about unique outcomes in the past he could keep on doing. His parents teamed up with Jason to talk about situations when they saw him overcome shyness. They reviewed the progress he made in counseling and the things he did to make it happen. Also, they discussed behaviors he could add that would give him more confidence. Finally, they talked about how Jason could use his faith in God as a means to overcome the Shyness Giant. The five stones he chose were faith, courage, action, persistence, and determination. Jason wrote these names on the stones on the activity sheet.

In the fourth step, Jason collaborated with the therapist, coming up with five action steps corresponding to each of the five stones. This became his strategy to defeat the Shyness Giant. In every social situation he entered, Jason would use these behaviors to defeat his giant by interacting with his peers.

To punctuate his decision to defeat the Shyness Giant, Jason and the therapist went outdoors and he carefully chose five large stones. The therapist asked him to take them home, paint them, and write on the stones the traits he was going to use to defeat the Shyness Giant. When he returned for the following session, he proudly displayed his newly decorated stones with the five traits painted on them.

In succeeding weeks, Jason reported new success in overcoming the Shyness Giant. He stated he was among the first to finish eating lunch at school so that he could be out on the playground early. Furthermore, he reported that he was playing kickball with his peers on the playground; he joined the children's choir at church and was talking more to other children. His parents described how Jason was defeating the Shyness Giant at church and when they visited him at school on Parents Day. Encouraged and challenged by Jason's progress, Jon and Sheryl were confronted with some of their own giants that were causing problems in their marriage. They agreed to enter marriage counseling to see if they could resolve their issues and reunite.

Weeks after termination, his mother reported that Jason's teachers had commented with amazement on his improvement in social settings. They noticed him interacting with students in class and on the playground and appearing more relaxed in social interaction. Likewise, his parents noticed continued improvement. They stated that when he came home from school he appeared more happy and positive about his experiences. Furthermore, he was becoming more active in children's activities at church. Later, Jason sent the therapist a thank-you card stating he was doing much better overcoming the Shyness Giant.

Suggestions for Follow-Up

This activity provides children with a valuable tool they can use to continue making progress after termination. In termination, therapists can celebrate the changes that have taken place with children and their families. Furthermore, they can talk about areas of growth that will need more attention. The activity sheet is a visual reminder of the behaviors children know will help them overcome the problem.

Explaining to children that they are the experts in solving their problems empowers them to continue to work after counseling is over. Furthermore, it helps children maintain an externalized view of the problem so that they can manage it better. This promotes self-confidence and builds self-esteem. Finally, involving family members depathologizes children, builds cohesion, and increases the likelihood of a positive outcome.

While this activity uses the biblical story of David and Goliath, many other stories are available for use in therapy with children and their families. Also, clients from other religious backgrounds have spiritual stories from their tradition they may find resourceful in overcoming problems. For example, teachings from the Quran can be used when counseling children of Islamic faith. The story of Siddhartha Gautama and his teachings on the four noble truths and the eightfold path may be helpful to children who practice Buddhism. Children of Hindu faith may be familiar with the Puranas: myths, stories, and legends within Hindu tradition. With a little imagination and creativity, combined with the narrative model, therapists and clients can design new methods of conquering problems using spiritual stories from any religion.

Contraindications

This activity is not useful for children who do not practice spirituality or come from non-Judeo-Christian backgrounds. However, with a little creativity, therapists can easily adapt this activity by using religious stories from other spiritual disciplines. Furthermore, stories of virtue from classic literature, such as Aesop's fables, the stories of Hans Christian Anderson, the Velveteen Rabbit, and others can be used in families that do not have spiritual values.

References

Dermer, S., Olund, D., & Sori, C. F. (2006). Integrating play in family therapy theories. In C. F. Sori (Ed.), *Engaging children in family therapy: Creative approaches to integrating theory and research in clinical practice* (pp. 37-65). New York: Routledge.

Freedman, J., & Combs, G. (1996). *Narrative therapy: The social construction of preferred realities.* New York: Norton.

Freedman, J., Epston, D., & Lobovits, D. (1997). *Playful approaches to serious problems: Narrative therapy with children and their families.* New York: Norton.

Helmeke, K. B., & Sori, C. F. (Eds.). (2006a). *The therapist's notebook for integrating spirituality in counseling I: Homework, handouts, and activities for use in psychotherapy.* Binghamton, NY: The Haworth Press.

Helmeke, K. B., & Sori, C. F. (Eds.). (2006b). *The therapist's notebook for integrating spirituality in counseling II: More homework, handouts, and activities for use in psychotherapy.* Binghamton, NY: The Haworth Press.

Miller, G. (2003). *Incorporating spirituality in counseling and psychotherapy: Theory and technique.* Hoboken, NJ: John Wiley & Sons.

Minuchin, S. (1974). *Families and family therapy.* Cambridge, MA: Harvard University Press.

Nichols, M. P., & Schwartz, R. C. (2004). *Family therapy: Concepts and methods* (6th ed.). New York: Allyn & Bacon.

Selekman, M. D. (2000). Solution-oriented brief family therapy with children. In C. E. Bailey (Ed.), *Children in therapy: Using the family as a resource* (pp. 1-19). New York: Norton.

Tuskenis, A. D., & Sori, C. F. (2006). Enhancing reliance on God as a supportive attachment figure. In K. B. Helmeke & C. F. Sori (Eds.), *The therapist's notebook for integrating spirituality in counseling II: More homework, handouts, and activities for use in psychotherapy.* Binghamton, NY: The Haworth Press.

Professional Readings and Resources

Freedman, J., & Combs, G. (1996). *Narrative therapy: The social construction of preferred realities.* New York: Norton.

Freedman, J., Epston, D., & Lobovits, D. (1997). *Playful approaches to serious problems: Narrative therapy with children and their families.* New York: Norton.

Helmeke, K. B., & Sori, C. F. (Eds.). (2006a). *The therapist's notebook for integrating spirituality in counseling I: Homework, handouts, and activities for use in psychotherapy.* Binghamton, NY: The Haworth Press.

Helmeke, K. B., & Sori, C. F. (Eds.). (2006b). *The therapist's notebook for integrating spirituality in counseling II: More homework, handouts, and activities for use in psychotherapy.* Binghamton, NY: The Haworth Press.

Miller, G. (2003). *Incorporating spirituality in counseling and psychotherapy: Theory and technique.* Hoboken, NJ: John Wiley & Sons.

Bibliotherapy Sources for Clients

Aesop. (1975). *Aesop's fables.* New York: Grosset & Dunlap.

Bennett, W. J. (1993). *The book of virtues: A treasury of great moral stories.* New York: Simon & Schuster.

The Holy Bible.

Horn, G., & Cavanaugh, A. (1980). *Bible stories for children.* New York: Simon & Schuster Books for Young Readers.

Williams, M., & Nicholson, W. (1958). *The velveteen rabbit.* New York: Delacorte.

HOW TO DEFEAT A GIANT

GIANT-DEFEATING STRATEGY

STEP #1: IDENTIFY YOUR GIANT: <u>SHYNESS</u>   (fill in the blank)

STEP #2: CHOOSE YOUR CHARACTER (check one please)
- ☐ SCARED SOLDIER
- ☐ COWARDLY KING SAUL
- ✔ DETERMINED DAVID

STEP #3: CHOOSE YOUR WEAPON
- ☐ OVERSIZED SUIT OF ARMOR
- ✔ MAKE-BELIEVE SLINGSHOT & FIVE SMOOTH STONES

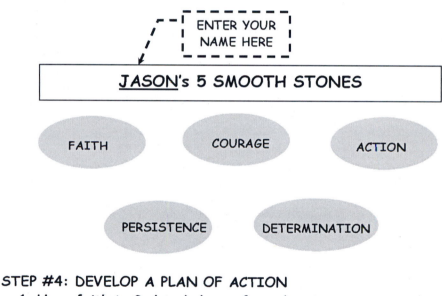

ENTER YOUR NAME HERE

JASON's 5 SMOOTH STONES

FAITH   COURAGE   ACTION

PERSISTENCE   DETERMINATION

STEP #4: DEVELOP A PLAN OF ACTION
1. Have <u>faith</u> in God to help me face the giant.
2. Pray every day for <u>courage</u> to face the giant.
3. Take <u>action</u> by standing up to the giant.
4. Be <u>persistent</u> to face the giant.
5. Be <u>determined</u> to conquer the giant.

Olund, D. J. (2007). How to defeat a giant: Using spiritual stories to empower children. In L. L. Hecker, C. F. Sori, & Associates, *The therapist's notebook, volume 2: More homework, handouts, and activities for use in psychotherapy* (pp. 229-236). Binghamton, NY: The Haworth Press.

HOW TO DEFEAT A GIANT

GIANT-DEFEATING STRATEGY

STEP #1: IDENTIFY YOUR GIANT:_____(fill in the blank)

STEP #2: CHOOSE YOUR CHARACTER (check one please)
- ☐ SCARED SOLDIER
- ☐ COWARDLY KING SAUL
- ☐ DETERMINED DAVID

STEP #3: CHOOSE YOUR WEAPON
- ☐ OVERSIZED SUIT OF ARMOR
- ☐ MAKE-BELIEVE SLINGSHOT & FIVE SMOOTH STONES

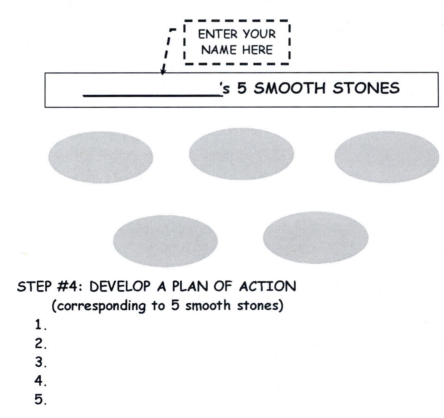

ENTER YOUR
NAME HERE

_____'s 5 SMOOTH STONES

STEP #4: DEVELOP A PLAN OF ACTION
(corresponding to 5 smooth stones)
1.
2.
3.
4.
5.

Olund, D. J. (2007). How to defeat a giant: Using spiritual stories to empower children. In L. L. Hecker, C. F. Sori, & Associates, *The therapist's notebook, volume 2: More homework, handouts, and activities for use in psychotherapy* (pp. 229-236). Binghamton, NY: The Haworth Press.

30

Spiritual Play Genogram

Catherine Ford Sori

Type of Contribution: *Activity, Handouts*

Objectives

The purpose of the spiritual genogram is to help clients identify and discuss religious beliefs and themes in their families of origin, as well as to clarify similarities and differences among family members' religious or spiritual beliefs and practices. This activity is an extension of Eliana Gil's (2003) family play genogram and may be used with individual adults, children, adolescents, and families.

Rationale for Use

Genograms

Genograms are a way of gathering and diagramming family histories across at least three generations with the purpose of helping clients see patterns and themes in their family of origin (McGoldrick, Gerson, & Shellenberger, 1999). Concrete, factual information is gathered regarding births, deaths, illnesses, occupations, education, ethnicity, immigration, abuse, and psychological problems. Often transgenerational patterns of distance, cutoffs, fusion, levels of differentiation, and triangles are revealed (Bowen, 1978). This information can guide the course of therapy in helping individuals resolve relationship problems from the past, as well as help people improve current relationships that are influenced by previously invisible legacies. The genogram is one of the primary tools used in Bowen systems theory and is often used in individual adult and couple sessions. Although the genogram may be used with families with adolescents, it is not typically used with families with young children, who often lack the language skills and attention necessary for prolonged history gathering.

Play Genogram

Eliana Gil created an ingenious method to make the genogram user friendly to both children and adults. The family play genogram activity (Gil, 2003; Gil & Sobol, 2000) was developed by Eliana Gil during her supervision of students at Monica McGoldrick's Multicultural Family Institute in New Jersey (see Sori, 2006). The family play genogram is an integration of sand tray, family play therapy, and Bowen systems theory. Instead of using the genogram to gather concrete facts, the family play genogram is a method of eliciting unconscious thoughts and feelings about individuals and relationships. By bringing often deeply buried emotions into conscious awareness, much rich emotional material often becomes available for processing. Because it in-

doi:10.1300/5550_30

volves using small figures called miniatures, it naturally appeals to children, adolescents, and most adults.

Gil (2003) states that there are two primary uses for the play genogram. The first is to use it as an in-session activity with individual children or adults; the client is asked to select a miniature that best represents his or her thoughts and feelings about each person in the family, and then place the objects on the corresponding space in the genogram. Clients then select miniatures to represent their relationship with each person in their family, and place these additional miniatures between themselves and the other family members.

The second use is the family play genogram (Gil, 2003; Gil & Sobol, 2000), which is done in the same manner. After the therapist draws a large genogram (on large construction paper) each family member is asked to select a miniature that best represents their thoughts and feelings about each person, and then place it on the genogram on the circle or square that represents each family member. As above, the clients are then asked to each select another miniature to represent their relationship with each family member, and to place those miniatures between each pair of dyads.

In the family play genogram, the therapist stands back to observe clients as they select their miniatures, and then notices the process of how family members interact with one another, and what their reactions are to the miniatures selected to represent various family members, as well as what is said about the miniatures. After the miniatures are selected and placed on the genogram, the therapist processes the play genogram by asking questions about the miniatures selected and the relationships among miniatures. The miniatures selected often have symbolic meaning for the clients. Often unconscious thoughts and feelings come into awareness as clients share about the figures selected, and transgenerational themes (such as cutoffs, triangles, levels of differentiation, and fusion) emerge. In processing this activity, Gil (2003) suggested:

> [C]linicians can express therapeutic curiosity and engage in a therapeutic dialogue congruent with their theoretical approach. Clinicians are advised to use open-ended versus closed questions, refrain from making interpretations and giving explanations, and take every opportunity to help expand the metaphors that are chosen, rather than moving away from metaphors too quickly. The true advantage of Play Genograms is that they provide an opportunity for deeper understanding of each individual's perception of self and others, which allows family members to see one another in a new light. Individual choices must be honored and protected. . . . This activity allows them to communicate with one another in different ways, and that everything which comes forward can be used toward some positive goal. (p. 51)

Gil (2003) also emphasized that the metaphors that emerge during this activity can guide the formation of treatment goals and the process of therapy. It is important to make a record of the information presented in the play genogram in terms of both notes and taking pictures that can be referred back to in the later stages of therapy.

Spiritual Play Genogram

Whereas many people have written about doing a spiritual genogram (e.g., Dunn & Massey, 2006), the spiritual play genogram is an integration of the spiritual genogram and the play genogram, and it can be used with children and adolescents, as well as individual adults and families. This activity can be used with clients of any faith or faiths.

In the spiritual play genogram activity, the therapist focuses clients' attention on the spiritual and religious beliefs and practices of family members over a period of at least three generations. Clients are asked to select miniatures to represent the spirituality or religious beliefs of each family member and then to discuss each person's beliefs and practices. In this way spiritual patterns that may have been transmitted across generations become revealed. It can be especially useful for families that may be reluctant to share family information in the usual talking format of a traditional genogram. In fact, it is a way to access the same relational information regarding triangles, cutoffs, fusion, and levels of differentiation. But by coming through the back door, much resistance can be bypassed, and rich emotional material can be unveiled. The spiritual play genogram can be useful to help clients identify with family members from past generations whose spirituality was a source of strength for them in times of trouble. As in the play genogram, the spiritual play genogram can also be used in two distinct ways: with individual child or adult clients, and with families.

Another benefit of the spiritual play genogram is that it may assist in the spiritual development of children and adolescents. For example, questions may arise for children while family members discuss their various religious beliefs, giving parents a chance to answer these questions or perhaps seek the counsel of a religious leader. This might also offer adolescents an opportunity to express views that may be different from their parents', opening up communication in this area. Clinicians could normalize that this is often a healthy stage of spiritual development. As families discuss the miniatures selected and how they view the spirituality of various family members, a deeper sense of spiritual heritage can develop, strengthening connections among those with similar views. At the same time, clinicians can ascertain how open the family is in allowing religious diversity. For example, this information can be useful in helping families when a family member has been cut off after choosing a different religious path from their family of origin.

Another area in which the spiritual play genogram may be helpful is undifferentiated spiritual development. For example, many people can harbor resentments over their religious upbringing and have cut off from their spiritual or religious development as a result of previous negative religious experiences. A spiritual play genogram can provide an avenue for healing and differentiation so that the client is free to pursue spiritual development as he or she chooses.

The spiritual play genogram activity may be especially useful with children and families who have experienced the death of a parent or other close family member. In discussing the miniatures selected by family members to represent the deceased, families can be helped to share their beliefs about God, death, heaven, angels, afterlife, and so on. This offers an opportunity for children to ask difficult questions and for clinicians to help parents clarify the difference between a physical death and the parents' beliefs about what happens to a spirit after death (see Biank & Sori, 2006a,b). Even if the death occurred a number of years ago, the unconscious meaning ascribed to a miniature often elicits feelings that have been repressed and unresolved. In one case, a young woman in an individual session chose a large superhero figure to represent her deceased brother. It was the largest figure on the genogram, and all the other characters were chosen in some relation to that figure—showing the centrality of this man's role in the family. As she discussed the figures in her spiritual play genogram, this client shared how the death of her brother had forever changed her family. She tearfully recalled how important he had been in her life, having served as her protector, and how she hadn't realized how much she still missed his reassuring presence in her life. She was comforted by their shared religious beliefs and her hope that she would one day be reunited with him in heaven.

Instructions

You will need a large collection of miniatures such as those used for sand tray, including many that represent religion or spirituality (see Handout 30.1 at the end of this chapter). Although professional miniatures may be purchased (see list of Web sites at the end of the chapter), clinicians can often purchase them inexpensively at dollar stores, garage sales, or bakeries (Gil, 2003). An alternative is to have clients do a collage, utilizing pictures cut from magazines instead of miniatures. You will also need:

Construction paper (about 22" × 28")
Camera
Chart to record miniatures (see Gil, 2003; or use notebook paper to list the miniatures selected by each person to represent each family member and dyadic relationships)

This activity should be done only after the clinician has joined well with clients. It can be explained as a way of obtaining a spiritual history or of helping clients explore spiritual issues or their spiritual heritage. Clinicians need to have a wide array of miniatures, and for this activity there should be many that have or suggest a spiritual theme. The therapist works with the individual client or family to draw a simple, three-generation genogram on large construction paper. In the family play spiritual genogram, each family member is then asked to select an object to represent each person's spirituality or religious beliefs, with the following instruction: "Each of you will choose a miniature that best shows your thoughts and feelings about the spirituality or religious beliefs of each person in the family, including yourself." The therapist observes the family dynamics as they select and place objects. It is important to notice as clients select miniatures, noting any hesitations over particular miniatures, figures selected but then put back, and any difficulty they may have in choosing an object to represent a particular family member. Gil suggests having modeling clay handy in case no appropriate miniature is found, so clients can mold their own figure, or allowing them to write words to represent a missing symbol (Gil & Sobol, 2000). When used with families it is especially important to note any family interactions and clients' level of involvement and enjoyment in this process (Gil & Sobol, 2000). The therapist may use Gil's (2003) chart to record family members' choices.

After all the miniatures have been placed on the genogram the clinician can engage the family in a discussion of the miniatures selected. Ask each person to tell you about each object. In processing the activity it is important to use open-ended questions, such as, "Tell me about this large angel you chose for your sister. What does it mean or represent to you?" (Caution: The therapist should not assume he or she knows the meaning of any particular miniature.) Observe how other family members react to each member's responses. Discuss the spiritual or religious meaning of each figure, noting similarities and differences among individual beliefs and the family's capacity to allow for differences.

It is important to question how various figures relate to the issue of spirituality or religion. Were any figures in conflict regarding this topic and, if so, how did that affect the spirituality or religious practices or beliefs of others? Clinicians can explore this by wondering about the relationships between two miniatures. For example, one client had selected a figure of a bear holding a book and reading to two small bears to represent her mother, and a miniature of a pot of gold to represent her atheist father, saying that "money was his God." The therapist remarked, "I wonder what it was like for the momma bear reading Bible stories to her bear cubs to be married to the pot of gold. And what was it like for the bear cubs to have a momma bear and a pot of gold for parents?" This led to a discussion of the conflicting values and loyalty conflicts the client had experienced both growing up and in adulthood, and how this had affected her spiritual growth. Also note patterns of spiritual beliefs across generations. Explore how these beliefs have helped individuals in the past and present, looking for sources of strength and resiliency.

Being careful to stay in the metaphor helps clients to discuss their thoughts and feelings more openly, because it is safer to talk indirectly about their family. It is important to ask clients to share what meaning an object holds for them and not to assume either a negative or positive connotation. For example, one girl chose a small gorilla in a treasure chest to represent her sister, who had recently committed suicide. The counselor could have assumed that her sister was a chest-thumping terror; however, when she asked what the gorilla was like, the girl shared that her sister had been fun to play with and was someone she looked up to.

In processing the spiritual play genogram, it is important to note both similarities and differences among family members' choices. It is also important to look for any patterns of religious or spiritual beliefs across generations. Clinicians may elicit stories of how these beliefs helped other family members through difficult times, thus possibly uncovering an untapped resource for a client who identifies with that family member. Looking for examples of how people used their spirituality to cope and helping clients to view it as a sign of resiliency can also benefit clients who are struggling in the present.

Finally, it is important to process what this activity was like for clients. What did they learn from the miniatures they selected, from those other family members chose, or from the discussion? What surprised them? What emotions were evoked regarding specific miniatures during the spiritual play genogram activity? See Handout 30.2 for a summary of how to introduce and process this activity.

Brief Vignette

The following is a vignette of how the spiritual play genogram was used with an individual adult.

Melissa was a widowed client in her midsixties who sought therapy to deal with issues of grief. She felt little purpose in her life since the death of her husband, even though she still enjoyed her part-time work as a children's librarian in a small rural community. In sessions she often spoke of how her strong Christian faith had been shaken at the sudden death of her husband. Prior to his death, her faith had been a tremendous source of strength and comfort to her. But since his death she found it difficult to pray, read the Bible, or attend church.

The clinician invited her to do a spiritual play genogram as an alternative to a traditional genogram, as well as a way to assess family patterns of spiritual and religious beliefs and practices, with the hope of finding additional resources that could be accessed to help the client adjust to the meaning of the death and its implications for her future life. A few of her key miniatures are discussed later (see Figure 30.1).

Melissa chose a rocking chair with a fancy hat on top to represent her maternal grandmother; these two separate items represented the hat her grandmother always wore to church each Sunday when Melissa was a child, and the rocking chair for how her grandmother would rock and sing her to sleep. She spoke of her grandmother's great strength and unyielding faith, even though her grandmother had lost both of her parents and all her siblings when she was only nine years old, and later had three offspring who died in early childhood. Although her grandmother was a Christian, Melissa selected a menorah to represent the relationship between her grandmother and herself, since her grandmother reportedly had some Jewish heritage, and Melissa and her late husband had attended a messianic (Jewish) Christian fellowship. Melissa closely identified with her grandmother and seemed to grow stronger as she discussed stories of how her grandmother's faith carried her through so many losses as well as the Great Depression.

For her father Melissa selected two miniatures. First she chose a figure of a learned man, which looked rather like a wise professor. She stated that her father was the parent who faithfully took her and her sister to church and Sunday school each week. He was a living example of a "good, Christian man who lived a moral and upright life." He had taught Sunday school, and one day when he asked his students who most reminded them of God, one young man had said, "Why you do, of course!" Melissa heartily agreed. The second figure was the Scarecrow from *The Wizard of Oz,* because her father bought her an Oz book for every birthday and Christmas, and read a chapter to her and her sister each night before bed. The Scarecrow represented a wise and loving figure, like God.

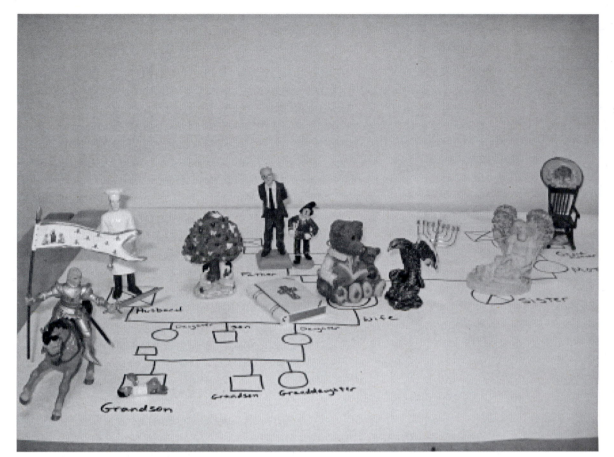

FIGURE 30.1. A spiritual play genogram showing miniatures selected to represent the client's thoughts and feelings about the spiritual beliefs and practices of some family members, as well as miniatures to represent the spiritual relationship between the client and key family members.

Melissa selected the figure of a chef to represent her deceased husband. She chose this because he enjoyed cooking for all their children and grandchildren whenever there were family gatherings. One way that he showed his nurturing love for family was through food. She also discussed their shared faith and how as a young couple they had been determined to raise their children in a Christian home. They had been very pleased that all of their children were Christians and, in fact, some were missionaries. She selected two figures to represent their relationship: One was an apple tree that said "love," with a male and female figure kneeling on each side of the tree. The other was a miniature of a Bible to represent their missionary children who were spreading their faith around the world.

Melissa's only sister had died as a young adult. For her Melissa selected a golden angel. She spoke of how even though she had gone to church as a child, Melissa had walked away from her faith in her twenties, when she was going through a very difficult period in her life. Melissa's sister had been the one to pray for her and ultimately was the one who led her back to the faith of her childhood through a life-changing spiritual decision. In looking back, Melissa recalled how much she had relied on God during that terrible time following the sudden and untimely death of her beloved sister. She realized that although she had suffered great pain, she had become stronger as a result of this experience, and her faith had deepened.

For herself Melissa selected two miniatures. The first was an eagle poised to take flight but with one broken wing. In discussing this, she stated that one of her favorite verses from the Bible was, "But those who hope in the Lord will renew their strength. They will soar on wings like eagles; they will run and not grow weary, they will walk and not be faint" (Isaiah 40:31, New International Version). She knew she had the strength to soar above the painful feelings and sense of loneliness that were holding her down, but was struggling, like the eagle with the broken wing. The second figurine she chose was a momma bear reading a book to a little bear. Melissa explained that this represented how she had read books and Bible stories to her children when they were growing up, and how she now loved to read *The Lion, the Witch, and the Wardrobe* from the Chronicles of Narnia by C. S. Lewis (1950) to her grandchildren. She shared what a tremendous joy they were to her and how important it was for her to spend time in meaningful activities with them.

For her oldest grandson Melissa selected two figures. The first was a knight on a horse, brandishing a sword and shield. Under the horse was a figure of a young boy lying on his back, reading a book. She said these represented the tremendous faith this young boy possessed. A year after attending a missionary camp he still said he couldn't wait to go back, and that when he grew up he wanted to become a missionary. To Melissa the knight represented King Peter in *The Lion, the Witch, and the Wardrobe,* while the boy lying on his back was her grandson reading the Bible.

The therapist pointed out how it appeared that she was the spiritual link between her grandmother, her father, her children, and her grandchildren. This brought excitement to Melissa's eyes and offered her a new, more determined purpose for this stage in her life. They also revisited what had been particularly helpful to her following her sister's death, with special attention to her spiritual and religious coping style (see Tuskenis & Sori, 2006). The therapist asked Melissa to share her beliefs about death, suffering, and an afterlife. After identifying some of her previously used spiritual coping tools, Melissa began a spiritual journal where she wrote down her thoughts and feelings, and sometimes wrote letters to God and to her late husband. She decided to spend more regular time with her grandchildren who lived close by and to take a vacation to visit her missionary children, to help them in their work and to spend time with those grandchildren. She also joined a women's Bible study group, where she began making some new friends who shared her beliefs, and with whom she would often pray.

Over time Melissa's feelings of grief lessened and she had a renewed purpose in life as she adjusted to widowhood. Melissa kept a picture of her spiritual play genogram on her refrigerator to remind her of both her spiritual heritage and her legacy.

Suggestions for Follow-Up

The clinician is encouraged to take two pictures of the spiritual play genogram: one that clients can take home, possibly to put on the refrigerator; the other for the clinician and family to refer back to throughout the course of therapy. For example, after doing this activity someone might want to emulate a grandmother's spirituality in being able to forgive someone and to reconnect with a distant relationship. After working on this relationship, the client might review the genogram and select different miniatures to represent the spirituality of that relationship. One woman after doing this activity asked if she could have her grandmother's well-worn Bible and received great insight and comfort in reading the marked passages and notes in the margin in her grandmother's handwriting. This helped her connect in a spiritual manner to her beloved grandmother and to identify with the legacy of strength and spiritual beliefs she had passed down to her granddaughter. This increased the woman's spiritual coping during a difficult time of loss and grief in her own life.

Contraindications

Clinicians should use caution in assessing clients for this activity. This is an excellent activity for spiritual or religious clients. Although it is useful to help people differentiate around the area of their spiritual beliefs, it may not be as useful for someone who is an atheist or agnostic, or who has no interest in spiritual issues. In addition, the activity may or may not be useful if the client's religious beliefs do not include an afterlife.

References

Biank, N., & Sori, C. F. (2006a). Helping children cope with the death of a family member. In C. F. Sori (Ed.), *Engaging children in family therapy: Creative approaches to integrating theory and research in clinical practice* (pp. 245-262). New York: Routledge.

Biank, N., & Sori, C. F. (2006b). Integrating spirituality when working with children and families experiencing loss of a parent. In K. B. Helmeke & C. F. Sori (Eds.), *The therapist's notebook for integrating spirituality in counseling II: More homework, handouts, and activities for use in psychotherapy* (pp. 67-82). Binghamton, NY: The Haworth Press.

Bowen, M. (1978). *Family therapy in clinical practice.* New York: Jason Aronson.

Dunn, A. G., & Massey, R. F. (2006). The spirituality focused genogram: A tool for exploring spirituality and the spiritual resources of individuals, couples and families in context. In K. B. Helmeke & C. F. Sori (Eds.), *The therapist's notebook for integrating spirituality in counseling I: Homework, handouts, and activities for use in psychotherapy* (pp. 77-88). Binghamton, NY: The Haworth Press.

Gil, E. (2003). Play genograms. In C. F. Sori, L. L. Hecker, & Associates, *The therapist's notebook for children and adolescents: Homework, handouts, and activities for use in psychotherapy* (pp. 49-56). Binghamton, NY: The Haworth Press.

Gil, E., & Sobol, B. (2000). Engaging families in therapeutic play. In C. E. Bailey (Ed.), *Children in therapy: Using the family as a resource* (pp. 341-382). New York: Norton.

Lewis, C. S. (1950). *The lion, the witch, and the wardrobe.* New York: Macmillan.

McGoldrick, M., Gerson, R., & Shellenberger, S. (1999). *Genograms: Assessment and intervention* (2nd ed.). New York: Norton.

Sori, C. F. (2006). Family play therapy: An interview with Eliana Gil. In C. F. Sori (Ed.), *Engaging children in family therapy: Creative approaches to integrating theory and research in clinical practice* (pp. 69-90). New York: Routledge.

Tuskenis, A. D., & Sori, C. F. (2006). Enhancing reliance on God as a supportive attachment figure. In K. B. Helmeke & C. F. Sori (Eds.), *The therapist's notebook for integrating spirituality in counseling II: More homework, handouts, and activities for use in psychotherapy* (pp. 43-63). Binghamton, NY: The Haworth Press.

Professional Readings and Resources

Gil, E. (2003). Play genograms. In C. F. Sori, L. L. Hecker, & Associates, *The therapist's notebook for children and adolescents: Homework, handouts, and activities for use in psychotherapy* (pp. 49-56). Binghamton, NY: The Haworth Press.

Helmeke, K. B., & Sori, C. F. (2006). *The therapist's notebook for integrating spirituality in counseling I & II: More homework, handouts, and activities for use in psychotherapy.* Binghamton, NY: The Haworth Press.

McGoldrick, M., Gerson, R., & Shellenberger, S. (1999). *Genograms: Assessment and intervention* (2nd ed.). New York: Norton.

Walsh, F. (Ed.). (1999). *Spiritual resources in family therapy.* New York: Guilford.

Bibliotherapy Source for Clients

Moore, T. (1992). *Care of the soul: A guide for cultivating depth and sacredness in daily life.* New York: HarperCollins.

Companies and Web Sites That Sell Miniatures

Feelings Company. www.feelingscompany.com.
Sandplay Toys. PO Box 372, San Geronimo, CA 94963. Phone: 415-0488-4052. www.sandplay-toys.com.
Self-Esteem Shop. 4607 N. Woodward, Royal Oak, MI. Phone: 1-800-251-8338. www.selfesteemshop.com.
Self Help Warehouse. www.selfhelpwarehouse.com.
World Toys and Miniatures. PO Box 20288, Oakland, CA 94620. Phone: 1-510-658-0858.

HANDOUT 30.1

MINIATURES FOR SPIRITUAL PLAY GENOGRAMS

Clinicians will need numerous miniatures from the categories below. In addition to clearly religious miniatures, more generic items should also be included, as clients may ascribe a religious or spiritual connotation to animals or other figures. Inexpensive sources for miniatures include stores that sell baking items, Zany Brainy, dollar stores, religious stores, the toy section in secondhand stores, and garage sales.

Animals	Structures	People	Religious symbols	Fantasy symbols	Vehicles	Miscellaneous
Farm animals, zoo animals, Wild animals (gentle & ferocious), dinosaurs, domestic animals, sea creatures, birds, insects, fantasy animals (e.g., unicorns, mermaids), snakes, lizards	Churches, synagogues, or other places of worship, ark, houses, schools, castles, haunted houses, forts, barns, hospitals, office buildings, windmills, jails	Families (different ethnicities, ages, occupations (e.g., glamorous, detective, teacher, police), babies, sports figures, dancers, brides and grooms, people (or animals) engaging in different activities (e.g., nurturing, playing), war figures	Religious books or scrolls, priests, rabbis, pastors, Catholic symbols (e.g., Mary), Jesus, crosses, Star of David, Ten Commandments, menorahs, Buddha, nativity scenes, angels, devils, ancient symbols, medicine men, ethnic religious symbols, dove, fish, lion, lamb, rainbow, praying hands, apple, sword and shield, armor, etc.	Witches, wizards, fairies, dragons, monsters, ghosts, fairytale figures (e.g., Wizard of Oz), cartoon figures, magic carpets, genies, magic wands, wishing wells	Cars, planes, trucks, boats, trains, ambulances or emergency vehicles, bulldozers, rockets or space ships, helicopters, buses, wagons, carts, motorcycles, bicycles, tanks, military vehicles	Representing death (e.g., tombstones), treasure chest, sun, moon, stars, diplomas, baby bottles, wine bottles, pill bottles, volcanoes, tunnels, caves, bridges, shells, food items, books, dishes, ethnic items, money, purses, mirror, stretchers, weapons, treasure box

Sori, C. F. (2007). Spiritual play genogram. In L. L. Hecker, C. F. Sori, & Associates, *The therapist's notebook, volume 2: More homework, handouts, and activities for use in psychotherapy* (pp. 237-247). Binghamton, NY: The Haworth Press.

HANDOUT 30.2

SPIRITUAL PLAY GENOGRAM

This activity is an integration of sand play, family play, and Bowen systems theory. It may be done within individual sessions with adults or adolescents, or with families.

Materials: Large collection of miniatures
Construction paper (about 22" × 28")
Videotape and/or still camera

Description:

- Use miniatures (or various size/color buttons or stones) and large paper to draw a simple three-generation genogram
- Have the client (or each family member) select an object to represent each person's spirituality or religious beliefs, as well as one to represent the relationships between dyads
- Observe the family dynamics as they select and place objects
- Lead the individual client or family in discussion of objects selected and why
- Listen for information about relationships, emotional connectedness, communication patterns, and structure of family (e.g., alliances)
- Note similarities and differences among family members' spiritual/religious beliefs and practices, and how this impacted relationships and spiritual development of individuals across generations.
- Note any conflicts, cutoffs, coalitions, and levels of differentiation regarding spiritual issues.
- Note how religion or spiritual beliefs or practices were a source of strength, resilience, or coping across the generations.

Preparation: Therapist draws a basic three-generation genogram of the family to fit the whole paper.

Procedures for Use with a Family:

1. Instructions: "Each of you will choose a miniature that best shows your thoughts and feelings about each person in the family's spirituality or religious beliefs, including yourself."
2. Construction: Each person simultaneously chooses miniatures and places them in appropriate place on genogram.
3. Observation: Therapist observes both the family process and possible metaphoric content of objects.
4. Recording: Use Gil's (2003) chart to record family members' choices. Take a picture, if possible, so the genogram can be reconstructed and reviewed in the future.
5. Processing: Ask each person to tell you about each object. What does it mean or represent to them? (Caution: Don't assume you know, and don't ask why they chose an object.) Observe how other family members react to each member's response. Discuss the spiritual/religious meaning of each figure, noting similarities and differences among individual beliefs and the family's capacity to allow for differences. Also note patterns of spiritual beliefs across generations. Explore how these beliefs have helped individuals in the past and present. Look for sources of strength and resiliency. Finally, process what it was like for each of them to do this activity. What surprised them? What did they learn? Was it enjoyable?

Adapted from Gil, E. (2003). *E. Gil Video: Family Play Therapy: Rationale and Techniques* (2001). Fairfax, VA: Starbright Training Institute for Family and Child Play Therapy.

Sori, C. F. (2007). Spiritual play genogram. In L. L. Hecker, C. F. Sori, & Associates, *The therapist's notebook, volume 2: More homework, handouts, and activities for use in psychotherapy* (pp. 237-247). Binghamton, NY: The Haworth Press.

SECTION VIII:
THERAPIST TOOLS

31

Family Strengths and Concerns Assessment

Belinda Stepnowski

Type of Contribution: *Handout*

Objectives

The Family Strengths and Concerns Assessment is an instrument designed to assist therapists working with individuals, couples, or families. Clients entering therapy may be hesitant to verbalize some of their concerns; this instrument provides a comprehensive list of concerns from which clients can communicate their problems to the therapist. In addition, clients may fail to consider some of the strengths that are inherent in themselves, their relationships, or their family. The questions on this instrument can bring those strengths into focus for both the client and the therapist.

The assessment guides therapists in a direction that will be the most beneficial for the clients and allows clients to voice their innermost thoughts and feelings. Furthermore, it can facilitate communication between therapist and client and help focus therapy quickly and productively.

Rationale for Use

When approaching therapy with an individual, couple, or family, a clinician must rely solely on information that the clients are willing or able to provide, particularly in early sessions when trust is initially developing. Often, individuals can be reluctant to offer personal information at first for various reasons, including privacy, fear that a partner or family member will become angry, or embarrassment. Likewise, some individuals may even withhold information in therapy in an attempt to remain in control of the situation. Finally, some clients are not good at expressing themselves verbally, so they may feel constricted when trying to communicate the issues surrounding themselves or their personal relationships to the therapist.

A written assessment makes fewer demands for verbal communication and allows individuals to express their concerns regarding numerous aspects of life, including personal feelings, sexual concerns, substance abuse issues, and problems involving mood, which may not be easily expressed. Moreover, since the assessment begins by having clients identify areas of strength in themselves and their relationships, positive feelings can easily be elicited as they recognize that they do indeed have some resources to compel them to progress in therapy. The therapist can then draw on these strengths to use as catalysts for therapy. If clients ever question their ability to progress past the problem, the therapist can review their strengths. These individual attributes can become resources for clients to utilize in their journey through therapy. Moreover, if the therapist emphasizes these strengths throughout the process of therapy, clients may learn to access them in the future when they encounter any dilemmas.

The Therapist's Notebook, Volume 2
doi:10.1300/5550_31

Likewise, it is pragmatic for the clinician to review the various concerns expressed by each client to ensure that all needs are addressed. Since clients may be hesitant to verbalize all of the concerns, the therapist should review these issues so the clients are assured that the atmosphere is safe to discuss distressing items. By looking at the concerns marked on the list, the therapist may be able to ascertain if evaluation is needed for a mental disorder.

Instructions

Provide all clients age thirteen and up with a copy of the Family Strengths and Concerns List and instruct them to begin completing each section. In the first portion, numerous strengths are listed. For each one, the client should select one of the following: (1) agree the attribute is a strength; (2) agree that some improvement could be made in this area; or (3) disagree that the characteristic is a strength. Then clients have an opportunity to list the top three strengths that are inherent in themselves, their relationships, or their families. This section gives clients an opportunity to recognize and highlight other positive attributes that may not have been included in the list.

Next, the clients should write in the three main issues that they would like to cover in therapy. Although it is quite possible that there are more than three, these will provide the therapist with a good direction to begin the course of therapy. Finally, the clients will go through the remainder of the list to identify whether any of the issues involve personal feelings, sexual activity, substance abuse, family roles, children, life transitions, mood, anger, relational problems, family, problems, or partner violence. The clients can mark each topic as a major concern, minor concern, or not a concern and, in turn, the therapist can utilize this to assess each idiosyncratic case that presents for therapy.

Contraindications

No contraindications are noted. In all instances of couple therapy, any concerns of domestic violence should be addressed separately.

HANDOUT 31.1

FAMILY STRENGTHS AND CONCERNS LIST

Name:_____ Date:_____

Please check the appropriate box for each item below.

	Strength	Needs Some Improvement	Needs Much Improvement
Communication open, plentiful			
Togetherness family outings, traditions			
Appreciation express thanks			
Encouragement providing support			
Division of Responsibilities clear/equal tasks			
Flexibility willing to compromise			
Affection/Love physical expression			
Community and Family Ties spirituality, extended family			
Commitment loyalty, responsibility			
Forgiveness willing to accept mistakes or apologies			
Shared Interests enjoying activities together			
Friendship closeness, companionship			
Security confidence, well-being			
Trust reliance, faith			

Stepnowski, B. (2007). Family strengths and concerns assessment. In L. L. Hecker, C. F. Sori, & Associates, *The therapist's notebook, volume 2: More homework, handouts, and activities for use in psychotherapy* (pp. 251-260). Binghamton, NY: The Haworth Press.

Warmth

    tenderness, kindness

Respect

    admiration, high opinion

Please list three strengths apparent in you and/or your family:

1. _____

2. _____

3. _____

Please list the three most important issues you would like to discuss throughout the course of therapy:

1. _____

2. _____

3. _____

Please check the appropriate box for each item below that causes you pain.

Personal Feelings	Major Concern	Minor Concern	Not a Concern
depressed mood/feeling blue			
feeling less pleasure in activities			
loss of energy/fatigue			
insomnia			
sleeping too much			
feelings of guilt			
feelings of worthlessness			
significant weight loss or gain			
thoughts of suicide			
thoughts of death			
difficulty concentrating			
fluctuations in appetite			
low self-esteem			
loneliness			
rejection			
undereating			
fear of gaining weight			
binge eating			
vomiting meals			
use of laxatives/diuretics			

other: _____

Stepnowski, B. (2007). Family strengths and concerns assessment. In L. L. Hecker, C. F. Sori, & Associates, *The therapist's notebook, volume 2: More homework, handouts, and activities for use in psychotherapy* (pp. 251-260). Binghamton, NY: The Haworth Press.

Sexual Concerns

	Major Concern	Minor Concern	Not a Concern
avoiding sexual contact			
absence of desire/arousal			
sexual abuse history			

Females

	Major Concern	Minor Concern	Not a Concern
lubrication difficulties			
problems achieving orgasm			
recurrent pain during intercourse			

other: _____

Males

	Major Concern	Minor Concern	Not a Concern
delay/absence of orgasm			
erectile difficulties			
premature ejaculation			
recurrent pain during intercourse			

other:_____

Substance Abuse Concerns

	Major Concern	Minor Concern	Not a Concern
excessive alcohol use			
amphetamines (diet pills, speed)			
marijuana use			
cocaine use			
hallucinogens (LSD, MDMA)			
inhalant use (gas, glue, paint)			
nicotine use			
opiates (morphine, heroin, codeine)			
use of multiple substances			
sedative/antianxiety substances			
legal problems: substance use			
failure to fulfill obligations			
social problems			
quitting substance use			

other:_____

Stepnowski, B. (2007). Family strengths and concerns assessment. In L. L. Hecker, C. F. Sori, & Associates, *The therapist's notebook, volume 2: More homework, handouts, and activities for use in psychotherapy* (pp. 251-260). Binghamton, NY: The Haworth Press.

Family Roles

	Major Concern	Minor Concern	Not a Concern
single-parenting problems			
disagreements: housework			
role arguments (who does what)			
stepparent and children			
parental responsibilities			
other:_____			

Child Concerns

	Major Concern	Minor Concern	Not a Concern
siblings not getting along			
new addition to family			
stealing			
truancy			
running away			
bed or pants wetting/soiling			
breaking rules			
wrong group of friends			
suspicion of alcohol/drug use			
academic performance problems			
suicide			
sexual behavior			
adjustment (divorce, school, etc.)			
disability			
legal problems			
obesity			
dating			
involvement with child protective services			
child custody proceedings			
foster care			
ADD/ADHD			
anxiety			
depression			
suicide			
loss			
problems with peers			
bullying			
other:_____			

Stepnowski, B. (2007). Family strengths and concerns assessment. In L. L. Hecker, C. F. Sori, & Associates, *The therapist's notebook, volume 2: More homework, handouts, and activities for use in psychotherapy* (pp. 251-260). Binghamton, NY: The Haworth Press.

Life Transitions

	Major Concern	Minor Concern	Not a Concern
divorce			
separation			
remarriage			
remarriage with children			
moving			
parenting a new child			
new job			
creating a partnership			
change in religion			
abortion			
miscarriage			
dissolving a partnership			
creating/integrating an LGTB family			

other: _____

Mood Concerns

	Major Concern	Minor Concern	Not a Concern
anxiety			
problems in social situations			
problems at work			
uncontrollable worrying			
restlessness			
irritability			
muscle tension			
difficulty concentrating			
panic attacks			
unreasonable fear of object			
unreasonable fear of situation			
avoidance of social situations			
repetitive behaviors			
stress due to traumatic event			
grief/mourning due to loss			

other: _____

Stepnowski, B. (2007). Family strengths and concerns assessment. In L. L. Hecker, C. F. Sori, & Associates, *The therapist's notebook, volume 2: More homework, handouts, and activities for use in psychotherapy* (pp. 251-260). Binghamton, NY: The Haworth Press.

Anger Concerns

	Major Concern	Minor Concern	Not a Concern
difficulty controlling temper			
excessive anger			
problems with conflict			
controlling			
breaking objects to relieve anger			
excessive hostility			
other:_____			

Relational Concerns

Parent/Child

	Major Concern	Minor Concern	Not a Concern
poor communication			
lack of trust			
lack of togetherness			
difficulty adjusting to new rules			
other:_____			

Partner

	Major Concern	Minor Concern	Not a Concern
emotional abuse			
physical abuse			
sexual abuse			
verbal abuse			
different perspectives clashing			
poor communication			
lack of trust			
disagree about raising kids			
differences in personality			
infidelity			
jealousy			
intellectual differences			
emotional intimacy			
affairs			
pornography			
lack of shared interests			
managing past intimate			
other: _____			

Stepnowski, B. (2007). Family strengths and concerns assessment. In L. L. Hecker, C. F. Sori, & Associates, *The therapist's notebook, volume 2: More homework, handouts, and activities for use in psychotherapy* (pp. 251-260). Binghamton, NY: The Haworth Press.

Sibling

	Major Concern	Minor Concern	Not a Concern
constant fighting			
arguing			
jealousy			
lack of trust			
lack of communication			
refusal to interact			

other:_____

Family Concerns

	Major Concern	Minor Concern	Not a Concern
physical problems/illness			
child custody conditions			
lack of commitment			
lack of togetherness			
poor communication			
finances			
extended family			
disability			
aging parents			

other:_____

Partner Violence Concerns

	Major Concern	Minor Concern	Not a Concern
slapping			
hitting			
pushing			
excessive and severe arguments			
threats			
isolation			
controlling partners			
degradation			
use of force			
use of weapons			

other:_____

Stepnowski, B. (2007). Family strengths and concerns assessment. In L. L. Hecker, C. F. Sori, & Associates, *The therapist's notebook, volume 2: More homework, handouts, and activities for use in psychotherapy* (pp. 251-260). Binghamton, NY: The Haworth Press.

Lesbian, Gay, Bisexual, and Transgender (LGBT) Concerns	Major Concern	Minor Concern	Not a Concern
sexual orientation			
gender identity			
coming out to others			
one partner more out than other			
parental acceptance of identity			
please specify:			
connecting to LGBT community			
religion/spirituality			
heterosexism/homo-negativity/ homophobia			

other: _____

Family Religious or Spiritual Issues	Major Concern	Minor Concern	Not a Concern
family religious differences			
spiritual or religious practices			
moral convictions			
problems stemming from religious backgrounds			

other:

Is there anything marked above that you do not want discussed with other family members?

YES   NO

If so, which items do you not want to discuss?

_____
_____
_____
_____
_____

Stepnowski, B. (2007). Family strengths and concerns assessment. In L. L. Hecker, C. F. Sori, & Associates, *The therapist's notebook, volume 2: More homework, handouts, and activities for use in psychotherapy* (pp. 251-260). Binghamton, NY: The Haworth Press.

32

Therapy Intake Form

Lorna L. Hecker
Catherine Ford Sori

Type of Contribution: *Handout*

Objectives

The Therapy Intake Form is designed to assist the therapist in the beginning stages of therapy. It is designed for each client to fill out independently. It can be used in individual, couple, family, or group therapy. This instrument is designed for adults. Although it is designed as a form that the client fills out independently, it may also be used as an intake interview instrument that the therapist uses as a guide to gather information regarding the present state of the client's significant relationships, as well as historical information that may have a bearing on therapy.

Rationale for Use

The Therapy Intake Form is an organization tool for the therapist to use to gather information regarding the client's significant relationships, both present and past. Family relationships are briefly explored. In addition, current relationship status is explored, as well as family background and current family concerns. The client is also queried about vocational issues. There is a checklist of mental health concerns and a checklist of physical health symptoms. The physical health symptoms checklist allows the clinician to make a referral to rule out physical conditions that may be causing or contributing to any mental health condition. Child concerns are also addressed. Last, the instrument allows clients to discuss their sense of how any previous therapy was or was not helpful and assesses their level of hopefulness for the present therapy.

Instructions

Clients should be allowed time prior to their first session to fill out the form as part of their intake paperwork. They should be instructed to fill out the form as best they can and ignore any questions that do not pertain to them. Each adult client should be given a form to fill out independently of other family members. Members of couples should always be given a chance to speak to the therapist independently so that the therapist can assess for domestic violence in a neutral environment. Clients who are fearful may not be honest in their reporting on the form for fear of reprisal.

Alternatively, some therapists may wish to use the form as an intake interview instrument, whereby they read the questions to the clients and record the information on the form themselves.

Contraindications

No contraindications are noted. Children should not be given the form.

Therapy Intake Form

Thank you for choosing us for your counseling service. To make your time with us more productive, please assist the professional staff by completing the questionnaire. The questions are designed to provide information for the purpose of knowing you better. The information you provide will be held in strict confidence. *Please fill out the form as completely as possible.*

Person Who Called for Therapy:

Last Name: _____   Home Phone: (____)_____

First Name: _____   Work Phone: (____)_____

Address: _____   Cell Phone: (____)_____

Zip Code: _____   Is it okay to leave messages?   Yes   No

Best days and times to reach you: _____

Sex: M   F   Transgender   Referral Source: _____

Age: _____   Date of Birth: _____

What is your race(s)?_____

What is your religion (if any)?_____

How religious are you? (circle) Not Religious   Moderately Religious   Highly Religious

What is your occupation? _____

Highest Level of Education: (circle)   Less Than 8th Grade   8th Grade

High School   GED   Some College   College Graduate

Advanced Degree   Other _____

Sexual Orientation: ____ Heterosexual (attracted to members of the opposite sex)

____ Homosexual (attracted to members of the same sex)

____ Bisexual (attracted to members of both sexes)

____ I am confused about my sexual orientation

Other _____

Hecker, L. L., & Sori, C. F. (2007). Therapy intake form. In L. L. Hecker, C. F. Sori, & Associates, *The therapist's notebook, volume 2: More homework, handouts, and activities for use in psychotherapy* (pp. 261-271). Binghamton, NY: The Haworth Press.

Relationship Status: (check)

Marital Status ☐ M ☐ S ☐ D ☐ W ☐ Sep ☐ Dom. Partners ☐ Cohabitating

Date(s) of previous marriage(s) or significant relationship(s):

Type of Relationship: _____

From: ___/___/____ To: ___/___/____ How did marriage/relationship

end?_____

Type of Relationship: _____

From: ___/___/____ To: ___/___/____ How did marriage/relationship

end?_____

Type of Relationship: _____

From: ___/___/____ To: ___/___/____ How did marriage/relationship

end?_____

Type of Relationship: _____

From: ___/___/____ To: ___/___/____ How did marriage/relationship

end?_____

About Your Partner (if Applicable):

Name of partner:_____

Is your partner employed?   Yes   No

If yes, where:_____

What does he/she do?_____

Do you have any concerns or questions about your partner or marital status that we should

be aware of, or that you would like to discuss?_____

_____

In two or three words, describe your partner: _____

In two or three words, describe your family: _____

Hecker, L. L., & Sori, C. F. (2007). Therapy intake form. In L. L. Hecker, C. F. Sori, & Associates, *The therapist's notebook, volume 2: More homework, handouts, and activities for use in psychotherapy* (pp. 261-271). Binghamton, NY: The Haworth Press.

About Your Children:

Name of Child	M	F	Age	Date of Birth	Ours	His	Hers	Adopted Foster

About Your Home:

Is anyone else living in your home? If yes, who is living in your home, what is your relationship to them, and what is your children's relationship to them?

_____

_____

Vocational History:

Employed _____   Unemployed _____

If employed, place of employment: _____

Part or full time:_____   Occupation:_____

How long have you had your present job?_____

Any problems at work?_____

Any specific problems while you were in school?_____

Military/veteran status: N/A:_____   Dates:_____

Position in service:_____   Stationed:_____

Did you serve in combat?_____

Comments:_____

Hecker, L. L., & Sori, C. F. (2007). Therapy intake form. In L. L. Hecker, C. F. Sori, & Associates, *The therapist's notebook, volume 2: More homework, handouts, and activities for use in psychotherapy* (pp. 261-271). Binghamton, NY: The Haworth Press.

About Your Family Background:

Please list your brothers and sisters and their ages:

Name	Age	Name	Age
_____	_____	_____	_____
_____	_____	_____	_____
_____	_____	_____	_____
_____	_____	_____	_____
_____	_____	_____	_____
_____	_____	_____	_____

Is your father living?_____

If not, date and cause of death:_____

Father's occupation:_____

Is your mother living?_____

If not, date and cause of death:_____

Mother's occupation:_____

Briefly describe the quality or nature or your relationship with your parents and note any questions or concerns you might wish to raise regarding that relationship (if any):

_____

_____

Problem Checklists:

Please check any of the following which may apply:

*Please put * by the items that are causing you the **most** difficulty*

Checklist #1

___Anxiety, tension, nervousness

___Heart palpitations or pounding

___Shortness of breath/rapid breathing

___High blood pressure/hypertension

___Frequent upset stomach/indigestion/nausea

___Excessive caffeine use

___Excessive alcohol use

___Excessive medication use

___Drug use

___Sexual functioning problem

Hecker, L. L., & Sori, C. F. (2007). Therapy intake form. In L. L. Hecker, C. F. Sori, & Associates, *The therapist's notebook, volume 2: More homework, handouts, and activities for use in psychotherapy* (pp. 261-271). Binghamton, NY: The Haworth Press.

___Muscle tension/spasticity/cramps

___Coldness or numbness in fingers

___Stiffness/aching/burning sensation in joints

___Dizziness or fainting spells

___Frequent or severe headaches

___Memory problems

___Inability to concentrate

___Crying spells

___Frequent wakening/early wakening

___Problems falling asleep

___Lack of appetite

___Infertility

___Hormonal imbalances (e.g., menopause, PMS)

___Pregnancy

___Miscarriage

___Abortion

___Diarrhea/constipation

___Urinary problems

___Chronic pain

___Chronic illness

___Excessive appetite

Checklist #2

___Loneliness

___Legal matters

___Sexual abuse

___Criminal behavior

___Fears and worries

___Inferiority

___Gender identity

___Internet relationships

___Shame

___Illness

___Infidelity of self

___Assertiveness

___Troublesome dreams

___Education

___Communicating

___Friends

___Suicidal thoughts

___Divorce

___Separation

___Stepfamily issues

___Temper

___Bereavement

___Finances

___Sexual concerns

___Gambling

___Despair

___Self-doubt

___Sexual response

___Decision making

___Unhappiness

___Disability

___Infidelity of partner

___Shyness

___Loss of faith in others

___Illness

___Parenting

___Education

___Anger with God

___Loss of faith in God

___Physical abuse

___Self-control

___Depression

___Insecurity

___Sexuality

___Pornography/cybersex

___Guilt

___Self-concept

___Ppremarital concerns

___Ambition

___Confusion

___Career/job

___Couple problems

___Dating

___Loss of meaning

___Disability

___Loss of love

___Adoption

___Eating disorder

Hecker, L. L., & Sori, C. F. (2007). Therapy intake form. In L. L. Hecker, C. F. Sori, & Associates, *The therapist's notebook, volume 2: More homework, handouts, and activities for use in psychotherapy* (pp. 261-271). Binghamton, NY: The Haworth Press.

If you are experiencing problems in your relationships with others, please indicate by checking all that apply:

Partner/Spouse_____   Child/Children_____   Parent(s)_____   Sibling(s)_____

Extended Family_____   In-Laws_____   Friends_____   Other_____

Comments:_____

_____

Child Concerns:

Identify by writing the initials(s) of the child (children) in the box next to the concern you or your partner have:

Bad Dreams	Health Problems	Moods	Worry	Fighting
Hyperactivity	Fears	Poor Attention	Arguing	Immaturity
Jealousy	Complaining	Sleep	Developmental Issues	Uncommunica-tive
Depression	Social Skills	Sadness	Stealing	Shyness
Sexual Abuse	Physical Abuse	Anger	Bed Wetting	Disobedience
Soiling	Lying	Attention Problems	Sexual Concerns	Learning Difficulties
Running Away	Drug/Alcohol Use	Impulsiveness	Schoolwork	Relations with Sibling(s) or Stepsiblings
Visitation Arrangements	Interference by Ex-Partner	Anxiety	Relationship w/Parent(s) or Stepparent(s)	Hair Pulling
Chores	Biting	Hitting	Talking Back	Truancy

Hecker, L. L., & Sori, C. F. (2007). Therapy intake form. In L. L. Hecker, C. F. Sori, & Associates, *The therapist's notebook, volume 2: More homework, handouts, and activities for use in psychotherapy* (pp. 261-271). Binghamton, NY: The Haworth Press.

Please state briefly any special concerns or questions about your children that you think we should discuss:

_____

_____

Family Concerns: If you answer yes to any of the following questions, please elaborate in the space provided.

1. Have there been any recent deaths in your family?	No	Yes	If yes, who, when, and from what?
2. Have you or a family member ever attempted suicide?	No	Yes	If yes, who, when, and how?
3. Has anyone if you family ever committed suicide?	No	Yes	If yes, who, when, and how?
4. Have you recently been concerned about anyone in your family harming themselves?	No	Yes	If yes, who?
5. Have you recently been concerned about anyone in your family harming others?	No	Yes	If yes, who?
6. Do you drink alcohol?	No	Yes	If yes, how much do you drink weekly?
7. Do you consume nonprescription drugs other than alcohol?	No	Yes	If yes, what drugs do you take and how often?
8. Do you take over-the-counter or prescribed drugs in a manner other than as directed?	No	Yes	If yes, what drugs do you take and how often?
9. Are you concerned about your use of alcohol or other drugs?	No	Yes	Why are you concerned?
10. Has anyone in your family expressed concern over your use of alcohol or drugs?	No	Yes	What have they said?
11. Have you recently been concerned about your spouse's/partner's use of alcohol or drugs?	No	Yes	Explain:

Hecker, L. L., & Sori, C. F. (2007). Therapy intake form. In L. L. Hecker, C. F. Sori, & Associates, *The therapist's notebook, volume 2: More homework, handouts, and activities for use in psychotherapy* (pp. 261-271). Binghamton, NY: The Haworth Press.

12. Have you ever been concerned about the way anger is managed in your family?	No	Yes	Explain:
13. Has anyone else expressed concern about the way anger is managed in your family?	No	Yes	Explain:

Medical Information:

1. Do you or any of your family members have any current medical conditions?
   Yes____   No____

   If yes, please note who and what the condition is:

   Who: _____

   Condition: _____

   Who: _____

   Condition: _____

   Who: _____

   Condition: _____

   Who: _____

   Condition: _____

   Do you or any of your family members have any physical disability or limitations? If so, what are they?
   Who: _____
   Disability/Limitation: _____

2. Please list any medications you or any family members are currently taking:

Person Taking Medication	Medication	Purpose	Dosage	Frequency	Prescribing Doctor

Hecker, L. L., & Sori, C. F. (2007). Therapy intake form. In L. L. Hecker, C. F. Sori, & Associates, *The therapist's notebook, volume 2: More homework, handouts, and activities for use in psychotherapy* (pp. 261-271). Binghamton, NY: The Haworth Press.

3. Should you have a medical emergency in session, whom would you like us to contact?

    Name: _____   Phone: _____
    Cell Phone: _____

4. Who is your medical doctor?
    Name: _____
    Address: _____
    _____

    Phone: _____

5. Have you or anyone in your family ever been hospitalized for psychiatric reasons? If so, who, when, and for what reason?

    Who: _____

    Dates of Hospitalization(s): _____

    Reasons for Hospitalization(s): _____

    _____

    Is this person currently under the care of a psychiatrist?   Yes   No

Previous Therapy and Therapy Expectations:

6. Have you ever had counseling or therapy before coming here?
    Yes___   No____   If yes, whom did you see and for how long?

    _____

7. If yes to 6, what was helpful for you in the previous counseling/therapy?

    _____

    _____

    If yes to 6, what was _not_ helpful in the previous counseling/therapy?

    _____

    _____

Hecker, L. L., & Sori, C. F. (2007). Therapy intake form. In L. L. Hecker, C. F. Sori, & Associates, _The therapist's notebook, volume 2: More homework, handouts, and activities for use in psychotherapy_ (pp. 261-271). Binghamton, NY: The Haworth Press.

8.   In your own words, briefly tell us why you are seeking therapy at this time:

_____

_____

_____

How would you know that therapy with us has been successful?

_____

_____

_____

9. Please rate your feelings regarding how hopeful you are that therapy will help:
        (circle your response)

| Hopeless | Somewhat Hopeless | Unsure | Somewhat Hopeful | Very Hopeful |

10.   Is there anything else you would like us to know?

_____

_____

_____

Thank you for your patience in answering these questions and for your cooperation!

Hecker, L. L., & Sori, C. F. (2007). Therapy intake form. In L. L. Hecker, C. F. Sori, & Associates, *The therapist's notebook, volume 2: More homework, handouts, and activities for use in psychotherapy* (pp. 261-271). Binghamton, NY: The Haworth Press.

33

Quick Depression Assessment

Catherine Ford Sori
Lorna L. Hecker

Type of Contribution: *Handout*

Objectives

The purpose of this handout is to provide therapists with a paper-and-pencil tool that can be used to initially assess depression or suicidality in adult clients. It provides a record of a depression screening that can become part of the client's file.

Rationale for Use

One of the most important skills for clinicians to master is assessing clients' levels of depression and risk for suicide. All professionals in the field of psychotherapy are trained to assess clients for depression as well as suicidality and are instructed to document such assessment in their case notes. The Quick Depression Assessment (QDA) is a one-page form that is designed to be an interactive tool between the therapist and client, where the therapist asks questions from the QDA and marks the sheet accordingly. This process allows the therapist to ask follow-up questions based on client responses. The symptoms being assessed in the top section of the QDA follow the acronym SWEETNERS, which stands for sleep, weight changes, energy level, enjoyment, thinking, negative thoughts, emotions, ruminations, and suicidality (see Handout 33.1).

The QDA provides a concrete record of a client's status that can be reviewed in supervision and at different times throughout the course of therapy. If given early in treatment it can serve as a baseline of depression, and the QDA can be readministered at the midpoint and end of treatment to assess and document clients' progress. In this way it is useful to focus treatment where needed. Above all, it serves to alert clinicians to the possibility that clients may be at risk for harming themselves and offers concrete evidence that the professional is following best practice standards in carefully assessing depression and suicidality in clients.

Instructions

Although all clients should be screened for depression and possible suicidality, this tool is particularly helpful when clients indicate they are struggling with depression on an intake form, such as the Therapy Intake Form (Chapter 32, this volume), or when they present with depression as a reason for initiating counseling. It is suggested that the QDA be used after the therapist has established sufficient rapport so that the client feels at ease answering the questions. In introducing the QDA, therapists should use a matter-of-fact tone of voice and indicate that the questions on this form are used routinely to assess clients who have indicated that they might be depressed. If depression markers are indicated, further evaluation is needed. Formal screening tools such as the Beck Depression Inventory (Beck, Rial, & Rickets, 1974) for adults or the Child Depression Inventory (Kovacs, 1985) for children are recommended.

Suggestions for Follow-Up

As previously mentioned, the QDA can be given at various points during the course of treatment, in order to assess how effective therapy is in reducing depression and suicidality. Sometimes others may notice that clients are improving, while clients themselves may not be aware that they appear to be less depressed and functioning better. Clinicians may elect to show clients their QDAs from different points of treatment, in order to highlight positive changes, punctuate what clients have done to get better, and articulate additional goals. It can be especially helpful to compare a QDA from the end of treatment to one taken early in therapy to help clients see how their answers have changed, as well as to articulate how they would know that they were slipping and might need to reinitiate treatment.

In the event that a client's answers indicate a high level of depression, therapists may suggest a referral to a physician to discuss the possibility of using medications to augment psychotherapy. In this case clinicians should be sure to obtain a release form from clients so they may consult with the physician regarding issues such as compliance with medication, treatment side effects, effectiveness, and so on. If a client is depressed, it is important for the clinician to get a list of any medications being used and to consider referring the client back to the prescribing physician to determine if any medications may be contributing to a depressed mood or causing side effects, such as sleep problems or weight fluctuations.

Whenever a client is suicidal, steps must be taken to ensure client safety. Safety plans have been detailed elsewhere (e.g., Lester, 2001) and in severe cases may include hospitalization of the client.

Contraindications

The QDA is designed to be used with adults and should not be administered to children. It should also be noted that the QDA is only meant as a brief assessment tool, as neither its reliability nor validity have been researched. In cases where a client is moderately or severely depressed or suicidal, or when a clinician may want to share information with another professional such as a psychiatrist, the authors recommend supplementing the QDA with an instrument that has high validity and reliability, such as the Beck Depression Inventory (Beck et al., 1974).

References

Beck, A. T., Rial, W. Y., & Rickets, K. (1974). Short form of depression inventory: Cross-validation. *Psychological Reports, 34*(3), 1184-1186.

Kovacs, M. (1985). The Children's Depression Inventory (CDI). *Psychopharmacology Bulletin, 21*, 995-998.

Lester, D. (Ed.). (2001). *Suicide prevention: Resources for the millennium.* Philadelphia: Brunner-Routledge.

QUICK DEPRESSION ASSESSMENT

Client: _____   **Date:** _____

Rate each symptom: 0 = none; 1 = mild; 2 = moderate; 3 = severe

S	=	Sleep (too little, too much)	0	1	2	3
W	=	Weight change	0	1	2	3
E	=	Energy level low	0	1	2	3
E	=	Enjoyment, lack of	0	1	2	3
T	=	Thinking (poor concentration)	0	1	2	3
N	=	Negative thoughts	0	1	2	3
E	=	Emotions (feeling sad, blue, anxious)	0	1	2	3
R	=	Ruminating (low self-worth, future, hopelessness)	0	1	2	3
S	=	Suicidal thoughts	0	1	2	3

Total Score: _____

ADD PERTINENT FACTORS RELATED TO:
       Family history of depression/suicide:
       Changes in sexual interest or performance:
       Daily or seasonal variations:

DOES CLIENT SAY HE or SHE IS DEPRESSED?   YES   NO

IF YES: ASK CLIENT TO RATE DEGREE OF DEPRESSION:

Not Depressed   Moderate Depression   Very Depressed

← ————————————————————————— →

1   2   3   4   5   6   7   8   9   10

PHYSIOLOGICAL SYMPTOMS:
Headache:____ Muscle Aches: ____ Backaches: ____ Fatigue: ____ Other: _____
(May need physician's assessment for illness, psychotropic medication evaluation)

ASSESS FOR SUICIDE RISK
Suicidal thoughts? Yes ____ No ____ How Often? _____ Describe: _____
Any previous attempts? Yes __ No __ When? _____
Treatment? _____
How was attempt made? _____
How did family react? _____
Does client currently have a plan? Yes __ No __ Describe: _____
Does client have means? (Describe): _____
Do not allow suicidal client to leave your office. Contact family member and have client
evaluated at a hospital.

_____   _____
Clinician's Signature   Date

Sori, C. F., & Hecker, L. L. (2007). Quick depression assessment. In L. L. Hecker, C. F. Sori, & Associates, *The therapist's notebook, volume 2: More homework, handouts, and activities for use in psychotherapy* (pp. 273-275). Binghamton, NY: The Haworth Press.

34

The Tiger Woods Analogy:
The Seven-Minute Active Listening Solution

Howard G. Rosenthal

Type of Contribution: *Activity*

Objectives

The purpose of this exercise is to make the therapist a better listener. Therapists often daydream or do not truly listen to the client's verbalizations. This activity truly abets insight and makes the therapist cognizant when he or she is not listening.

Rationale for Use

Most therapists wrongly assume that when they daydream or simply aren't listening, the client will not notice. Moreover, the helper will often rationalize that even if his or her listening skills are subpar, it will not impact the counseling relationship or the outcome of treatment. This experiential paradigm will demonstrate beyond a shadow of a doubt that the treatment is indeed negatively impacted by such behavior.

Instructions

This activity is best conducted in a classroom setting or at a workshop; however, a dyad is all that is necessary. One helper plays the role of the therapist or counselor while the other plays the role of the client.

First, the person who will play the client leaves the room with the activity leader and is told that he or she should rate the helper on a continuous scale of 0 to 100. A rating of 0 is terrible; 50 is average; and a rating of 100 means the counselor is doing a near-perfect job. Thus, the client might rate the counselor as a 6, a 72, or perhaps a 97.

The client is cautioned that he or she should be very honest and not let the fact that he or she is an acquaintance of the helper impact the rating. The client is told that there will be two brief sessions lasting approximately seven minutes each. The client is instructed to tell the counselor a real or fabricated problem using similar verbiage for each of the two sessions or trials (i.e., the problem remains the same).

It is important that the client does not tell the helper that he or she is being rated on the trials. In addition, the ratings are not revealed until the leader brings up the subject.

Next the helper is taken to another location (e.g., the hall or an adjacent room) and is given instructions. The helper is reminded that there are times in everyday life when we pretend to be listening to somebody but we really aren't. Perhaps we are cooking dinner, waxing our car, or dust-

The Therapist's Notebook, Volume 2
© 2007 by The Haworth Press, Inc. All rights reserved.
doi:10.1300/5550_34

ing our furniture, while the phone is lodged in our ear. The activity leader then says something like, "Can you remember a time like that?"

Invariably the helpers laugh and say something like, "Yeah, when my mother-in-law calls."

The leader then tells helpers that they should purposely let their mind wander during the first trial. "Think of where you are going to lunch, that new handbag you want to buy, where you will go on vacation." This paradoxical technique (Haley, 1991), which is stressed in strategic psychotherapy, is also applicable when training helpers. Helpers are instructed not to use any of the basic counseling skills (e.g., empathy, summarizing, etc.) during this part of the activity. Helpers are also told not to tell the client what they were instructed to do even if the client guesses, which is rare.

Opposite instructions are provided for Trial 2. Here the counselor is literally told, "Now I want you to do the opposite of Trial 1. No matter how boring your client is, I want you to hang onto every word. Absolutely, positively refuse to let your mind wander."

The two trials of about seven minutes each are conducted. The leader then reveals that the helpers have been rated and clients reveal their scores. The ratings for Trial 1 are nearly always pathetic, hovering below 50 and often in the single digits. Once in a while a client will even inquire if a negative rating is permissible.

In contrast, Trial 2 ratings are generally healthy and can often hit the mythical ceiling of 100.

The leader then has the helpers reveal their roles for the two trials.

Processing the Activity

The individuals who played clients are asked to explain their feelings and thoughts in relation to their ratings. The leader can ask relevant discussion questions such as these:

> Did you feel discounted? What was going through your mind during Trial 1? If you went to a real agency or a private practice and a therapist treated you this way during the first session, would you return for a second session? How was Trial 2 different? Describe what was specifically helpful for you during Trial 2.

Brief Vignette

The following is an example of this training activity using two master's-level therapists who worked for a local counseling agency. Mandy played the role of the therapist, while Kelly took on the role of the client. Kelly's ratings of Mandy were somewhat typical: 14 for Trial 1, and 93 for Trial 2.

Kelly told Mandy that the rating of 14 "was a gift" and that despite the therapist's directions to be brutally honest, she would have given her a zero or perhaps a negative number if she didn't think it would hurt her feelings. Kelly revealed that she felt angry, discounted and insignificant during the first trial:

> Look Mandy, you seemed to be more interested in looking at the surroundings in the room than you did about hearing my difficulties. Not only would I refuse to see you again, but also I would report your lack of competence to the person running the counseling center. If I had been a real first-time client, I doubt whether I would have ever made an appointment with another helper. I want you to know that the effects of that session would not have ended at the conclusion of the interview.

During Trial 2, however, Kelly reported feeling important, prized, and the center of attention. "You came across like you really cared, and that meant a lot," she told Mandy. "I was inclined to listen to your input. You seemed competent and truly concerned."

Mandy admitted she was surprised by the damage inflicted in the first trial by a short seven-minute interview. She further expressed guilt and insight, mentioning that on a number of recent occasions in her actual practice she had been daydreaming more about the new house her family was moving into than her clients' difficulties. "I guess I never gave it much thought," admitted Mandy. "I just assumed that my clients wouldn't know the difference, but my ratings tell a different story. I must admit that this will have an immediate impact on my counseling technique."

The Tiger Woods Analogy

The quintessential message in the follow-up stage is the Tiger Woods Analogy. It is extremely useful and puts the entire exercise in perspective. The leader says to the participants something like the following:

> Let's say I was attempting to sink a four-foot putt and I missed it. There's a good possibility of that happening. Nevertheless, it is also possible that Tiger Woods could miss it too. Sure, he's a terrific player, and he's much less likely than me to miss it, but even he misses an occasional four-foot putt. Now let's say Tiger and I both go for that same four-footer again. What will most likely transpire?
>
> Well, the chances are good I will miss it the same way I did the first time. Tiger, on the other hand, being a consummate professional, will adjust and most likely sink the putt the second time around. Why? Simply put, he's a world-class professional and when he makes a mistake he adjusts.
>
> As counselors and therapists, we are all fallible human beings. We make mistakes. There will always be times when we are daydreaming, not listening to the client as well as we should, or mentally putting together our order for Cantonese cuisine that we will consume after our last client finishes the session. The idea of this exercise is not to totally prevent these occurrences from happening. Again: they will occur, just like Tiger misses an occasional short putt. The idea, nevertheless, is that the exercise will make us cognizant; give us insight into our shoddy therapeutic technique.
>
> The bottom line is that although we as imperfect humans (and therapists) will still make the mistake of not listening in an ideal manner, we will be much more likely to remember this activity—see the harm that it causes—and bring ourselves back to an ideal state of active listening. Unlike a neophyte who will not recognize the behavior, we—like Tiger on his second putt—will adjust our active listening skills and transform a poor or mediocre session into a valuable experience for the client.

Suggestions for Follow-Up

Following this activity, helpers can be encouraged to videotape or audiotape their sessions and rate themselves on the same 0-100 point scale on how well they use their listening skills.

Contraindications

None noted.

Reference

Haley, J. (1991). *Problem-solving therapy* (2nd ed.). San Francisco: Jossey-Bass.

Professional Readings and Resources

Cate, S. (1999). *Active learning exercises for social work and the human services.* Boston, MA: Allyn & Bacon.

Egan, G. (1990). *The skilled helper* (4th ed.). Pacific Grove, CA: Brooks/Cole.

Meier, S. T., & Davis, S. R. (2005). *The elements of counseling* (5th ed.). Pacific Grove, CA: Thomson Brooks/Cole.

Rosenthal, H. (2005). *Before you see your first client: 55 things counselors, therapists, and human service workers need to know.* New York: Brunner-Routledge.

Index

Page numbers followed by the letter "f" indicate a figure; those followed by the letter "t" indicate a table.

3HC (hugging, holding, huddling, and cuddling), 47, 48-50, 51-53, 55

AA (Alcoholics Anonymous), 121, 124t
Abuse
    childhood, 159-160, 177-183
    concerns and fears, 40, 258t, 266
    information gathering on, 237, 258t
    by partner, 252, 259t
    verbal, 38, 111, 258t
Academic performance, problems with, 60, 61, 256t
Accepting, 29, 36
Acknowledgments, 152, 154, 155
Action, stone representing, 232
Actions, responsibility for, 121
Actions interaction with feelings, 75, 121, 123t, 124t
Active imagination activity, 125, 126-127, 129, 130t
ADD/ADHD, 230, 256t
Adlerian lifestyle interview questions, 106
Adolescents
    career options for, 87
    case studies of, 94-97, 111-112
    communication in, 75, 111, 112
    horticulture studies on, 148
    spiritual development of, 239
Adult children relationships with parents, 105-106
Adult incest survivors, 159-163
Adult (persona), 177, 178, 179, 180, 181-183
Adventure-based therapy, 69
Aesop's fables, 233
Affection, assessing, 253
Affection, attitudes toward, 50, 51, 52
Affectionate versus sexual behavior, 49
Affective processes, 69, 70
Afterlife, 243, 244
Aging, concerns about, 41
Alcohol dependence, 120, 121, 148, 255t, 256t, 268t
Alcoholics Anonymous, 121, 124t
Alliances, 69
Allison (fictional child of divorce), 200, 201, 211-222
Altered consciousness, 139, 140
Alternate-hand journaling, 180-183
Anderson, Hans Christian, 233

Anger
    issues, 252, 258t
    management skills, 124t, 269t
    post-divorce, letting go of, 191
    problems, 119-120, 121, 124t
Animals in therapy, 101
Anne (fictional counselor), 207-208, 209, 210
Anxiety
    assessing, 257t, 265
    in children, 256t
    disorders, 139, 140
    in parents of ill children, 57
    reducing, 120, 124t
    struggling with, 230
Approximations, shaping by successive, 115-117
Arguments
    analyzing, 13, 16
    feelings during, 19
Art in therapy. *See also* Drawing in therapy; Flowers in therapy
    for child abuse survivors, 180
    externalization, facilitating through, 81, 109
    healing, role in, 37, 169, 170, 171-172
Assessment instruments, 251-254, 254t-260t, 273-274, 275
Assimilation, cultural, 131
Atheists, 240, 244
Attachment theory, 4
Attention-deficit/hyperactivity disorder, 230, 256t
Auditory images, 140
Automatic thoughts, 119, 120, 121

Beauty (element of holiness), 170, 171, 176
Beck Depression Inventory, 274
Bedrooms, avoiding, 48
Behavior
    adaptive, developing, 230
    consequences of, 119, 120, 121, 123t, 124t
    contract, 116
    evaluation of, 30
    interventions and modification, 115-117
    negative, identifying and overcoming, 119-120, 121-122

Behavior (continued)
    nonverbal, 50, 133
    nurturing, 112
    positive, promoting, 229
    repetitive, 257t
    therapy, 115
Belief systems, 229, 233
Bible stories, 230-231, 232-233
Bibliotherapy, 194, 223, 226
Binuclear family, 189
Biologically based emotions, 4
Bipolar disorder, 121
Blaming, 29, 36, 111
Board games in therapy, 59, 60-61, 63t-65t, 66f-67f,
        102
Body image, 151, 153, 154
Body signals, negative, 28
Bowen systems theory, 238, 247
Brady Bunch (TV family), 198
Bragging versus acknowledging accomplishments, 152
Breast cancer patients, 173
Bribing/rewarding, 29, 36
Bridging Game for Siblings, 59, 60-61, 63t-65t, 66f-
        67f
Brief strategic therapy, 115
Buddhism, 233
Burnout, 148

Cancer
    in children, 57, 58, 59-61
    patient support groups, 173
    relaxation and visualization exercises for patients
            with, 139
Career options, exploring, 87-91, 88f
Career-related messages, 151
Caring habits, 29, 30, 34, 36
Catherine (child abuse survivor), 181-183
CD, blank as therapeutic prop, 96
Change, negative consequences of, 120, 121
Checkbook as therapeutic prop, 97, 100
Child custody, 197, 256t, 259t
Child Depression Inventory, 274
Child (persona), 177, 178, 179-183
Childhood abuse, 159-160, 177-183
Children
    communication in, 75, 77-78
    concerns regarding, 256t, 261, 267t
    conflict, reactions to, 200
    death, dealing with, 77-78
    depression in, 139, 256t, 267t
    horticulture studies on, 148
    illness impact on, 57-58, 60-61
    spiritual development of, 239
    as symptom bearers, 229
Children of divorce
    adjustment of, 187
    case studies, 201

Children of divorce (continued)
    communication in, 82-84, 199, 200, 201, 209-210
    experiences of, 199-201
    literature for, 189, 201, 203-222, 223
    parents, relationship with, 189, 190, 200, 224
    self-blaming for divorce, 189, 224
    in stepfamilies, 193, 196-197, 198
Choice theory, 34
Choice Theory: A New Psychology of Personal
        Freedom (Glasser), 29
Chris (child abuse survivor), 178
Chronically ill children, family relationships of, 57-58,
        60-61
Church attendance, 232, 233, 241
Church groups, 149
Classic literature, 233
Client postures, 70
Clock as therapeutic prop, 95, 97, 99
Coalitions, assessing, 69
Cognitive-behavioral theory, 119
Coins as therapeutic prop, 95, 100
College options, 87
Communication. See also Emotions and feelings,
        communicating
    assessing, 253, 258t
    instruments, 251, 252-254, 254t-260t
    negativity, interrupting during, 23-24
    patterns of, 69, 70
    problems in, 71
Community support groups, case studies of, 161-162
Compassion (element of holiness), 170, 171, 176
Complaining, 29, 36
Computer disk as therapeutic prop, 96, 99
Conflict
    children's reactions to, 200
    handling, 107
    intragroup, reducing, 162
    parental, impact of, 187
    personification of, 111-112, 111f
    positivity, increasing during, 21
    problems with, 258t
    resolution of, 69
    in values, 240
Congruence, 4
Connecting Spaces, 69-70, 71-72, 74
Conscious and unconscious mind, communication
        between, 125
Context of 3HC (hugging, holding, huddling, and
        cuddling), 47
Contextual meanings, exploring, 70
Control over self versus others, 30
Coping ability, 139, 200, 230
Coping tools, spiritual, 243
Counselors, rating of, 277-279
Couples, Connecting Spaces activity for, 70
Couples Drawing Together (activity), 3, 5-8, 9
Courage, 232
Coursework connection to career goals, 87, 89, 90

Co-workers, relationships with, 162
Creative Career Constellation, 87-91, 88f
Crises, post-trauma, 163
Crisis intervention groups, 149
Criticizing, 29, 36
Cross-cultural world, 131-132, 135
Crown (element of holiness), 170, 171, 175
Cuddling in intimate relationships, 48, 55. *See also* 3HC (hugging, holding, huddling, and cuddling)
Cue words and phrases, 22, 23
Cultural assimilation, 131
Cultural diversity groups, 149
Culturally appropriate therapy, 131
Culture, home versus host, 131-132, 136
Cystic fibrosis, 58

Darlene (bereaved client) (case study), 173
Darrell (student) (case study), 89-90
David and Goliath (Bible story), 230-231, 232-233, 235f-236f
Deadly habits, 29, 30, 34, 36
Death
    child abuse as type of, 178, 179
    children's attitudes toward, 58, 63t, 65t
    familial, questioning concerning, 268t
    flowers evoking themes of, 148, 149
    of parent, 173, 239
    religious beliefs concerning, 239, 243, 244
    of sibling, 239, 240, 242
    of spouse, 241
    stories about, 77-78
    thoughts of, 254t
Deconstructive approaches in narrative therapy, 230
Deep breathing, 139
Defensive states, 177
Defensiveness, decreasing, 5, 7, 111
Delia and Dave (case study), 12-14
Depression
    assessment of, 273-274, 275
    childhood, 139, 256t, 267t
    concerns, 266
    feelings accompanying, 120
    in parents of ill children, 57
    personification of, 111f
    physiological factors in, 147-148
    reducing, 274
Depth psychological orientation, 125
Destroyer (persona), 177, 178, 183
Determination, 232
Developmental damage, repair of, 183
Developmentally disabled, groups for, 149
Diabetes, 58
Diane (child abuse survivor), 180
Dictionary of Occupational Titles (DOT), 90
Dieting, 151
Diffuse physiological arousal (DPA), 22

Dinosaur's Divorce, 189
Disability, 256t, 259t, 266, 269
Dissociation, 127, 140
Divorce, concerns about, 257t, 266
Divorce, emotions evoked by
    children's stories, encouraging, 199, 200, 201, 205, 206, 210, 213-214, 215-217
    gingerbread figure activity, 82-84
    grieving, 189
    movies addressing, 223
Divorced parents
    fighting between, 203-204, 205-206, 207-208
    relationships between, 187, 190, 191, 198
    tips for, 187-188, 189-191, 199-200
Divorcing family (case study), 82-84
Doctoral student (case study), 126-127
Domestic violence, 22, 261
DOT (Dictionary of Occupational Titles), 90
DPA (diffuse physiological arousal), 22
Drawing in therapy
    for child abuse survivors, 180
    for couples, 3, 5-8, 9
    for families, 82, 83
    for single people, 173
Dream figures, 125, 126-127, 129
Driver's license as therapeutic prop, 95, 100
Drug dependence, 121, 148, 255t, 256t, 268t
Duration of 3HC (hugging, holding, huddling, and cuddling), 47

Earnest (eleven-year-old) (case study), 50-52
Eating disorders, 181, 254t, 266
Eco-map, 160-163, 165f
Educational groups, 149
Ego strength, 127
Eightfold path, 233
Eight-year-old child of divorce (case study), 82-83
Elnora (child of divorce), 201
Embracing, levels of, 47
Emotional abuse, 258t
Emotional climate, 49
Emotional honesty, 4
Emotional intelligence, 200
Emotional softening, 21
Emotional styles, 3
Emotionally focused activities, 11
Emotionally focused therapy (EFT), 4, 15
Emotions and feelings. *See also* Divorce, emotions evoked by; Primary emotions; Secondary emotions
    clarifying, 109
    coping with, 121
    debilitating, overcoming, 229
    exploring, 120
    identifying, 149
    issues involving, 252
    and relationships, 166-168

Emotions and feelings *(continued)*
 thoughts and behaviors, link to, 75, 121, 123t, 124t
 unconscious, eliciting, 237
Emotions and feelings, communicating
 in art, 37
 by children and adolescents, 75, 76, 77-79, 82, 189, 209-210
 conflict, handling of, 112
 with drawing, 6, 7-8
 Finding a Connection activity as aid in, 11-14
 with flowers, 147, 148
 by parents, 225
 in writing, 209-210, 251
Encouraging, 29, 36
Escape, avenues for, 121, 124t
Exercise bike, riding, 115, 116
Experiential education, 69
Experiential therapy, 4
External control, 29, 30
External feelings, 12, 17f. *See also* Secondary emotions
Externalizing
 activities, 86f, 109, 110
 disorders, 52
 problems, 81-82, 109-110, 230, 232

Faith
 challenges to, 241, 242
 internalizing, 230
 stone representing, 232
Families of origin
 affection, attitudes toward, 50, 51
 projection onto current family, 95
 understanding, 105, 107-108, 237
Family
 background, 261, 265
 communication patterns, 231
 disordered, 229
 identity, rules, and rituals, 197
 LGTB, 257t
 meetings, 197
 moving, patterns of, 133, 135
 negative messages from, 151, 153, 154
 nurturing behaviors, 112
 outings, 83
 post-divorce, 189, 217, 219, 220, 222, 223, 225, 226. *See also* Stepfamilies
 structure, assessing, 231
 systems, 69, 231
 traditions, 136
Family play genogram, 237-238
Family Strengths and Concerns Assessment, 251-254, 254t-260t
Feeling Head activity, 75-79
Feelings. *See* Emotions and feelings
Fight-or-flight response, 22
FILM (function, information, limitations, and modifications), 94

Finding a Connection activity, 11-15
First-married families versus stepfamilies, 193, 197, 198
Flashbacks, 163
Flowers in therapy
 for couples, 37, 38-41, 39f, 40f, 44
 for groups, 147-149
Focus groups, 149
Fondness and admiration system, 3-4, 5, 7
Forgiveness, assessing, 253
Foster care, 256t
Foundation (element of holiness), 170, 171, 176
Four noble truths, 233
Frequency of 3HC (hugging, holding, huddling, and cuddling), 47
Friends and friendships
 adolescent attitudes toward, 94-97
 assessing, 253
 of incest survivors, 162
 negative messages from, 151, 153, 154
 wrong group of, 256t
"Friendship License," 95
Function, information, limitations, and modifications (FILM), 94

Games in therapy, 59, 60-61, 63t-65t, 66f-67f, 102
Garage, cleaning, 115, 116
Garbage, taking out, 152-155
Gender differences in sex versus affection preference, 49
Gender identity, 260t, 266
Gender stereotypes, 49
Generosity, 125
Genograms, 237-244
George, Milo, and Reeves (postdivorce family) (case study), 225
Gerontology clients, horticulture studies on, 148
Getting Together and Staying Together: Solving the Mystery of Marriage (Glasser), 29
Giant, defeating, 230-231, 232-233, 235f-236f
Gil, Eliana, 237, 238, 240
Gingerbread Figure Activity, 81, 82, 83-84, 86f
Glasser, William, 29, 30
Glory (element of holiness), 170, 171, 176
Goal or intent of 3HC (hugging, holding, huddling, and cuddling), 47
Gottman, John, 3, 4, 7
Grandparent-grandchild relationships, 241, 243
Greta (child abuse survivor), 179
Grief
 assessing, 257t
 in children of divorce, 189
 dealing with, 149, 241, 242, 243
 unresolved, 133, 136
Growth, 139, 140
Guided imagery exercises, 139, 140, 143-145

Hats as therapeutic prop, 96
Healing
    art and metaphor role in, 169, 171, 172
    of child abuse survivors, 183
    genogram as avenue for, 239
    guided imagery role in, 139, 140
Helen (incest survivor), 161-162
Hindu faith, 233
Holding, 47, 48
Holiness, elements of, 170, 171, 175-176
Homeopathic therapy, flower and plant use in, 147
Hopelessness, feelings of, 120, 121, 124t, 170
Horticulture, 147, 148
How to Defeat a Giant, 230-231, 232-233, 235f-236f
How to Win As a Stepfamily (Visher), 194
Hugging, significance and types of, 47-48. *See also*
        3HC (hugging, holding, huddling, and
        cuddling)
Humor, 69

Identity
    of hidden immigrants, 132, 133, 135
    rebuilding after trauma, 172, 183
Imagination activity, 125, 126-127, 129, 130t
Immigrants, hidden, 131-133, 135-136
Immigration, genogram information gathering on, 237
Inattention, 50-51
Incest survivors, 159-163
Index cards as therapeutic prop, 99
Infidelity, 12-13, 14, 258t, 266
Inner resources, 140
Inner self projection onto external object, 93
Insight role in therapy, 119, 122
Inspiration, 37
Intensity of 3HC (hugging, holding, huddling, and
        cuddling), 47
Interactions
    family, 240
    negative, 21-24, 26-28, 33, 111
    with others, 159
    parent and child, 229
    positive, 21, 231, 233
Interactive approach to therapy, 5
Interests, personal connection career goals, 87, 88-89,
        90
Intergenerational therapy, 105-108
Internal dialogues, 120
Internal family systems, 69
Internal feelings, 12, 18f, 19. *See also* Primary
        emotions
Internalizing disorders, 52
Internet Movie Database, 226
Interrupting, refraining from, 28
Interrupting of negative interactions, 21-24, 26-28, 33
Interviews
    of immigrants, 132, 133, 135-136
    initial, 29, 30-31, 32-33, 34

Interviews *(continued)*
    intake instrument, 261
    of parents, 105, 106-108
    structured, 29, 30-31, 32-33, 34, 52
    vulnerability, assessing through, 5
Intimacy, 71
Intimate relationships, touching in, 47
Introduce, do, and review (process), 94
Introspection, 147, 149
Islam, 233

Jason (fictional child of divorce), 200, 203-210
Jason (nine-year-old) (case study), 231-233
Jessica (child abuse survivor), 178, 180-181
Johnson, Susan, 3, 4, 7
Judgment (element of holiness), 170, 171, 175-176
Judy (fictional counselor), 217-219, 220-221
Jung, Carl, 125

Kabbalah, 169, 170, 171, 172, 174
Katie and Patrick (case study), 32-34
Kelly (client) (role play), 278
Kevin and Angela (case study), 38-42
Keys as therapeutic prop, 96-97, 101
Kinesthetic experiences, 140
Kingship (element of holiness), 170, 171, 176
Kinship Care Practice Project, 160

Lana (child abuse survivor), 180
Laura (child abuse survivor), 180
Lawn, mowing, 116
Leah (sixteen-year-old girl) (case study), 111-112
Legal system, 190
Lesbian, gay, bisexual, and transgender (LGBT) issues,
        257t, 260t
Lesbian couples, case studies of, 6-7
Life, broadened perspective of, 125
Life events, 148, 160, 166
Life reviews, 148
Life transitions, 88, 135, 252, 257t
Lifestyle interview questions, 106
Limbic system, 147-148
Linda and Carolyn (case study), 6-7
The Lion, the Witch, and the Wardrobe, 243
Lisa (incest survivor), 162
Listening
    habit of, 29, 36
    sharing and, 83-84
    strategies, 28
    in therapy, 277-279
Love maps, 3, 5, 7
Lovers following divorce, 190
Loving-kindness (element of holiness), 170, 171, 173,
        175

Loyalty conflicts, 240
Luria, Isaac, 170

Mandy (therapist) (role play), 278-279
Maribel (single mother of three) (case study), 50-52
Marriage
    between religious and nonreligious persons, 240
    childhood illness impact on, 57
    counseling, 112, 233
    external control in, 29
    of incest survivors, 162
    own versus parents', 106, 107
    problems, 111, 112, 231
    religious faith role in, 242
    status and history, 263
    thoughts and feelings regarding, 38-42
Mask, feelings behind, 19
Media, negative messages from, 151, 153, 154, 155
Medical conditions, 269
Medications, 274
Meditation, 173
Melissa (widow) (case study), 241-243
Memory, positive, 139
Memory, stimulating, 147
Mental disorder, evaluation for, 252
Mental garbage, 153-154
Mental health concerns, 261
Mental oasis, 139
Mental treasures, 155
Methamphetamine dependence, 121
Mike and Beth (case study), 107
Miniatures, 238, 239-240, 241, 242, 242f, 246t, 247
Miss Anne (fictional counselor), 207-208, 209, 210
Miss Judy (fictional counselor), 217-219, 220-221
Missy (child abuse survivor), 179
Mistakes, apologizing for, 112
Mistakes, correcting, 279
Money as therapeutic prop, 95, 96, 100, 101
Mood, problems and issues involving, 251, 252, 254t, 257t
Mosaic, creating, 172, 173
Movie clips for post-divorce families, 223-225, 226
Mrs. Doubtfire (movie), 224, 225
Music in therapy, 102

Nagging, 29, 36
Narrative therapy, 69, 81, 109, 113, 230, 232
Nature in therapy, 37-42, 44, 101, 102
Needs, partner's, helping meet, 20f
Negative behavior, identifying and overcoming, 119-120, 121-122
Negative body signals, 28
Negative interactions
    interrupting, 21-24, 26-28, 33
    patterns of, 111
    risk factors for, 24

Negative messages, impact of, 151, 153, 154-155
Negative thoughts
    assessing, 273, 275
    ridding self of, 151, 154
Negativity, decreasing, 21, 155
Negotiating disagreements, 29, 36
Newlywed couple (case study), 23-24
Nonblaming perspective, 109, 111
Nonverbal behavior, 50, 133
Nonverbal cues, 22, 27
Nonverbal expression, 76, 189

Objects, common in therapy, 93-97, 99-102, 125, 126
Obstacles, overcoming, 230
Occupational Outlook Handbook (Bureau of Labor Statistics, 2004-2005), 89, 90
Occupational therapy, flower and plant use in, 147
Olfactory memory, 147, 148
Organizational structure, 69
Outcomes, recalling unique, 230
Outspokenness, 111, 112

Paper currency as therapeutic prop, 96, 101
Paradoxical intervention, 115, 117
Parent and child
    activities for, 70
    interactions, 229
    relationship between, 105-106, 107, 108, 162, 258t, 265. See also Children of divorce: parents, relationship with
    religious life, 241
Parenting. See also Divorced parents
    affection in, 51, 52
    of babies, 32, 33
    of chronically ill children, 57
    concerns, 266
    differences around, 71
    of new child, 257t
    responsibilities, 256t
    thoughts on future, 39, 41
Parents
    aging, 259t
    background on, 265
    interviewing, 105, 106-108
    single, 256t
Partner relationships, 258t, 263
Partner violence, 252, 259t
Pediatric cancer patients, 57, 58, 59-61
Peer pressure, 94, 96-97
Pencil-and-paper instruments, 5
Persistence, 232
Personal introspection, 147, 149
Personal responsibility, accepting, 30

Personality
  flower representing, 148, 149
  integration of, 125
  socialization, theory of, 48
Pets, death of, 77-78
Physical health, promoting, 41, 42
Physical health symptoms, 261, 265-266, 275
Picture albums, 199, 200-201, 220
Plants in therapy, 97, 147
Play genograms, 237-238
Play therapy, 231
Playfulness in therapy, 5
Pocketbook as therapeutic prop, 97, 101
Poetry, 181-183
Positive, focusing on, 30-31, 32-33
Positive behavior, promoting, 229
Positive interaction, increasing, 21
Positive messages, 151
Positive task, focusing on, 31
Positive thoughts, 152-153, 154, 155
Post-traumatic stress disorder (PTSD)
  assessing, 257t
  in parents of ill children, 57
  in siblings of cancer patients, 58
  symptoms, 14-15
  treating, 139
Primary emotions
  expressing, 7, 12, 13, 14
  nature of, 4, 11
Problem bag, 110, 111f, 112
Problems, facing and interacting with, 109
Procrastination, overcoming, 115-117
Projection of family of origin onto current family, 95
Projection of inner self onto external object, 93
Props in therapy, 93-97, 99-102
Psychiatric hospitalization, 270
Psychological growth, promoting, 148
Psychological problems, genogram information
  gathering on, 237
Psychosis, 127
Punishing, 29, 36
Puranas, 233
Purse as therapeutic prop, 97
Purse snatcher (dream figure), 126-127

Quick Depression Assessment (QDA), 273-274, 275
Quran, 233

Rages at self, 50
Rational-emotive behavior therapy, 115
Reality orientation, 127
Reality therapy, 29, 30
Rebecca (incest survivor), 162
Reed and Susi (case study), 71-72
Relapse prevention for negative interactions, 24

Relational dyads, activities for, 70
Relationships. *See also relationship categories*
  assessing, 160, 161-162, 165f, 166-168, 251, 252,
    258t
  between divorced parents, 187, 190, 191, 198
  body image impact on, 151
  boundaries in, 69
  building, 31, 33-34
  genogram representation of, 238
  of hidden immigrants, 132, 135, 136
  of incest survivors, 159-160, 161-162
  intimate, touching in, 47
  perceptions of, 30-31, 32-33
  sexual, 121
  skills, 159
  status of, 261, 263
  in stepfamilies, 196, 197, 256t
  trauma impact on, 159-160, 169
  verbally abusive, 38
Relaxation exercises, 139, 143-144
Religious background, 262
Religious beliefs, 237, 239
Religious differences, 239, 240, 260t
Religious issues, 260t
Religious values, 229, 233
Remarriage, 257t. *See also* Stepfamilies
Repatriation, 131, 132
Resiliency, 229, 241
Resistance to 3HC (hugging, holding, huddling, and
    cuddling), 49-50
Respecting, 29, 36
Responsibilities, division of, 253, 256t
Ring as therapeutic prop, 95, 101
Role expectations, 69
Role play, 277-279
Roles, issues involving, 252, 256t

Sadie (child abuse survivor), 178
Safety, sense of, trauma impact on, 169
Sally (alcoholic) (case study), 121
Sally (incest survivor), 162
Sarah (incest survivor), 161
Satir, Virginia, 4
Scapegoating, avoiding, 109
School, problems in, 50-51, 52, 60, 61, 256t
School-to-college transitions, 88
School-to-work transitions, 88
Secondary emotions, 11, 12
Self
  sense of, 169
  splitting of, 177-178
  trauma impact on, 169-170, 171, 173, 177-178
Self-acceptance, 37, 125, 153
Self-assignments for therapists, 116
Self-awareness, expanding, 125, 126, 127
Self-blame, avoiding, 109

Self-blame for divorce, 189, 224
Self-confidence, 230, 233
Self-control versus external control, 30
Self-dialogue, 180-183
Self-differentiation, 149
Self-disclosure, 162
Self-discovery, promoting, 140
Self-disgust, 179
Self-enhancement, church groups on, 149
Self-esteem
    behavior, negative impact on, 120
    in children, 229, 230, 233
    in children of divorce, 189
    improving, 151
    procrastination impact on, 115
    programs on, 149
    trauma impact on, 169
Self-exploration, 42
Self-help book, Kabbalah as, 174
Self-image
    assessing, 254t
    child abuse impact on, 179, 181
    controlling, 154-155
    incest impact on, 159
    of women, 151
Self-loathing, 179
Self-mutilation, 120
Self-parenting skills, 178-179
Self-perception, genograms as aid in understanding, 238
Self-perception, improving, 160
Self-protection, 7
Self-reflection, 37
Self-regulatory skills, 229
Self-soothing, 22, 24, 26
Self-understanding, increasing, 125
Self-worth, procrastination impact on, 115
Separation anxiety, 189
Seven Caring Habits, 29, 36
Seven Deadly Habits, 29, 36
Sexual abuse, 258t, 266, 267t
Sexual behavior, 48, 49, 120, 124t, 256t
Sexual concerns, 252, 255t, 256t, 266
Sexual orientation, 260t, 262
Sexual relationships, inappropriate, 121
Shared custody, 197
Sharp tongue, 127
Shirt as therapeutic prop, 96, 101
Shoes as therapeutic prop, 95, 101
Shyness, 232-233, 266
Sibling relationships
    affection in, 50-51
    illness impact on, 57, 58, 59, 60-61
    problems in, 256t, 259t
Siblings, activities for, 70
Siddhartha Gautama, 233
Single-parenting problems, 256t
Situation Trigger Worksheet, 120, 121, 123t-124t

Sixty-year-old woman (case study), 127
Skinnerian behavior modification, 115
Sleep problems
    assessing, 273, 275
    disorders, 139, 140
    medication-related, 274
    in parents of ill children, 57
Snake (dream figure), 127
Social expectations, 151
Social interaction, 231, 233
Social problems, 255t, 257t
Social situations, avoidance of, 257t
Social skills, developing, 148
Social support, 160, 162
Solution-focused therapy, 69
Solutions, arriving at, 14, 20f
Solving circle, 31, 34
Soul, 175
Special place
    creating, 139, 143, 144-145
    drawing, 140
Spiritual beliefs, 247
Spiritual development, 149, 239, 247
Spiritual introspection, 147, 149
Spiritual issues, 260t
Spiritual journal, 243
Spiritual patterns, 238-239, 247
Spiritual play genogram, 237, 238-244, 242f, 246t, 247
Spiritual stories, 230-231, 232-233
Splendor (element of holiness), 170, 171, 176
Stepfamilies, 193-194, 196-198, 256t, 266
Stepmom (movie), 224, 225
Stepparent-stepchild relationships, 196, 197, 256t
Stories, alternative, developing, 81, 113, 230
Stories of virtue, 233
Storytelling, 75-76, 77-78
Strategic family therapy, 69
Strength (element of holiness), 170, 171, 175
Strengths, assessing, 229, 251, 252, 253-254
Stress
    dealing with, 133, 136
    physiological factors in, 147
    reducing, 139
    traumatic event, due to, 257t
    work-related, 173
Structural family therapy, 69
Substance abuse, 251, 252, 255t, 256t. *See also*
        Alcohol dependence; Drug dependence
Successive approximations, shaping by, 115-117
Sue (hidden immigrant) (case study), 132-133
Suicide
    attempted, 268t, 275
    commission of, 240
    risk for, 256t, 273, 274, 275
    thoughts of, 254t, 266, 275
Support groups, case studies of, 161-162
Support system, 133

Support within couples, 29, 36, 71-72
Survival tactics, 177, 178, 179
SWEETNERS (sleep, weight changes, energy level,
    enjoyment, thinking, negative thoughts,
    emotions, ruminations, suicidality), 273, 275
Systems theory, 4

Tactile experiences, 140
Target behaviors, developing, 119, 120
Target persons of 3HC (hugging, holding, huddling,
    and cuddling), 47
Tension Traverse, 69
Term paper, writing, 115, 116, 117
Therapeutic alliance, 22
Therapeutic change mechanism, 21
Therapist-client collaboration, 21-22
Therapist-client role play, 277-279
Therapists, rating of, 277-279
Therapists, self-assignments for, 116
Therapy
    effectiveness, assessing, 274
    history of previous, 261, 270-271
    intake form, 261-271, 273
Thoughts
    alternative, creating, 120
    behaviors, impact on, 119, 121, 123t
    negative, 151, 154, 273, 275
    positive, 152-153, 154, 155
    unconscious, 237
    versus feelings, 75
Threatening, 29, 36
Tiger Woods Analogy, 279
Time stress, personification of, 111f
Time-outs, 22, 23-24, 26, 27
Tolerance toward others, 125
Tony (twelve-year-old) (case study), 77-78
Tracy (incest survivor), 162
Transgenerational patterns, 237, 238-239, 241, 247
Transitions, 88, 135, 252, 257t
Trash, taking out, 152-155
Trauma
    healing from, 169, 171, 172, 183
    relationships, impact on, 159-160, 169
Treatment, response to, 139
Trigger events and situations, 119-120, 121
Troy (child abuse survivor), 179

Trust
    capacity for, 159, 169, 253, 258t
    as caring habit, 29, 36
    fostering, 160

Unconscious thoughts, 237
Undecided major, 87
Understanding (element of holiness), 170, 171, 175
Unprotected sex, 120, 124t
Useful Process Questions, 72, 74

Verbal abuse, 38, 111, 258t
Verbal cues, 22, 23
Verbal expression, 76, 189, 251
Vessels, broken (metaphor), 169, 170, 171-172, 173-
    174, 175-176
Video games, playing, 88f, 90
Videotapes of clients, 231-232
Visher, Emily and John, 194
Visitation, 197, 215, 219, 221, 223, 267t
Visual images, 140
Visual memory, 147, 148
Visualization exercises, 139, 140, 143-145
Vocational issues, 261

Wallet as therapeutic prop, 97, 101
Want ads, therapeutic use of, 155
Weight changes, 273, 274, 275
Wellness, groups on, 149
Welty family (case study), 59-61
Who Wants to Be a Millionaire? (game show), 231-232
Will (element of holiness), 170, 171, 175
Williamson, Donald, 105
Wisdom (element of holiness), 170, 171, 175
Wobbly Woozy, 69
Women, self-image of, 151
Women incest survivors, 161-162
Words, power of, 154
Words versus activities, 53
Written assessment, 251-254, 254t-260t, 273-274, 275
Written homework assignments, 50, 53

Yoga class, 173

Dear Customer:

Please fill out & return this form to receive special deals & publishing opportunities for you! These include:
- availability of new books in your local bookstore or online
- one-time prepublication discounts
- free or heavily discounted related titles
- free samples of related Haworth Press periodicals
- publishing opportunities in our periodicals or Book Division

❑ OK! Please keep me on your regular mailing list and/or e-mailing list for new announcements!

Name _____

Address_____

STAPLE OR TAPE YOUR BUSINESS CARD HERE!

_____

*E-mail address _____
*Your e-mail address will never be rented, shared, exchanged, sold, or divested. You may "opt-out" at any time.
May we use your e-mail address for confirmations and other types of information? ❑ Yes ❑ No

Special needs:
Describe below any special information you would like:
- Forthcoming professional/textbooks
- New popular books
- Publishing opportunities in academic periodicals
- Free samples of periodicals in my area(s)

Special needs/Special areas of interest:

_____

_____

_____

_____

Please contact me as soon as possible. I have a special requirement/project:

_____

_____

_____

_____

The Haworth Press Inc.

PLEASE COMPLETE THE FORM ABOVE AND MAIL TO:
Donna Barnes, Marketing Dept., The Haworth Press, Inc.
10 Alice Street, Binghamton, NY 13904–1580 USA
Tel: 1–800–429–6784 • Outside US/Canada Tel: (607) 722–5857
Fax: 1–800–895–0582 • Outside US/Canada Fax: (607) 771–0012
E-mail: orders@HaworthPress.com

GBIC07

Visit our Web site: www.HaworthPress.com